International Politics
and the Sea:
The Case of Brazil

Westview Replica Editions

   This book is a Westview Replica Edition. The concept of
Replica Editions is a response to the crisis in academic and
informational publishing. Library budgets for books have been
severely curtailed; economic pressures on the university presses
and the few private publishing companies primarily interested in
scholarly manuscripts have severely limited the capacity of the
industry to properly serve the academic and research communities.
Many manuscripts dealing with important subjects, often representing the highest level of scholarship, are today not economically viable publishing projects. Or, if they are accepted for
publication, they are often subject to lead times ranging from
one to three years. Scholars are understandably frustrated when
they realize that their first-class research cannot be published
within a reasonable time frame, if at all.

   Westview Replica Editions are our practical solution to the
problem. The concept is simple. We accept a manuscript in camera-
ready form and move it immediately into the production process.
The responsibility for textual and copy editing lies with the
author or sponsoring organization. If necessary we will advise
the author on proper preparation of footnotes and bibliography.
We prefer that the manuscript be typed according to our specifications, though it may be acceptable as typed for a disserta-
tion or prepared in some other clearly organized and readable
way. The end result is a book produced by lithography and bound
in hard covers. Initial edition sizes range from 400 to 600
copies, and a number of recent Replicas are already in second
printings. We include among Westview Replica Editions only works
of outstanding scholarly quality or of great informational value,
and we will continue to exercise our usual editorial standards
and quality control.

International Politics and the Sea:
The Case of Brazil
Michael A. Morris

Because Brazil's emergence as a major power is paralleled by its emergence as an ocean power, the country is a particularly important example of the ocean policies of developing states. Ocean affairs have become increasingly important for Brazilian foreign policy, and Brazil, in turn, has come to occupy a distinctive position in bilateral, regional, and global negotiations for a new ocean order.

This book surveys all aspects of Brazilian ocean policy: domestic influences, naval affairs, offshore petroleum exploration, shipping, and fishing. National ocean policy is related to international politics through analysis of Brazil's participation at international maritime conferences and its maritime relations with other states. The final chapter compares Brazil's ocean policy with policies of other states, both developing and developed.

Michael A. Morris is assistant professor of political science at Clemson University. He has been visiting associate professor at the Sociedade Brasileira de Instrucão in Rio de Janeiro, and for three years was research associate at the Foreign Policy Research Institute.

International Politics and the Sea: The Case of Brazil

Michael A. Morris

Universitas
BIBLIOTHECA
l'avensis

Westview Press / Boulder, Colorado

To my father, Delyte Wesley Morris,
Educator, Administrator, and Humanitarian

A Westview Replica Edition

Published in 1979 in the United States of America by
     Westview Press, Inc.
     5500 Central Avenue
     Boulder, Colorado 80301
     Frederick A. Praeger, Publisher

Library of Congress Catalog Card Number: 79-5040
ISBN: 0-89158-456-0

Printed and bound in the United States of America

Contents

Acknowledgements

Special thanks go to two scholars who had con-
fidence in this study when it was no more than an
idea. Professor Carlos Astiz of the State University of New York at Albany encouraged and assisted
me in this project from the earliest stage. Professor Candido Mendes of the Conjunto Universitário
Candido Mendes gave support and encouragement for a
stay in Rio de Janeiro, Brazil. Research support
also was given by the Organization of American States
and the Faculty Research Committee of Clemson
University.

Thanks are also due for the two typists of the
final manuscript, Martha Morris and Judy Payne.

My wife, Rekha, shared the experiences of this
study with me, and gave me encouragement throughout.

Scores of interviews were conducted in the
United States, Brazil, and several other Latin
American states for this study. Appreciation is expressed to all these individuals, mostly unnamed in
this study at their request, for their time and interest. It was particularly through these interviews
that ocean politics emerged as a process involving
people and groups, not just abstract interests.

Earlier versions of some parts of this study
have appeared in published form: (1) "Trends in
U.S.-Brazilian Maritime Relations," Inter-American
Economic Affairs, 17 (Winter 1973), 3-24. (2)
University of São Paulo Occasional Paper: "A Nova
Posição do Brasil no Mundo" (The New Position of
Brazil in the World), Geografia e Planejamento, 11
(1974). (3) "The Domestic Context of Brazilian Mari-
time Policy," Ocean Development and International
Law: The Journal of Marine Affairs, 4 (1977), 143-
169). (4) "Brazilian Ocean Policy in Historical
Perspective," Journal of Maritime Law and Commerce,

xi

10 (April 1979), 349-393. (5) "Brazil at the Third
United Nations Conference on the Law of the Sea,"
Ocean Development and International Law: The Journal
of Marine Affairs, 6 (1979), 131-177. (6) "Mudança
e Continuidade nas Relações Navais Brasileiras-
Americanas" (Change and Continuity in U.S.-Brazilian
Naval Relations), Revista Marítima Brasileira (the
official journal of the Brazilian Navy), (1979).
    The narrative of this study carries through
1978.

1. The Sea In Brazilian Foreign Policy

Brazil is one of the few viable Third World candidates for a relatively rapid transition from developing, somewhat dependent status to developed, major power status. Not only does Brazil appear to be crossing the threshold from underdevelopment to development, but it also seems headed toward the rank of a major power.[1]

Progress toward developed, major power status ultimately depends on Brazil's own continuing domestic and international growth, although developments in the international system and in key diplomatic relationships with other states also set limits on growth and upward mobility. Brazil's gradual movement upward in international status has coincided with some fundamental changes in the international system and in key diplomatic relations with other states, especially the United States. U.S.-Brazilian relations have traditionally been close, with the United States occupying a central position in Brazil's diplomatic constellation. More recently, fundamental changes in U.S. global strategy and hemispheric policy have coincided with changes in Brazilian policy to alter considerably the traditional contour of bilateral relations. International system changes have tended to reinforce these developments. Changes on each of these international dimensions, all relatively favorable to Brazil's rise, may be characterized as follows: (1) the international system has been evolving from a bipolar toward a multipolar order; (2) Brazilian foreign policy has been evolving from a position of weakness toward a position of strength; and (3) U.S.-Brazilian relations have been evolving from a state of relative dependency and inequality towards one of greater independence and equality.

Change in each area, however, has been uneven: the international system is still largely bipolar in

1

the military sphere; Brazilian foreign policy is
still hampered by important areas of weakness; and
U.S.-Brazilian relations are still influenced by a
legacy of dependency. And some other changes have
tended to brake Brazil's growth.

Change and continuity in this foreign policy
environment have therefore affected Brazil's rise in
complex ways. Brazil's position in the world is improving, in the sense of being more extensive and
independent than previously, but change and continuity intermingle. In order to clarify these relationships, key factors of change and continuity in
the international system and their economic, political, and military implications for Brazil will be
noted briefly. Trends in Brazilian foreign policy
have been shaped by and have also shaped this international environment, and will be subsequently
analyzed. Key characteristics of the international
system and of Brazilian foreign policy constitute
the setting for the topic of this book, trends in
Brazilian ocean policy. In a final section of this
chapter, Brazilian ocean policy is related to this
larger policy setting and the organization and ra-
tionale of the book are set forth.

CHANGE AND CONTINUITY IN THE INTERNATIONAL SYSTEM

Certain aspects of the international system remain unaltered: the nuclear balance is still shaped
by the two superpowers; the Soviet Union and China
are still basically antagonistic to the United
States; and Japan and Western Europe are still the
United States' most valued allies. The international system is nevertheless shifting gradually
from a bipolar order toward a multipolar one. The
resurgence of Japan and a united Europe have contributed toward economic multipolarity and the new
pragmatism of China has contributed to political
multipolarity. The achievement by the Soviet Union
of nuclear parity, the commercial challenge posed by
Japan and the European Common Market, and the gradual expansion of Chinese influence have all contributed to a relative decline of U.S. power. The
emergence of multipolarity has then involved changes
in the positions of all five major poles of power
in the international system--the United States,
the Soviet Union, Japan, a united Europe, and China.

Some aspects of the emerging new order augur
well for peace. The United States and the Soviet
Union have eased their cold war competition by seek-

ing détente, and the United States and China have
moved toward rapprochement. Other aspects of the
evolving international system are ridden with conflicts. Serious problems have arisen between the
Soviet Union and its former ally, China, just as
U.S. relations with Japan and the European Common
Market have been troubled by failure to forge mutually satisfactory economic relations. And Third
World states are generally growing more restive with
the existing order.

The shift from a bipolar system toward a multipolar one has important economic, political, and
security implications for Brazil's position in the
world.

Economic implications

The international economy has been relatively
congenial to Brazil's gradual emergence as a developed state, although there have been increasing
difficulties in sustaining growth since the 1973-
1974 oil crisis. A growing world economy and consequent availability of capital have had a highly
positive effect on Brazil's economy. Greater world
economic multipolarity has provided additional foreign sources of trade, investment, and finance,
which played a key role in the 1968-1973 economic
boom and have helped sustain growth since then. The
United States is still Brazil's largest single
trading partner and foreign investor and trade and
investment between Brazil and the United States
have been growing in absolute terms, but at a slower
rate than that of Japan and Western Europe. The
U.S. share of cumulative foreign investment in
Brazil has declined from about one-half in the early
1960s to about one-third of total foreign investment
in the country at present, and the U.S. share of
Brazilian trade fell as well from 33.7 per cent in
1964 to between a fourth and a fifth of the total
in recent years. Western Europe and Japan together
now share over one-third of Brazilian trade and
about half of foreign investment in Brazil. In
recent years, petroleum has averaged about a quarter
of total imports, mostly from the Middle East.[2]

The declining U.S. share of trade and foreign
investment is, in part, simply a natural concomitant
of greater economic multipolarity. However, the
decline also reflects problems in the bilateral relationship. For Brazil, important aspects of present bilateral relations were shaped during the period

3

of greater Brazilian dependence on the United
States, so that greater economic multipolarity, by
lessening reliance on its traditionally dominant
ally, has been welcomed.

Brazilian vulnerability to external economic
conditions still remains considerable, and the
Brazilian ability to shape these conditions continues to be relatively limited. Recent external developments with unfavorable implications for Brazil
include uncertain economic conditions in the developed states and soaring oil prices. In fact, the
increasing openness of Brazil's economy and greater
reliance on foreign investment, commerce, and technology tend to make it more vulnerable than previously to such adverse developments in the international economy.

New forms of dependency, however, may be more
acceptable than the traditional ones. Brazil's
economic dependency is much more diffuse than previously, since no one state occupies a dominant position in its foreign economic relations. Rapid
transition to developed status in a multipolar order
still involves national dependence on the world
economy, because of the importance the Brazilian
economic model places on external economic relations as an engine for domestic growth. But most
developed states are themselves subject to similar
vulnerabilities because of increasing global interdependence.

Some recent studies have recognized that
Brazilian dependence in general and on the United
States in particular has varied over time on a
number of levels. Viewed from such a dynamic perspective, Brazilian dependence has tended to de-
crease in recent years as national economic power
and diversification of foreign economic relations
have accelerated.[3]

Domestic developments have complemented the
relatively favorable global setting to project
Brazil into a more prominent international position.
An impressive array of natural and human resources
is being mobilized to support increasingly diversified industrial and agricultural production.
Brazil's potential for major power status has long
been acknowledged, but only with increasing mobiliza-
tion of national resources has a significant rise in
international influence appeared attainable.
Brazil's gross national product, over $100 billion
dollars annually by the late 1970s, is already about
three times that of the nearest South American com-

petitor, is larger than that of any other developing
state, and ranks tenth in the world. Greater economic power is supporting an increasingly active
foreign policy, with resultant expansion of Brazilian
influence in the international arena.

However, the transition to developed, major
power status, even if relatively rapid, promises to
last until at least the end of this century.
Brazil's development has been most uneven, with rapid
industrial growth in south-central Brazil taking
priority over balanced regional development and income redistribution. Per capita national income of
somewhat over $1,000 falls far short of that in the
leading industrial states. Domestic development and
international influence will be hindered as long as
fundamental disparities in the economy are not cor-
rected.

Political implications

Multipolarity has tended to increase diplomatic
flexibility for Third World states, especially the
larger, more dynamic ones, such as Brazil. New
poles of power have increased alternatives and cold
war competition has become more diffuse and has
shifted from the military toward the economic and
political spheres. As Brazil continues to emerge
as a major power in this setting, it is increasingly
recognized to occupy a distinctive position between
the First and Third Worlds. But Brazilian access to
key decisions affecting the contours of the global
order still remains difficult. As an aspirant major power, Brazil has objected to this lack of access or "freezing of [the structures of] world power,"[4] although such freezing of power appears less
characteristic of the emerging multipolar order than
of the preceding bipolar one.

The United States has indeed recognized Brazil's
new status as the predominant power in Latin America
on repeated occasions, and has sought to adjust the
bilateral relationship accordingly. The transition
to greater Brazilian independence and equality in
the bilateral relationship has been facilitated,
since the United States and Brazil continue to share
important common interests and both sides favor
compromise in resolving differences. Differences in
perspective continue, however, about the implications
of Brazil's growth and emergence as a major power for
the United States.

Brazilian policy-makers continue to value close

relations with the United States, but recognize that
national growth tends to diversify foreign relations,
lessen dependency, and lead to distinctive Brazilian
interests which do not necessarily correspond with
U.S. interests. Increasingly vigorous pursuit of
distinctive Brazilian interests therefore may contribute to a regional order, and indeed to a world
order, unlike that envisaged in U.S. policy.
Brazilian concern with the freezing of power illustrates just such a difference of perspective.

U.S. policy, in contrast, still harbours a
paternalistic attitude, since Brazil's growth seems
to be regarded more in terms of relieving U.S.
responsibilities on U.S. terms than as an autonomous
process of national self-assertion. A key implication of the Nixon Doctrine's emphasis on accommodation between the five major world power centers and
relative U.S. disengagement from the Third World was
encouragement of regional orders compatible with
U.S. interests.[5] In this scheme, Brazil, as the only
emerging major power in Latin America, would be dele-
gated U.S. regional responsibilities and would assist integration of a stable regional order into a
five power world order. Subsequent U.S. administrations have continued to stress order in the Third
World on U.S. terms while finding it difficult to
commit sufficient resources to assist the evolution
of compatible regional systems. Accordingly, the
U.S. has continued to look to strong regional allies,
including Brazil, for support as regional poles of
power and stability, but with uneven results.

Military implications

Security considerations, especially cold war
competition between the two superpowers, tended to
shape international politics during the bipolar era.
The Third World acquired considerable importance as
a cold war battleground, and security interests
seemed to require a substantial U.S. commitment to
economic development of developing states. For
example, bilateral relations both before and after
the 1964 coup included close collaboration between
the Brazilian and American militaries and sizable
assistance for development. Superpower détente and
the emergence of multipolarity have contributed to
subsequent U.S. reassessment of its global security
interests and commitment to Third World development.
Superpower military competition has become less
prominent and traditional U.S. concern with commu-

nist threats to the Third World has been deemphasized. As on the economic front, bilateral military ties have accordingly declined relative to other international military contacts. Compatible regional powers, as noted, are still encouraged to take up the slack left from a diminished U.S. world role to establish stable regional orders.

Brazilian policy-makers have welcomed a more benign international security environment, but they have explicitly rejected seeming regional implications of recent U.S. policy of spheres of influence and Brazilian regional hegemony. Instead, they have moved to diversify military contacts and envisage self-sufficiency in the longer-run. Development of a mutually acceptable image of Brazil's more influential position in the world is perhaps the most basic challenge posed by change for the bilateral relationship.

TRENDS IN BRAZILIAN FOREIGN POLICY

In spite of differences in emphasis, all military governments since the 1964 coup have shared certain common aims, which differ in several important respects from those held by preceding civilian governments. A more active foreign policy has been promoted to assist domestic economic development and enhance national security.[6] Although this foreign policy orientation is primarily concerned with supporting domestic concerns, especially economic development and national security, correction of uneven regional development and income disparities is not stressed. In sum, "foreign policy has become a conscious instrument of an increasingly conscious national development policy."[7] In the long run, the attainment of major power status is expected to result from Brazil's domestic and international growth. Eventual attainment of developed, major power status may shift the central concern of Brazilian foreign policy from domestic development toward international prestige and influence, but such a trend is still inchoate.

Considerable continuity in the conduct of Brazilian foreign policy by successive military governments since 1964 has flowed from common objectives. Continuity in foreign policy will characterize the new Figueiredo administration as well, which is to take office on March 15, 1979, according to the Foreign Minister-designate, Ramiro Elisio

Saraiva Guerreiro. Of particular interest for this study, Sr. Saraiva Guerreiro has been a leading member of the Brazilian maritime community, including head of the Brazilian delegation to the Third United Nations Conference on the Law of the Sea.

A general foreign policy approach endorsed by the successive military governments, albeit with differences of emphasis, may be described through four major characteristics. These four characteristics, taken together, have adapted the aspirations of an emerging major power well to the situational constraints and opportunities of an emerging multipolar order.

Diversification

A concerted program to diversify markets and products for export has been carried out in order to boost economic development at home while lessening diplomatic dependence on the United States and economic dependence on specific commodities. Brazilian dependence on coffee, for example, has declined considerably in the past decade. The share of coffee in Brazilian exports fell from 53 per cent in 1964 to less than 20 per cent in recent years, while the proportion of industrial exports rose in the same period from 5 per cent to about one-third of the total. Changes in the international system, especially the emergence of economic multipolarity, have facilitated diversification of export markets as well. Trade diversification has been especially marked in the cases of Western Europe and Japan, as noted, and relations with Latin America, other developing states, and the socialist states are also being intensified.

The first military government of Castello Branco did maintain particularly close relations with the United States, while all subsequent military governments have pressed diversification more and have not hesitated to defend national interests vigorously when in conflict with those of the United States. In retrospect, even the foreign policy of Castello Branco was not subservient to the United States, and instead seems to have regarded especially close cooperation with the United States as necessary in dealing with the domestic political and economic crisis.

Expansion of interests

While Brazilian foreign policy remains largely

8

oriented toward support of internal needs--to assist
domestic development and enhance national security--
Brazil's domestic and international growth is tending to expand Brazilian international interests.
This includes Brazil's emergence as an aid donor and
heightened Brazilian concern with achieving a direct
participant role in decisions on global economic,
political, and military issues. The diversification
policy, too, tends to expand Brazilian international
interests.

This expansion of interests has been largely
benign, in spite of arguments to the contrary. Some
nationalist circles in Spanish America, for example,
have argued that increasing Brazilian involvement
in Bolivia, Paraguay, and Uruguay demonstrates
imperialistic designs. The broad Escola Superior de
Guerra definition of national security does lead to
concern about possible instability in the border
areas, although Brazil's growing international involvement has largely been limited to expansion of
economic and political interests. As noted, Brazil
has rejected any hegemonic designs in Latin America,
either on its own or in association with the United
States. The impact of Brazil's growth is nevertheless being felt most directly in neighboring Latin
American states, since Brazil has not been con-
fronted with a freezing of the structures of power
on a regional scale, as has tended to occur on a
global scale.

Greater assertiveness of interests

The transition from bipolarity to multipolarity
has not altered many features of the international
system which Brazil regards as inimical to its progress toward developed, major power status. Brazil
has expressed its dissatisfaction with unfair or
biased economic, political, and military structures
embedded in the existing international order, and
has clearly defined positions critical of the status
quo. For example, Brazil has criticized the existing
structure of world trade, especially trade barriers
in the developed states, as making the transition
toward development difficult. Disarmament and arms
control efforts, such as the non-nuclear proliferation treaty, have been criticized as often serving
the interests of the established great powers. The
sudden concern of the developed states with pollu-
tion--maritime or land-based--has been regarded as
self-serving as well and possibly inimical to

9

developing states' interests.

Concerted efforts have been made to generate change, via bilateral and multilateral channels. In multilateral forums, the injustice of the freezing of power and the obligation of "collective economic security"[8] have been emphasized to mobilize Third World support against the developed states. Even though Brazil aspires to leave developing for developed status, it has increasingly emphasized its affinity of interests with Third World states in forging a more equitable international system. More recently, however, some radical Third World interpretations of the New International Economic Order have posed some awkward policy dilemmas for Brazil, which favors more moderate, pragmatic approaches to change.[9]

Policy dilemmas posed for an emerging major power situated between the First and Third Worlds, such as Brazil, have been evident as well in bilateral dealings with developed states. Greater assertiveness of Brazilian interests has been geared toward reshaping traditional relationships with the United States, and, more broadly, toward gaining greater access to and influence in the international order. But Brazil's desire for change is relative, since the bulk of Brazil's international relationships have been and are likely to remain with developed states, even with diversification. Pressure for change accordingly tends to be limited to modifying the rules of the game to permit easier access to the rich men's club, rather than overturning the rules, as some Third World states less well endowed than Brazil appear to want.

Some initiatives in foreign policy by civilian governments in the early 1960s resemble the above foreign policy developments--diversification, expansion of interests, and greater assertiveness of interests--more in appearance than in substance. In the early 1960s, Brazil was in a position of relative economic weakness, so that foreign policy initiatives were sustained largely by rhetoric or ideology. A successful broadening and defense of Brazilian interests internationally had to be undertaken from a position of strength, which occurred from the late 1960s and early 1970s.

Pragmatism

Pragmatism has increasingly displaced ideology as a foreign policy consideration. During the first

10

years of military government after the 1964 coup,
there was great concern with alleged communist subversion from Cuba and elsewhere, just as leftist
ideological considerations tended to influence
foreign policy during the last years of civilian
government. The subsequent decline of the notion
of ideological frontiers," articulated by the first
military government of Castello Branco, permitted a
reassertion of Itamaraty's (the Brazilian foreign
ministry) traditional low-key, moderate approach to
diplomacy. While the Geisel administration has been
more avowedly pragmatic and less ideological than
the preceding military governments, they, too, tended
to take pragmatic foreign policy postures on non-
cold war matters.

TRENDS IN BRAZILIAN OCEAN POLICY

International aspects of Brazilian ocean affairs fall within the purview of Brazilian foreign
policy, so Brazilian ocean policy reflects the four
foreign policy characteristics sketched above, and
operates within the constraints and opportunities
of the international system. The applicability of
the four foreign policy characteristics to Brazilian
ocean policy may be noted explicitly.
First, Brazil's international maritime relations, long involving primarily the United States,
have been diversifying rapidly over the past decade.
Second, over the past decade, Brazilian maritime
interests have likewise expanded quite rapidly and
Brazil has emerged as a significant maritime power.
Third, this rise in maritime status internationally has not been easy and has required greater
assertiveness of maritime interests. The traditional
ocean order includes "freedom of the seas" and liner
conferences, which have appeared as examples of
"freezing of power" from the perspective of an
aspirant power such as Brazil. This required
changing the existing ocean order and reshaping maritime relations with developed states, but at the
same time, Brazil has been reluctant to endorse radical planks or interpretations of the New International Economic Order as they apply to the maritime
sphere, particularly the deep seabed. For example,
Brazilian policy-makers have cited opposition of
developed states to a strong international deep
seabed authority as an example of the freezing of
power, although Brazil has been willing to compromise,

11

in contrast to radical states, by favoring a major role for multinational corporations as well.

So in applying the first three foreign policy characteristics (diversification, expansion of interests, and greater assertiveness of interests), Brazilian ocean policy has generally been pragmatic, the fourth characteristic. Another example of pragmatism in ocean affairs is the extension of the territorial sea to 200 miles in 1970, which has been considered as "a true archetype of a new style of foreign policy" since distinctive Brazilian interests were subsequently asserted successfully, without a confrontation with the United States, due to circumspect diplomacy.[10] It is significant that this analysis by a left-leaning critic of the military regime scores current Brazilian foreign policy pragmatism as "opportunism," but still acknowledges the change in Brazilian posture vis-à-vis the United States from deference to assertiveness of interests and positive results achieved therefrom.

Brazil's emergence as a maritime power therefore parallels and is part of broader Brazilian emergence as a major power, and is examined in detail in subsequent chapters. But ocean affairs are also distinctive, so that trends in Brazilian ocean policy are not merely derived from trends in Brazilian foreign policy, as affected by the international system.

Analysis of Brazilian ocean affairs in subsequent chapters will call attention to maritime trends and events which are distinctive, as well as those which are derivative in nature or linked to broader issues. Ocean affairs in general, like Brazilian ocean policy in particular, are distinctive in at least five ways, justifying a separate focus.

First, ocean affairs overlap both domestic and foreign policy and constitute a relatively cohesive, distinguishable universe or sub-system of national events. Domestically, a maritime community manages interrelated maritime interests, including naval affairs, shipping, and ocean resources, with the navy involved in all aspects of maritime affairs. Internationally, defense and pursuit of maritime interests involve interaction between national ocean policies and participation in international maritime conferences and negotiations, all with their own particular traditions and dynamics. A maritime environment therefore often conditions ocean politics in ways distinctive from politics involving land masses.

Ocean policy not only exhibits distinctive patterns, but also is having an increasing impact on both national and foreign affairs. The distinctive, increasingly important impact of ocean policy on the domestic and international fronts respectively constitute points two and three.

Second, the increasing importance of ocean policy for domestic affairs justifies extended examination of Brazilian maritime affairs. Domestically, the growth of maritime power and interests, including naval and merchant marine growth, more intensive exploitation of ocean resources, and a 200-mile territorial sea since 1970, has had an increasing impact on national development. The navy's responsibility for development and security of the country's extensive riverine network has linked maritime affairs to national integration as well.

Third, the increasing international importance of maritime affairs justifies extended examination of ocean policy. Ocean affairs occupy an increasingly important position in international politics and in foreign policy because of technological, economic, and political changes. New resource extraction possibilities and greater ocean uses have evoked complex national and international responses. At the global level, changes have generally been unsettling as demands for a new ocean order have escalated. Developed states, as the primary beneficiaries of the old ocean order, have faced a challenge of accommodating change with traditional policies. Developing states have faced the dual challenge of promoting a new global ocean order more compatible with their interests and forging a national ocean policy, for all practical purposes, for the first time.

Fourth, Brazil is a particularly important example of these challenges for Third World ocean policies, because its emergence as a major power is paralleled by its emergence as a maritime power. Ocean affairs have become increasingly important for Brazilian foreign policy, and Brazil, in turn, has come to occupy a distinctive position in bilateral, regional, and global negotiations for a new ocean order. Although national ocean policy has evolved erratically, Brazil has been prominent among developing states in building maritime capabilities across a broad front. Consequently, Brazil is increasingly coming to stand between the First and Third Worlds in the maritime sphere.[11]

Fifth, the increasing outreach of Brazilian

ocean policy involves complex interaction with other national ocean policies of both developed and developing states, and invites comparisons with them. The development of a comprehensive profile of Brazilian ocean policy throughout the course of this study hopefully will encourage other overviews of national ocean policies, especially those of Third World states which have been few and far between, and will generate fruitful comparisons. Many Third World states, of course, have been too burdened with other problems to develop an ocean policy or only have very limited maritime potential. Depending on definition, this study indeed may be the first comprehensive profile of the ocean policy of a significant Third World state.

A comprehensive survey is made in subsequent chapters of all aspects of Brazilian ocean policy, including domestic influences, participation at international maritime conferences, naval affairs, ocean resources, and shipping. The first portion of the study presents a general overview of Brazilian ocean policy (Chapters 2 through 6), with later chapters presenting more specific profiles of major maritime sectors (Chapters 5 through 8). Chapters 5 and 6 on the navy overlap both portions of the study, since the navy at once is responsible for overall coordination of maritime affairs and is itself a major maritime sector. The two parts of the study are further integrated, because the first, general portion of the study presents many findings on which the later, sectoral chapters build, while the later part of the study indicates how ocean policy is expressed through specific sectors. A final chapter compares findings about Brazilian ocean policy with other states, both developing and developed.

NOTES

1. Considerable attention has been focused in recent years on Brazil's emergence as a major power. See, for example, the following works and others cited therein: William Perry, Contemporary Brazilian Foreign Policy: The International Strategy of an Emerging Power, Foreign Policy Papers, Vol. 2, No. 6 (Beverly Hills, California: Sage Publications, 1976); and Ronald M. Schneider, Brazil: Foreign Policy of a Future World Power (Boulder, Colorado: Westview Press, 1976). For an analysis by this author of Brazil's emergence as a major power, particularly how Brazil's growth has been projecting the

country more actively into international affairs and some of
the consequences of this new role, see the University of São
Paulo Occasional Paper by Michael A. Morris, "A Nova Posição
do Brasil no Mundo," Geografia e Planajamento 11 (1974). This
author was also the Coordinator of a major research project
in two volumes on the related topic, "Brazil's International
Role in the Seventies," at the Foreign Policy Research
Institute during 1972-1973.

2. See, for example, recent issues of the following reports:
U.S., Department of State, Background Notes: Brazil; and U.S.,
Department of Commerce, Foreign Economic Trends and Their
Implications for the United States: Brazil. Also see a re-
cent synthesis by Werner Baer and Carlos Von Doellinger,
"Determinants of Brazil's Foreign Economic Policy," in Latin
America and World Economy: A Changing International Order, ed.
Joseph Grunwald (Beverly Hills, California: Sage Publications,
1978), pp. 146-161. U.S. aid is not discussed here, since the
United States is phasing out its bilateral development assistance programs to Brazil. Increased Brazilian capabilities
and greater U.S. aid emphasis on multilateral rather than
bilateral channels are responsible for this change. The
United States does remain the largest donor to multilateral
lending institutions, from which Brazil is a major recipient
of assistance, but this has not presented problems for
bilateral relations with Brazil, in part because the U.S.
exercises much less control over multilateral aid than
bilateral aid.

3. Robert A. Packenham, "Trends in Brazilian National De-
pendency Since 1964," in Brazil in the Seventies, ed. Riordan
Roett (Washington, D.C.: American Enterprise Institute for
Public Policy Research, 1976), pp. 89-115. Gregory F.
Treverton, "Latin America in World Politics: The Next
Decade," Adelphi Papers 137 (Summer 1977): 31.

4. J. A. de Araújo Castro, "O Congelamento do Poder Mundial,"
Revista Brasileira de Estudos Políticos, 33 (1972).

5. George Liska acknowledged that the Nixon Doctrine was de-
liberately ambiguous about this point, but that its logic led
it to be vitally concerned with the emergence of stable regional orders in the developing world which would dovetail
with entente between the five major world powers. Liska concluded that these U.S. policy preferences would very likely
survive the Nixon administration, since the Nixon Doctrine re-
tained important aspects of past administrations' foreign
policies while reshaping policy in response to new world
events. George Liska, "The Third World: Regional Systems
and Global Order," in Retreat From Empire?: The First Nixon

Administration, ed. Robert E. Osgood (Baltimore: The Johns Hopkins University Press, 1973), pp. 279-343.

6. The Escola Superior de Guerra (National War College) doctrine linking development and security—development is necessary to overcome national weaknesses which ultimately threaten security, while security provides the necessary stability for development—has had a profound impact on policy-makers. See Chapters 2, 5, and 6 for more details on ESG doctrine as related to ocean affairs.

7. Brady B. Tyson, "Brazil," in Latin American Foreign Policies: An Analysis, eds. Harold Eugene Davis and Larman Wilson (Baltimore: The Johns Hopkins University Press, 1975), p. 223.

8. Collective economic security has been presented as the economic counterpart to the collective security obligation of the United Nations Charter. That is, just as all states must cooperate in opposing aggression, so, too, must they cooperate in overcoming underdevelopment. See Sergio Armando Frazão, "Desenvolvimento Econômico e Expansão no Mundo de Hoje: O Conceito de Segurança Coletiva," Revista Brasileira de Política Internacional 55-56 (Sept.-Dec. 1971). This article was originally presented as an address to the XXVI Session of the United Nations General Assembly.

9. Wayne A. Selcher, Brazil's Multilateral Relations: Between First and Third Worlds (Boulder, Colorado: Westview Press, 1978), pp. 16-17, 75-76. Also see Chapter 4 of this book.

10. Carlos Estevan Martins, Brasil-Estados Unidos dos 60 aos 70 (São Paulo: CEBRAP, 1972), pp. 56-58. Also see Celso Lafer and Félix Peña, Argentina y Brasil en el sistema de relaciones internacionales (Buenos Aires: Ediciones Nueva Visión, 1973), especially page 114.

11. The Brazilian Navy's representative on the Brazilian delegation to the Third United Nations Conference on the Law of the Sea has emphasized that Brasilian maritime interests are not typical of either those of developing or developed states, so that Brazil should not identify exclusively with either group. Murillo Souto Maior de Castro, "O Direito do Mar e o Problema do Mar Territorial," Revista Marítima Brasileira 93 (July-September 1973): 86. On this same point, see also an editorial from O Estado de São Paulo, "O que se espera da diplomacia brasileira," June 11, 1971, page 3.

2. Brazilian Ocean Policy in Domestic Politics

The sea has had a major impact on Brazilian history via maritime colonization, coastal settlements linked by the sea, and overseas commerce. Brazil's 4,500 mile maritime frontier along the littoral and around the islands is the most extensive of any South American or South Atlantic state and is one of the longest in the world. Brazilian waters, since the extension of the territorial sea in 1970 from 12 to 200 miles, comprise over 900,000 square miles, almost one-third of Brazil's enormous land area.

The prominent geographical characteristics of the extensive Brazilian littoral and its likewise extensive territorial sea may be summarized briefly. The littoral stretches southeastwardly from the Oiapoque river at 4°N, on the northern border with French Guiana, past the mouth of the Amazon, then round the Brazilian bulge, where the South American and African land masses are but some 1,600 miles distant. The high seas separating the two continents are narrowed still further by national waters, which on the Brazilian side include the 200-mile territorial sea off the northeastern bulge (35°W) and adjoining national waters beyond surrounding the Fernando de Noronha archipelago (32°25'W) and São Pedro and São Paulo rocks (29°22'W). The coastline with its 200-mile territorial sea then proceeds southwestwardly, with an isolated pocket of territorial sea beyond the 200-mile limit surrounding the islands of Trinidade and Martin Vaz lying at 20°30'S, to the Chui rivulet on the border with Uguguay at 34°S.

Brazil's prominent position in the South

Atlantic has nevertheless not led it to become a
maritime-oriented states. Systematic efforts have
not generally been made to utilize the ocean in support of national policies. With undeveloped continental open spaces, Brazil, unlike the mother
country, Portugal, did not feel compelled to turn
toward the sea to survive. Nor has Brazil pursued
national greatness via both land--and maritime--
based power, like its northern neighbor of similar
continental dimensions, the United States.

Increasing efforts have been made during the
past decade to utilize ocean space and the resources
of the sea for national policy ends. Domestic
changes help explain new Brazilian approaches to
the sea. The domestic context of Brazil's emerging
ocean policy will be discussed from three perspectives. Basic national policy guidelines will be
examined first, with particular attention given to
their influence in shaping ocean policy. Bureaucratic politics has shaped, but also has been shaped
by, these guidelines, and will be examined in a
subsequent section. International politics, too,
has played an important role in shaping Brazilian
ocean policy, and its relationship to the domestic
context will be explored in a final section.

POLICY GUIDELINES

Brazilian military thought has been of central
importance for the policy process since early 1964,
when the armed forces overthrew the civilian Goulart
government. The roots of current military doctrine
can be traced to the National War College (Escola
Superior de Guerra, ESG), which was established a-
long US lines in 1949 for advanced career training
of promising officers from all three armed services.
American influence on ESG thought in the early years
was extensive, directly via US advisors and US
counterinsurgency doctrine as well as through more
diffuse channels such as frequent advanced training
of Brazilian officers in the United States and heavy
reliance on US weapons. Military ties with the
United States have remained close over the years,
but a rather distinctive EGS doctrine linking development and security gradually emerged.

The basic tenet of ESG national security doctrine is that development and security are inextri-
cably linked. On the one hand, satisfactory economic
development cannot be achieved without internal order

and well-prepared and equipped armed forces. Conversely, national security can only be broad-based if a healthy economy is able to generate resources for societal demands and military necessities. From this premise, it is concluded that national policies should seek to harmonize both developmental and security needs as far as possible. Policy measures taken to speed up economic development and modernize and expand the armed forces are consequently considered to be complementary.

Events leading up to the 1964 coup d'état confirmed the validity of the central development-security postulate of military thinking according to successive military governments. By 1963 the economy was encountering extremely serious problems and political agitation was rising on both the right and the left, threatening a breakdown of order. As interpreted by ESG doctrine, economic development was being compromised by the lack of political order while national security was being undermined by impending economic chaos and an ambiguous governmental stance toward communism. The first military government of Castello Branco, moreover, was dominated by leading ESG figures and concepts. Successive military governments did modify certain specific ideas and policies associated with ESG thinking, such as the immediacy of the military threat of communism and the consequent need for an intimate alliance with the United States. The central ESG doctrine linking development and security issues nevertheless "permeated all major military groups in Brazil" and was "accepted as a basic new fact of political and military life."[1] Many influential civilians have participated in ESG courses as well, which helped shape a common way of thinking about national problems among ruling elites after 1964.

Numerous benefits have flowed from the development-security guideline for national policies. Political order imposed from above helped stabilize the economy from 1964-1967 and prepared the ground for sustained high economic growth rates in subsequent years. The rationalistic bent of military thought led to an increase in planning and some simplification of formidable bureaucratic procedures. Pragmatism, too, was evident in the military willingness to develop different balances between security and developmental factors according to the concrete circumstances of different situations. Foreign participation has been encouraged in many areas of the economy, for instance, in order to boost industrial production. In some other areas, especially

19

those regarded as directly related to security, national self-sufficiency has been stressed. Such pragmatic, rationalistic manipulation of developmental and security policies, at times with an emphasis on conservative measures and at other times on nationalistic onces, tended to have positive economic results, particularly during the first decade of military rule.

Unfortunate results have also been derived from the security-development binomial. With security and development regarded as interdependent, doctine justifies the perpetuation of military rule. The new, broad definition of security tended to expand the mission of the military in politics beyond the traditional "moderating" role of intervening temporarily to protect constitutional order. Internal security and civic action missions in the 1950s marked the incipient trend toward the expansion of political functions of the military. This was accentuated by the economic and political crisis of the early 1960s and led to direct military rule in 1964. Military rule began as an interim solution to impose order and permit a relatively rapid return to democracy. By the late 1960s, the military, with the cooperation of technocrats, had come to take on the much more extensive tasks of reshaping both the economy and the political system to provide conditions for continuing growth and stability. A return to democracy is still promised, although now, this apparently refers to the controlled development of a new political class which can carry on some non-disruptive political tasks at the margin of an authoritarian system.

Security and development without representative politics has taken its toll on civil liberties and the lower classes. The absence of checks and balances has led to a wide variety of authoritarian measures, from censorship and suppression of political dissent to repression where threats to national security have been perceived. Without the tugs and pulls of diverse political forces, significant income redistribution measures have been postponed in a country of great regional and class disparities.

Since history reconfirms the validity of the security-development doctrine to those in power, both its negative and positive aspects tend to be perpetuated. The ESG has played a leading role in inculcating this line of thinking in upper-level military officers and technocrats. Officers at the rank equivalent to Colonel or Brigadier General from

all three services, along with prominent government
and private sector members, participate in the year-
long ESG course aimed at developing and applying the
security-development doctrine. Attendance at the
ESG, a recent study concludes, is the best indicator
of an officer's prospects of reaching three-or four-
star rank. Biographical information of the most
senior army Colonels and Brigadier Generals indicates a high degree of attendance at the ESG, while
those ranking Colonels who have not been selected
for the National War College are more likely to be
retired than promoted. Nearly all full Generals
have attended the ESG and those few Divisional
Generals who had not attended that institution were
not expected to receive a further promotion. The
same considerations hold true for navy and air force
officers of equivalent rank.[2]

Brazilian national security doctrine then helps
unite the views of all three armed services, but it
also has required adaptation to the peculiarities of
each service. In the case of the navy, the basic
security-development policy guideline has been broadly adapted to the requirements of maritime policy.
Brazilian waters, naval writers stress, are an important resource for national development and generate corresponding security requirements, especially
since the territorial sea was extended to 200 miles
in 1970.[3] Developmental components of maritime
policy include the merchant marine, the shipbuilding
industry, ports, fishing, and mineral exploration
while the security component or "naval power" ("poder
naval") refers to the navy. Balanced development of
the fleet and the merchant marine, provision of
corresponding civilian and military infrastructure,
and inculcation of a national maritime mentality
should all be undertaken to strengthen the development and security components of maritime policy,
together referred to as "maritime power" ("poder
marítimo").

Such overlaps of national security and development in maritime affairs have tended to expand
the traditional activities of the navy, just as they
have expanded the role of the armed forces in national life in general. The security implications
of civilian maritime activities, especially maritime
transportation, led to increasing navy involvement
after the 1964 revolution imposed new policy guidelines.[4] The navy also has become involved in other
maritime areas where no other group was able to perform necessary functions, such as maritime instruction, hydrography, oceangraphic research, and support

for development of isolated riverine and coastal settlements. The increasingly active position of the navy in maritime affairs has been accompanied by an extensive program of weapons modernization, a trend evident in the other armed services as well.

Policy evolution of developmental and security activities relating to the sea therefore broadly reflects that of national developmental and security policies. More detailed elaboration of maritime policy from the security-development premise, however, has not been feasible for two reasons.

First, the security-development policy guideline is linked only in logic but not in spirit to maritime affairs. The maritime and terrestrial dimensions of national development and security, in accord with the logic of doctrine, should be part of a single process.[5] But the terrestrial in fact has dominated national priorities since at least the fall of the Empire in 1889, often at the expense of maritime affairs and ultimately of national well-being.

A recurring plea in navy writings is that Brazilians acquire a maritime mentality to appreciate the importance of the sea for national development and security, such as that which existed under the Empire.[6] Subsequent efforts to develop maritime activities have been sporadic during most of this century, as in the shipbuilding industry. This contrasts with a series of national development strategies for coordinating and stimulating terrestrial activities for industrialization, including road but not riverine or maritime transportation. Since economic realities frequently recommend more balanced development, particularly since the 1973-1974 oil crisis, historical responsibility for the priority of land transportation has been attributed to the predominance of the army over the navy in politics throughout this century.[7] More immediately, the Escola Superior de Guerra has been associated with the army and its national security doctrine is rooted in land-based counterinsurgency theory. Analysis of the writings of the prominent army intellectual, General Golbery do Couto e Silva, illustrates some of the difficulties in reconciling army and navy thinking.

Golbery made a heavy imprint on ESG thinking through his teaching and writings during the school's formative decade of the 1950's. Since then he has occupied extremely influential positions in successive military governments.[8] Central to his

thought is that security threats emanate from one
continental land mass to threaten another. On the
one hand, no likely security threats to Brazil are
presented by the geopolitical land mass circumscribed by a sweeping internal semicircle ("hemiciclo interior") encompassing North and South
America and part of Antarctica. Brazil's major task
on the South American continent is instead to speed
up national integration and project its influence
peacefully in surrounding states. On the other hand,
the Eurasian land mass lying beyond the Western
hemisphere constitutes an enormous, external geopolitical area ("hemiciclo exterior") from which
security threats to Brazil are likely to emerge.
The South Atlantic is important both as a barrier to
aggression via vulnerable African states and as a
vital channel of communication for the West in
countering encroachments from Eurasia.

Maritime power, in Golbery's thought, is clearly
derivative from and subordinate to land power. It
only deserves mention as an element in repelling
land-based aggression or as a possible detraction
from the central task of building up land power.
Reflecting the traditional opposition in classical
geopolitical thinking between land and sea power,
Golbery concludes: "It is between the two (internal
and external geopolitics) that a great Brazilian
dilemma is situated, much more important tomorrow
than even today--that of antagonism between continental forces and maritime attractions".[9]

Recent work of another Brazilian general, Carlos
de Meira Mattos, on geopolitics and Brazil does hold
some interest for ocean affairs. Meira Mattos
shares the same basic outlook and orientation as
Golbery, and he, too, was associated with the ESG as
head of the political affairs section. His thought
accordingly been regarded as updating Golbery's
similar influential vision of a decade previously.[10]
Befitting an army general, Meira Mattos clearly has
followed Golbery's lead in stressing land masses as
focal points for threats and responses. He went a
step further, however, in a 1975 book by citing navy
writers approvingly who have stressed the importance
of the sea for Brazil.[11] Then in a 1977 book, Meira
Mattos put considerable stress on the importance of
the South Atlantic for Brazil, and even proposed a
South Atlantic strategy.[12]

In an interview with this writer, General Meira
Mattos indicated that greater stress in his later
work on ocean affairs did not represent any funda-

mental change in orientation but rather represented
pragmatic adaptation to changing circumstances. He
still acknowledged in the interview that continental
concerns of Brazilian geopolitical thought have not
permitted serious analysis about the implications of
the importance of the sea. Hopefully, he added, his
latest book would help call attention to this traditional omission even though it does not reflect the
majority position within the armed forces.[13]

Not only is the marriage of land-based and
ocean strategy a minority position, as Meira Mattos
admitted, but the marriage is precarious even in
his own work. Brazil's destiny, according to Meira
Mattos, is to open up the hinterland, whose development was held back by dependence on maritime communication until a highway network was developed
which could facilitate "the continentalization of
the South American hinterland."[14]

While Brazilian geopolitical thought has not
integrated maritime issues with its major focus on
land masses, "Argentine geopolitical thinking is
much more ocean-oriented than Brazilian."[15] In apparent recognition of this unsatisfactory state of
affairs, the ESG recently has begun to refine a
national military doctrine for combined use of the
three services.[16] The ESG will also begin to rotate
its directorship between all three services from
1979, when Admiral Carlos Henrique Rezende de
Noronha will become the first ESG head since 1964
from the air force or navy.[17]

Second the ESG security-development doctrine
has been excessivly abstract to provide specific
direction for maritime policy. The Escola Superior
de Guerra does help prepare a homogeneous elite of
high-level civilians and military officers for
directing broad national policy defined by the
doctrine. But, adds the navy officer responsible
for advanced instruction at the Naval War College
(Escola de Guerra Naval), the ESG is not oriented
specifically toward navy problems. Each service
instead has unique problems and has devised specific
doctrinal elements or approaches for dealing with
them. Unlike the Escola Superior de Guerra, for
example, where attendance is voluntary at the upper
career level, all eligible navy officers must at-
tend courses at the Naval War College during three
different periods of their careers, when a common
approach to technical and doctrinal questions
peculiar to the navy is developed.[18]

But the navy's maritime power doctrine leaves

much to be desired as well. The maritime power
doctrine is almost as abstract as the related
security-development doctrine, and has not proved
to be a sufficiently detailed guideline for maritime
policy either. To the extent maritime policy has
been fleshed in, specific, concrete measures, not
ambitious, abstract policy guidelines are responsible.

Specific measures related to policy coordination undertaken by or affecting the navy are especially important, since it has emerged as the central
policy-maker in domestic maritime affairs. Proposals for a Ministry of Defense to coordinate defense matters, for example, have emanated from the
army but would have a direct impact on the navy
policy coordination role. Both the navy and the
air force have consistently opposed the proposed
measure, which they have feared would facilitate
army interference in their respective service affairs.[19] As matters stand, most navy problems are
generally resolved within the navy hierarchy, which
culminates in the office of the Navy Minister. The
Navy General Staff (Estado Maior da Armada) is
largely limited to planning functions and the Armed
Forces General Staff (Estado Maior das Forças
Armadas), while directly linked to the president and
superior in the policy hierarchy to the Estado Maior
da Armada, is mostly limited in power to recommenda-
tions. Like the proposed Ministry of Defense, the
Armed Forces General Staff has been mistrusted by
the navy due to traditional army predominance in
the body.

Another measure, a master plan (Plano Diretor
da Marinha), was inaugurated in 1963 within the navy
to encourage both long- and short- term planning by
setting basic overall objectives from which biennial
plans would be derived. Only by 1967 did the master
plan system begin to be organized effectively and
implemented by the various operational sectors of
the navy, and serious problems continue to hinder
planning.[20]

Efforts to coordinate Brazilian maritime affairs began to extend to other departments as well
in the late 1960s, with the navy usually playing a
leading role. In 1968, the Interministerial Commission on the Exploration and Utilization of the
Seabed and Oceans (CIEFMAR) was created to formulate
and coordinate a Brazilian policy for the recently
inaugurated United Nations debates on the seabed
beyond the limits of national jurisdiction. Since
the scope of the commission was foreign, not domes-

tic, affairs (to develop a Brazilian policy for international negotiations on the law of the sea), it was chaired by the Ministry of Foreign Relations. Nine other governmental agencies besides the Ministry of Foreign Relations (Itamaraty) had interests in the area and were included in the commission's membership.[21]

In June 1970, a few months after the territorial sea was extended to 200 miles, a second body, the Interministerial Study Commission for Matters Related to Brazilian Policy on Ocean Resources, was created to formulate and coordinate a national maritime policy. Since the purpose of the Study Commission was to develop a marine resources policy for areas within national jurisdiction (internal waters, the continental shelf and the territorial sea), the navy, rather than Itamaraty, occupied the presidency. In contrast to CIEFMAR, the Study Commission was streamlined to include only six governmental agencies as permanent members, two of which were divisions of the navy.[22]

Provisions were made for coordination between the international negotiating stances developed in CIEFMAR and the domestic policy initiatives in the area of maritime resources taken by the Study Commission. The Study Commission, however, has only met infrequently and has not played an important role in shaping an interdepartmental maritime policy.[23] And its mandate was limited to marine resources, so that important areas of maritime affairs, such as ports, shipbuilding, and the merchant marine were left either to take isolated policy initiatives or to flounder.

A similar interministerial Commission for Resources of the Sea, chaired as well by the Navy ministry, was created in 1974 with higher level representation from nine governmental agencies.[24] But progress has again been slow in improving maritime policy coordination, and only marine resources were the object of policy coordination. There has been no effective overall policy coordination of maritime affairs, it is recognized, and a confused network of legislation governs activities in the different maritime sectors.[25]

In spite of the absence of an effective national maritime policy, important activities have been taken in various maritime sectors. But without effective overall direction, uneven development, distortions and overlaps inevitably occurred.[26]

Several conclusions about the mixed record of

policy guidelines for maritime affairs stand out. Only recently has the sea, and especially Brazilian waters, been recognized as an important resource for national development requiring an integrated maritime policy. The enlargement of the territorial sea to 200 miles in 1970 extended the scope of maritime affairs and accentuated the importance of developing a national maritime policy. Both general and specific policy guidelines in the late 1960s and early 1970s, however, failed to produce an effective maritime policy. Implicit or explicit guidelines for a maritime policy have included: the inauguration of planning procedures in the Navy Ministry; interdepartmental committees for coordination of maritime policy; the general security-development and maritime power policy guidelines; and more specific, sectoral policy guidelines. All have had important shortcomings, but they did lay the foundation for eventual development of a national maritime policy. Sectoral guidelines, in particular, were developed and began to stimulate maritime activities by the late 1960s, with more decisive results in the 1970s. But here, too, progress was uneven and did not resolve the problem of overall policy coordination.

Difficulties in formulating and implementing an effective maritime policy are in part interwined with the problem of underdevelopment. Establishment of clear priorities, rational planning within and between ministries, and tailoring of policies to specific requirements and limited resources are all complicated by underdevelopment. Brazil is making considerable progress toward achievement of developed status, so that more satisfactory resolution of these basic policy dilemmas is in the offing. And it is well to recall that even developed states have had great difficulty in forging well-coordinated maritime policies. Setting of priorities and policy management in maritime affairs is an especially complex undertaking with potentially great implications for various sectors of the economy, so that it tends to become involved in the politics of numerous agencies and interest groups. Marine policy making in the United States, for example, has been the arena for political infighting between numerous groups, both private and governmental, as recurring attempts have been made to evolve appropriate machinery for coordinating national ocean affairs.[27]

BUREAUCRATIC POLITICS

Maritime policy guidelines in Brazil and the representative democracies do share, as we have just seen, certain general strengths and weaknesses. They do help rationalize the policy process, although decision-making still reflects the political vagaries of specific junctures. But here the parallel ends. Bureaucratic politics shaping Brazilian policies during the last decade of military rule has been authoritarian and largely hidden from the outside observer, especially disagreements in officer opinion. The policy veil over Brazil's closed political system nevertheless can be penetrated sufficiently to discern the general nature of the domestic forces at work.[28]

Responsibility for overall direction of maritime policy has been concentrated in the hands of the navy on the domestic front and in the foreign ministry and the navy on international questions, with ultimate approval by the president and his closest army advisors. The navy is the only specialized maritime sector which also shares policy-making power on basic international ocean questions with Itamaraty. Since responsibilities of the navy go beyond the relatively narrow military missions of its sector to encompass overall direction of maritime policy, it becomes involved in maritime affairs on both the domestic and international fronts.

Until quite recently, the relatively limited interest of maritime affairs has contributed to concentration of decision-making power. Even maritime constituencies, such as fishing, have been largely unorganized and have taken only a fleeting interest in broad maritime policy matters. The 1958 and 1960 Geneva international law of the sea negotiations, for example, appeared far removed from economic, domestic concerns of the Brazilian maritime community. Petrobrás, the state oil monopoly, only began extensive oil exploration and extraction on the continental shelf in the 1970s. Maritime affairs have come to affect a variety of Brazilian interests, as the number of agencies included in the 1968, 1970, and 1974 interministerial coordinating groups indicated. These participating agencies of the maritime community have supplied technical advice as well as specific guidelines for their respective sectors, but they have not shared responsibility for developing broad guidelines of Brazilian maritime policy.

28

The political realities of military rule since
1964 have perpetuated concentration of decision-
making power, with the navy broadly representing
domestic maritime interests, Itamaraty and the navy
handling Brazil's international maritime interests,
and the president and top-level army advisors retaining ultimate policy responsibility. Interest
group and partisan politics have been rigidly controlled, so that civilian influence on policy has
generally been exerted via technocrats or in coalition with military groups. The crucial decision to
extend the territorial sea to 200 miles in 1970,
including its historical background and aftermath,
illustrates these general relationships of domestic
forces shaping maritime policy.

Public justification and policy realities of
the 1970 decision to extend the territorial sea
have diverged sharply. The decision has been presented as responsive to the national will and as a
logical extension of the security-development doctrine. Both claims are misleading.

The territorial sea extension has been justified
plausibly in terms of its contribution to development and security (added wealth; broader area under
national control), but the security-development
policy guideline is much too ambiguous and abstract
for the 1970 decision to have been derived logically
and rationally from it. The security-development
doctrine, after all, had occupied a position of
prominence since the military took over the reins of
power in 1964 without implying a 200-mile corollary.
Nor was the Escola Superior de Guerra an advocate of
the 200-mile formula prior to the 1970 decision.[29]
Stepan concludes that " . . . despite the new pro-
fessionals' agreement on the inseparability of internal security and national development, the contrast between Peru and Brazil has helped point out
that the ideology itself leaves unspecified most
concrete policy decisions."[30]

Without a solid basis in doctrine, the 200-mile
thesis lacked broad support. The 1970 decision to
extend the territorial sea was taken precipitately,
without consulting majority opinion either within
the military or of the public at large. Analysis of
the historical background of the decision to extend
the territorial sea reconfirms this conclusion.

During the 1950s and most of the 1960s, no
maritime issue, including the breadth of the territorial sea, ever became a live issue for national
political debate, save the 1963 French-Brazilian

Lobster War. Law of the sea discussions during these
two decades were largely limited to preparations for
the 1958 and 1960 Geneva conferences and possible
ratification of the conventions concluded there.
Brazilian policy regarding the breadth of the territorial sea was conservative throughout and policy-
makers were even hesitant to extend the territorial
sea to twelve miles, which was apparently permitted
by the Geneva contentions.[31]

Brazil's delay in considering ratification of
the Geneva accords consequently did not mask a revisionist law of the sea policy. The Geneva accords were first presented to Congress for ratification in 1962, but were not brought to a vote due
to the inadvisability of debating a potentially divisive question at a time of internal political instability. Disinterest and caution--to wait and see
other states' responses to the conventions--contin-
ued to postpone consideration of ratification. By
1968, when the Brazilian executive finally brought
up ratification of the conventions before Congress
again, the United Nations Seabed committee had already begun to reconsider key Geneva issues which
eventually would lead to a third law of the sea conference. Brazil still did not embrace the growing
revisionist trend in the law of the sea, although
it was evident by this time that adherence to the
conventions would remain far from universal. Executive relations with Congress, if stormy, illustrate the still relatively conservative law of
the sea position.

The concern of the executive at the time, due
to ambiguities of the Geneva territorial sea provision, was to keep a 12-mile territorial sea option
open rather than to move toward a 200-mile option.
The executive accordingly stipulated to Congress in
late 1968 that adherence to the Convention on the
Territorial Sea and the Contiguous Zone could only
be approved after the decree for a 12-mile territorial sea had been issued. This proviso evoked
congressional ire due to its peremptory nature
rather than any desire for more radical measures.
Congress tended to be even more conservative than
the executive on the territorial sea issue, and
authorized the president to adhere to the Geneva
conventions on October 15, 1968 (Legislative Decree
number 45). This 1968 congressional initiative
authorizing adherence to the Geneva conventions left
ratification and definitive endorsement of narrow
territorial sea limits as a standing policy option

until 1970. But ratification was overtaken by events. On April 25, 1969, at a time when a mandatory recess had been imposed on Congress, the territorial sea was extended as planned from 6 to 12 miles by executive decree. An earlier executive decree of November 18, 1966 had enlarged the territorial sea from 3 to 6 miles with an additional six-mile continguous zone, when Congress was also in mandatory recess.

With military governments in power since 1964, the role of Congress in national affairs, of course, had declined drastically. Congress, even at a time of democratic governments during the 1958 and 1960 Geneva negotiations, had not exerted an important influence on Brazilian law of the sea positions. Congress was not represented on the Brazilian delegation at Geneva, for example, which was composed of representatives of the navy, foreign relations, mines and energy, and agriculture ministries. Congress, like the executive, was largely disinterested in law of the sea matters during the 1950s and 1960s. A 200-mile territorial sea was only proposed in Congress for the first time in 1967, a full fifteen years after the pioneering 200-mile Declaraction of Santiago on the Maritime Zone. Several Brazilian legislators interested in maritime affairs repeatedly advocated a 200-mile territorial sea in the late 1960s, but were avowedly voices in the wilderness.[32] The congressional majority, long hesitant in supporting 200-mile legislation, did respond positively when the government finally decided to take this measure. On other issues, especially civil rights, Congress had been critical in the late 1960s and several times had been cleansed by the executive. By 1970 a more pliable legislative body quickly approved nationalistic 200-mile legislation.

Legal and political obstacles to the extension of the territorial sea to 200 miles were also substantial before 1970 within the executive branch of the government. The Foreign Relations ministry had continued to hew to the traditionally cautious Brazilian law of the sea posture, and had been hesitant to give its support to a measure rejected by predominant legal opinion in the country. Majority navy opinion as well did not favor the measure before 1970. Admiral Paulo Moreira de Silva, the influential Director of the Navy Research Institute and President of the Foundation of Studies of the Sea, has recounted the favorable reaction of the great bulk of high-level navy officials to his

31

lobbying in favor of a narrow territorial sea prior
to 1970.[33] One of the most active lobbyists for the
200 miles, Professor Élio Monnerat, has reported as
well that he only made some progress in late 1969 in
gaining acceptance of the measure by naval officers
since most were either actively opposed or uninterested in an extensive territorial sea.[34] The air
force, after the navy, would be the armed service
most directly affected with controlling an extensive
territorial sea and was likewise reluctant to undertake this burden with insufficient matériel. By late
1969, Monnerat's sponsorship and subsequent approval
of a 200-mile resolution before a joint meeting of
the Brazilian Association of Maritime Law and the
Brazilian Society of Aeronautical and Space Law
(SBDAE) helped sway air force opinion in favor of
the 200 miles.[35]

Itamaraty's legal objection, majority navy and
air force opinion, and the standing congressional
resolution favoring adherence to the Geneva conventions were all put aside by the government leadership in late 1969. By the end of 1969, the government leadership began to prepare a legal basis for
extending the territorial sea to 200 miles. At the
request of the navy, Clóvis Ramalhete, the eminent
Brazilian jurist of the Hague Permanent Court of
Arbitration, submitted a legal opinion on December
30, 1969 about the right of states to extend the
territorial sea. The opinion concluded that the 200-
mile rule had emerged as a regional norm and that
Brazil was competent to take the measure unilaterally.

Ramalhete did provide the doctrinal basis for
the 200-mile decision. His opinion subsequently
evoked the remark from the navy minister, Barros
Nunes, that "I had the cannons; Ramalhete gave me the
ammunition". But Ramalhete has recognized that
since he was one of the few Brazilian jurists at the
time to publicly support the 200 miles, a prestigious legal justification for an extension of the
territorial sea was expected rather than an impar-
tial overview of the issue. The request for his
opinion indicated that the government had already
decided to remove legal obstacles blocking the
measure.[36]

With presidential acceptance of the Ramalhete
opinion, measures were subsequently taken on lower
governmental levels to flesh in the 200-mile decision already taken from above. The navy and
Itamaraty created an informal Work Group composed of

officials from both ministries to study the repercussions of altering Brazil's territorial sea regime.
The Work Group first met on January 5, 1970, with
the ostensible aim of objectively studying territorial sea alternatives: "To consider as a matter of
priority the question of the territorial sea, with
respect to the repercussion of any decision about
this on the regime of other marine spaces". In
fact, with the Ramalhete opinion in hand and presidential intentions clear, the Work Group was able to
establish a smaller group to draft 200-mile legislation at a second meeting on January 13. The drafting group subsequently submitted the draft 200-mile
legislation with article-by-article commentaries to
the Work Group, which in turn approved the document
with some minor modifications by the end of the
month and forwarded it to the Navy and Foreign Relations ministries.[37] After an additional month of
deliberations about likely domestic and international repercussions, these two key ministries jointly
submitted a statement of purposes favoring the 200-
mile draft legislation to the president (DNU 56/
502.72 of March 9, 1970). On the following day,
March 10, 1970, the president requested the opinion
of the National Security Council about the security
implications of a 200-mile territorial sea. The
Secretary-General of the National Security Council,
army general João Batista de Oliveira Figueiredo,[38]
subsequently reported unanimous approval by council
members of the measure in a statement of purpose
(number 011/70), which held that foreign challenges
could be managed while vital domestic interests
would be advanced. President Médici then signed the
attached draft legislation on March 25, 1970.

A final step was added to the legislative process to stimulate support for the 200 miles. A
second opinion by Ramalhete on February 27, 1970
about the legal modality of extending the territorial sea had concluded that the president alone
rather than Congress has competency in this area.
The executive failed to heed this second opinion,
and submitted the decree-law to Congress for final
approval on April 9, 1970. Ramalhete has confirmed
the impression that his second opinion was rejected
in order to build up public support for the territorial sea extension by involving the legislature in
the decision.[39] Amidst a wave of public support
for the executive 200-mile decree, the measure was
promptly approved by Congress, with the support of
both parties, by May 1970.[40]

Manipulation of public opinion by the government nevertheless occurred at a relatively late date. Public support for the 200 miles had been building up even before the governmental leadership decided on the measure at the end of 1969. During the fall of 1969, much of the press of the major cities along the littoral had become militant about alleged abuses by foreign fishermen beyond the 12-mile territorial sea. The image painted by the press of sophisticated foreign factory ships using predatory fishing practices to unfairly strip away part of the national patrimony--perhaps engaged in or related to spying operations as well--lent the 200-mile territorial sea issue a political impact overshadowing strictly economic considerations. National pride increasingly became committed to the defense of a broad expanse of ocean, regarded as Brazilian waters, beyond the traditionally narrow territorial sea. Ramalhete and Monnerat have both referred to animated encounters subsequent to their pro-200 mile presentations over television and in the press with porters, taxi-drivers and others of a low social station, normally uninterested in maritime affairs.[41] The conclusion of one navy admiral appears correct that public opinion was increasingly in favor of the 200 miles in late 1969 and anticipated support for the measure by the navy, which was not associated with the press campaign.[42]

But the influence of the press during late 1969 should not be exaggerated. It is certainly erroneous to claim, as some have, that public agitation for the 200 miles led the government to extend the territorial sea. Had the government been united against a 200-mile territorial sea, it could have proscribed any public discussion of the matter during 1969, just as it had censored discussion of other issues from time to time, such as torture. Government indecision about the 200 miles until the end of 1969 instead allowed rival civilian-military factions to take their case directly to the press and lobby for support.

The narrow territorial sea group, on the one hand, did begin to lose adherents in late 1969. But even within the press, Brazil's most prestigious newspaper, O Estado de São Paulo, criticized the 200 miles as contrary to traditional national respect for the law, and newspapers in the interior generally ignored the issue. Throughout the 1960s and probably until the government openly lent its support to the 200 miles in early 1970, majority public opinion received direction from key maritime

34

elites favoring narrow territorial sea limits
(Itamaraty, Congress, most of the air force and
navy, and the bulk of Brazilian jurists) or simply
ignored the issue.

On the other side, the nationalistic rhetoric of
the pro-200 mile school found an increasingly effective forum in the press and gained new recruits
within and outside the government. The government
leadership welcomed an issue which appeared to catch
the popular imagination, even though some months
elapsed before any decision was taken on the matter.
Examination of the national political situation at
the end of the 1960s helps explain the ambivalence
of the governmental leadership toward the 200 miles.

When the 200 miles first began to emerge as a
popular nationalistic issue in late 1969, the military regime was experiencing severe political difficulties. Economic performance was improving, but
the political system had become increasingly authoritarian. Military rule, portrayed in 1964 as a
transitional regime to prevent economic and political chaos and restore conditions for democracy, had
become transformed by the end of the decade into a
modernizing, authoritarian regime of indefinite
duration.[43] This transformation created severe
strains within the military and in civil-military
relations.

Significant crises within the military occurred
in October 1965 and December 1968, as well as during
the period under consideration here, September-
October 1969, when President Costa e Silva's illness
caused a succession crisis until General Emílio
Garrastazú Médici was appointed president by an interim junta.

On the civilian side, pressure was increasing
for political liberalization to match economic progress. During 1964-1967 a harsh stabilization program helped put an inflation-ridden, deficit-prone
economy back in order, although at the expense of
the lower classes. The economy was able to register
an 8 percent growth rate during 1968-1970 and even
faster growth rates in subsequent years, but this
was still not accompanied by political and social
reforms. In part, dissent took a violent form as
urban guerrillas stepped up terrorism, which was
met with severe governmental repression, including
instances of torture. Others became increasingly
disenchanted with military rule, as a return to
democracy no longer appeared probable.

Nationalism was stimulated on several fronts by

35

the newly installed Médici government to help mobilize support for an unpopular regime. Nationalism
about the 200 miles was used to help mobilize support for an unpopular regime.[44] At first the government permitted 200-mile propaganda without committing itself to the measure. After the 200-mile decision was made, an increasingly popular issue was
consciously transformed by the government into a
broad-based nationalistic campaign. Foreign protests about the 200 miles continued to generate widespread national indignation, especially until the
United States and Brazil reached a modus vivendi on
the issue in a shrimp agreement on May 9, 1972.

Brazilian participation in the world soccer
finals in June 1970 was also used to drum up intense
nationalistic feeling. President Médici emerged as
an ardent soccer fan during the march of the Brazilian team to its third world championship, rooting
with such nationalistic slogans as "no one can hold
back Brazil" ("ninguém segura o Brasil"). Amazonian highway development was developed into another nationalistic campaign about the same time.
On March 5, 1970--ten days before the 200-mile territorial sea decree--President Médici announced that
the Amazon would be integrated into national life
to the benefit of all through a first stage intensive construction program of two highways on an
east-west, north-south axis.

Measures were also taken to develop a consensus
within the government to complement these nationalistic measures for recruiting popular support. Once
the government leadership finally opted for the 200
miles, both disciplinary methods of converting the
governmental maritime policy elites and appeals to
self-interest were used. Army relations with the
navy, the key domestic maritime policy elite, illustrate the use of the carrot and the stick by the
government leadership in the decision to extend the
territorial sea.

As for the stick, in the 200-mile decision the
president and his closest army advisors took the
initiative over the head of majority navy opinion
and silenced critics. The army has occupied a predominant role in the post-1964 military regime, and
this predominance, usually latent in maritime affairs, was directly exercised in the 1970 decision
to extend the territorial sea. The manifold implications of a very substantial territorial sea extension for domestic economic and political affairs, as
well as foreign policy, led the president, an army

general, and his closest advisors, mostly high-level army officers on active duty or detached service, to become deeply involved in the decision.

This rough distribution of decision-making powers in maritime affairs, with the army retaining residual responsibility for key matters and specialized bodies handling more routine affairs, characterizes power realities in the military regime for most other important issues as well. Technocrats, for example, play a major role in running the economy, but the top military leadership appears responsible for determining policy guidelines for economic matters with profound political implications. Such overall political decisions about the economy have included low priority for income redistribution and emphasis on high rates of growth. The army orientation of the government is reinforced by numerous army officers, either on detached service or retired, who occupy leading positions in many civilian ministries and agencies. Their navy counterparts, in contrast, are concentrated in governmental ministries (ie, Department of Transportation) or sectors of the economy (shipbuilding) related closely to maritime affairs.

Divisions within the navy on the territorial sea issue contributed to the navy's subordinate role in the 1970 decision. The vice-president at the time, an admiral, Augusto Hammon Rademaker Grunewald, did not play an important role in the decision, and, as noted, the bulk of the navy favored narrow territorial sea limits. On the other hand, veteran supporters and recent converts to the 200 miles in the navy lobbied actively within as well as outside the government in 1969, and helped convince the army leadership of the expediency of the measure. Once the decision was made, the navy also continued to coordinate routine domestic maritime affairs, including implementation of the 200-mile decree. The air force played an even less prominent role in the 1970 decision and, unlike the navy, was not represented in the Work Group which fleshed in the 200-mile legislation.

The lopsided distribution of decision-making powers between the army, navy, and air force in the 1970 decision to extend the territorial sea did not generate inter-service conflict, due to the presence of the carrot as well as the stick. Everyone has something to gain, or so it seemed, from an additional 188 miles of ocean space and resources. Army predominance in the military regime generally has been accompanied by respect for institutional interests of the other services, and in this case, extra benefits were held forth for the two services most directly affected by any extension of the territorial sea, primarily the navy but also the air force.

Institutional benefits of the 200 miles for the navy and the air force included a potential expansion of tasks and weaponry. The previous concern of many navy officers about undertaking the burden of patrolling and defending an extensive territorial sea with insufficient matériel was offset by the prospect held forth of continuing increases in weaponry to perform new roles. This prospect has been fulfilled as the navy and air force arsenals have since been beefed up and roles have expanded.[45]

The navy moved actively on its own as well to reap the benefits of a broad territorial sea. The pro 200-mile group within the navy, which up to 1970 argued that development required a broad swath of national ocean space and weaponry adequate for its control, pushed for a larger navy budget after the territorial sea extension.

The carrot held out by the 200 miles promised to help alleviate past grievances as well as attenuate recurring budgetary tug-of-wars. A debate over navy and air force responsibilities for national defense had been aggravated in 1960, when the navy received an aircraft carrier, purchased in 1956 from Great Britain and then modernized in Dutch shipyards. The navy regarded the aircraft carrier, christened Minas Gerais, as an essential addition to the fleet, allegedly starved for funds since World War II, and as a stimulus to naval aviation.[46] Feelings ran just as high in the air force, which regarded control of fixed-wing planes operating from the Minas Gerais as vital to its continued growth and institutional well-being as a relatively new branch of the armed services. The Castello Branco government in 1965 finally settled the jurisdictional dispute over naval aviation in favor of the air force, which would control fixed-wing planes and pilots while the navy would only control helicopters. Adoption of a 200-mile territorial sea five years later consequently came to be greeted eagerly by the navy, which stood to gain much more in terms of tasks and weaponry than it had lost in the naval aviation hassle. Air force officers also by and large came to regard the 200 miles with optimism, since patrolling and defending an extensive territorial sea required ex-

panded tasks and weaponry while leaving naval aviation largely under the jurisdiction of the air
force.

Nationalism, like institutional benefits, was
important in preventing intra- and inter-service
conflict. It will be recalled that nationalistic
support was building up in the navy and air force
in late 1969 for the 200 miles, so that by early
1970 divisions over the issue were more within each
of the armed services than between them. The nationalistic presentation of the 200-mile decree in
early 1970 helped attract support from middle-level
officers from all services, who in the 1965 and 1968
internal military crises had effectively pressured
the government leadership in a more authoritarian,
nationalistic direction. Popular enthusiasm for the
200 miles also had its effect on the undecided in
all three armed services, who proudly saw the military's image, tarnished in the late 1960s, transformed temporarily into a vanguard of nationalism.
In contrast, supporters of a 12-mile territorial sea
were associated pejoratively with foreign powers
allegedly exploiting Brazilian fishing and were portrayed as against nationalist and regionalist 200-
mile aspirations.

The rapidity of the conversion of the navy and
the air force to support of a 200-mile territorial
sea suggests that views in favor of a narrow territorial sea were not held strongly by most officers.
Arguments in favor of a 12-mile limit were predominantly negative and uninspiring--insufficient
weaponry to defend and patrol 200 miles; adverse
reactions of stronger foreign powers in the case of
a territorial sea extension; adherence to generally
recognized legal norms, etc. Institutional and
nationalistic arguments for the 200 miles were emo-
tive and capable of rapidly mobilizing support within the armed services. The nationalistic and
institutional dividends of the 200 miles indeed
have proved so convincing that no revanchist movement for a 12-mile limit exists in any of the armed
services.

No other issue has been as divisive within the
navy during the period of military rule since 1964
as the 1969-1970 territorial sea debate, and even
this division did not prove long-lasting. Navy
opinions have also differed over roles to be performed in the South Atlantic, as noted later in
this chapter and at greater length in Chapter 6, but
at no point have deep, lasting divisions appeared

regarding this issue.

The army has been more prone since 1964 toward competing factions and recurring internal debates about basic policy orientation, in large part because it has been involved directly in key issues of political economy. The "Brazilian model" has been a subject of hot debate abroad since its inception, and at home, too, basic policy priorities and approaches have increasingly come to be questioned, including within the armed forces. The list of such contentious subjects includes the role of the state, the role of multinational corporations, income distribution, and political participation. While the military government was able to stimulate and guide nationalism on the 200-mile issue, by the late 1970s, on these other issues, nationalists and others tended to become increasingly critical of official policy and isolate the government politically.

Disagreements over issues essentially extraneous to traditional military roles have consequently tended to be reflected in the armed forces, especially within the army. Since the navy's responsibility has generally been limited to maritime affairs, it has often been spared the divisiveness of many such extra-institutional debates.

The extension of the territorial sea, however, has not resolved certain aspects of rivalry between the three armed services. In spite of new tasks and weaponry involving the 200 miles, the navy and the air force have remained subordinate to the army. This subordination does not rankle the air force to the extent it does the navy. The air force, after all, only grow out of army and naval aviation during World War II, while the navy historically played a key role in Brazilian military affairs.[47]

The navy, with the assistance of foreign officers under contract, played a decisive role in defeating Portuguese forces for independence in the early nineteenth century. On several occasions during the rest of the century, the navy also undertook domestic operations in support of national unity and foreign operations in the River Plate area. During the Empire, from independence until 1889, the pro-monarchical navy was in a relatively privileged position, since the army often had to depend on the navy for mobility during an era of rudimentary land transportation in most of the national territory. The political balance between the armed forces was altered in 1889, when a predominantly army movement overthrew the Empire. Subsequent navy feelings of neglect led to unsuccessful naval revolts in 1891 and 1893, and the aristocratic leaning of the navy lingered.[48] Army-navy differences have not broken down into armed conflict clearly along service lines since 1893, but service rivalry has continued with ups and downs, as the army has maintained a dominant position in the armed services.

Until the military coup of 1964, service rivalry was conditioned by the traditional moderating role of the army, which involved temporary army intervention to protect constitutional order. While this role accorded the army special powers, it also limited the army's direct intervention in the political system to removal of the president from office followed by Congress' rapid approval of the act. This traditional limitation on the army's direct involvement in politics was respected by civilians and the military alike, and consequently tended to prevent effective resistance by officers in the navy or air force to the moderating function.[49] Between the armed services, rivalry during this period mostly involved competition for budgetary and task prerogatives. Navy resentment over the failure to fare better in the competition was evident in nostalgia for the favorable position enjoyed during the Empire.

During the troubled period immediately preceding the 1964 military coup, all services became so concerned over threats to institutional unity that ideological sources of disunity were contained. For example, the revolt of air force and navy noncommissioned officers and enlisted men in September 1963 and the enlisted men's naval mutiny of March 1964 were instances of ideologically-related insubordination within services rather than inter-service rivalry. Since the civilian, left-leaning Goulart government apparently condoned such indiscipline for its own political ends, these threats to the military institution contributed to unity of officers of diverging ideological orientations from all three services for a coup. The navy nevertheless has been less politically active during this century than the army, and hesitated to throw its support behind the revolt initiated by the army on March 31, 1964 until the following afternoon. This navy hesitancy has been a source of some army resentment.[50]

Since Goulart chose not to risk a civil war by trying to mobilize his allies within all three armed services, there was very little armed opposition to

41

the army-led revolt. U.S. involvement in the coup
has been rumored all along, but only recently has it
been documented that the United States had a con-
tingency plan, Operation Brother Sam, for a naval
carrier task force group and an air lift to support
the coup, if required.[51]

Direct military rule from 1964 and the greatly
expanded role of the army as director of the political system created a new context for service rivalries. The army, in alliance with technocrats, was
now directly responsible for allocating budgets and
tasks, resolving interservice conflicts, and determining grand strategy for the economy and the
political system, including the armed forces. This
has had mixed effects on inter-service relations.

Army determination of crucial policy decisions
for the military, as indicated, does grate the navy
in several ways: less navy autonomy than in the nineteenth century and less ability to resist army
interference in navy affairs than before 1964; navy
resentment about the adverse determination of the
jurisdictional dispute over naval aviation and about
recurring army proposals for a Ministry of Defense;
and imposition of land-based development/security
doctrine on the navy. Ultimate army responsibility
for the political failures of military rule, especially the refusal to allow effective popular
representation, also has tended to have a direct,
adverse impact on the prestige of all three services.

But if the army is ultimately responsible for
the political failures of military rule, so is it
for economic successes. The successes of military
rule, especially in economic affairs, have provided
greater resources for all three armed services and
higher priority for their needs. Even on the
political front, there have been certain armed
services' benefits from military rule. The severe
constraints on partisan politics imposed by the
military ended the tradition of many civilian poli-
ticians in Brazil to seek out and cultivate inter-
and intra-service factions to support their positions.

Many of these characteristics of contemporary
army-navy relations have surfaced as the 200-mile
territorial sea has been put into practice. The
standard distribution of service responsibilities,
with the army leadership retaining ultimate control
of grand strategy and vital policy decisions--in
this case, the extension of the territorial sea--
and the navy coordinating more routine maritime af-

fairs, began well. Due to the institutional and nationalistic benefits of the 200-mile decision, the navy, as noted, quickly lent its support to the measure. But while the 200-mile territorial sea seemed appropriate in 1970, hard-line aspects of the policy and its implementation led to subsequent army reassessment of the measure.

The policy was hard-line since it asserted full state sovereignty over 200 miles of ocean space. This claim was more extreme than either those of most other South American states made prior to 1970, or those of the Caribbean states which developed the more moderate patrimonial sea doctrine after 1970.[52] The navy, moreover, soon came to recognize and accept its vested interest in maintaining the new military responsibilities associated with protection of state sovereignty 200 miles off the coast. This led the navy to favor severe limitation of foreign activities in the area. Hard-line navy implementation of the 200 miles threatened to compound international difficulties and produce Brazilian isolation in global law of the sea negotiations.[53] Domestic problems also arose from navy determination to severely limit foreign participation in the 200 miles. For example, the navy opposed the request--eventually granted from above-- of Petrobrás, the state oil monopoly, to permit international petroleum companies through risk contracts to assist oil exploration of the continental shelf.

For international, domestic, and institutional reasons, the army no longer welcomed as readily what had become a gratuitous expansion of navy and air force roles. Political expediency in 1970 had led to one measure highly favorable to maritime interests, the extension of the territorial sea, and another highly favorable to ground transportation interests, the Amazonian highway construction program. By the mid-1970s, the army leadership ironically felt compelled to move toward a more pragmatic interpretation of the 200 miles and to consider a more balanced transportation scheme for opening up the interior because of the exigencies of the oil crisis. The 200-mile interpretation, if becoming more pragmatic by the mid-1970s, was still ambitious. Open endorsement of a compromise formula such as a patrimonial sea or economic zone was politically difficult so soon after a vigorous, nationalistic campaign for full sovereignty over 200 miles,[54] and in any event a more comprehensive territorial sea concept remained popular for security

43

reasons.[55]

The foreign ministry could not remain aloof from the 200-mile debate and its aftermath. Its concern about adverse international repercussions of a greatly expanded territorial sea had led it to join forces with naval officers who were reluctant to assume the added security responsibility of controlling 200 miles with inadequate weaponry. Itamaraty, however, also had an interest in avoiding adverse foreign policy consequences which threatened to result from low navy morale following the naval aviation reverse. An anti-communist South Atlantic defense pact linking Brazil with Portugal and South Africa held forth the prospect of institutional benefits and new naval responsibilities, and began to gain support within the navy in the late 1960s.[56] Such an alliance among South Atlantic conservative powers would have had a disastrous effect on Brazilian relations with developing states, and began to shed new light on the 200 miles for Itamaraty. The 200 miles threatened to lead to foreign policy disputes, but it at least promised to deter any such defense pact by offering alternative, more immediate benefits for the navy. Since 1970 the navy indeed has been absorbed in asserting control over the broad new swath of ocean space and talk of a South Atlantic naval alliance with Portugal and South Africa died out until the overthrow of the conservative Portuguese dictatorship in April 1974. A revival in the mid-1970s of the idea of a South Atlantic naval alliance in response to Soviet involvement in the independence movement in Angola and in the South Atlantic is discussed in Chapter 6.

So Itamaraty came to support a 200-mile territorial sea, but lent its traditional voice of moderation to pragmatic 200-mile interpretations. Accommodations between the United States and Brazil regarding fishing and naval access were later worked out, which left the Brazilian 200-mile territorial sea claim intact.[57]

By mid-decade, some important shifts in Brazilian ocean policy were occurring. The precipitate, political nature of the 1970 territorial sea extension--essentially a political decree followed by political mobilization--had begun to have unexpected effects by the mid-1970s. The resources of the sea out to 200 miles were increasingly recognized to be of greater, more protracted interest than more fleeting nationalistic or political benefits. A 200-mile territorial sea continued to be

44

claimed, although with more pragmatic implementation. What had begun as a political sea was increasingly becoming an economic sea. But downgrading of nationalistic rhetoric and politics in the 200-miles did not lessen the navy's new interest in 200-mile security interests. As Chapter 6 shows, security interests in the 200 miles have remained important throughout.

FOREIGN POLICY, DOMESTIC POLITICS, AND OCEAN AFFAIRS

The web of domestic and international ocean politics frequently is so tightly interwoven that certain maritime policy problems tend to recur in very different contexts. Since 1970, for example, U.S. ocean policies have evolved from stress on military-strategic interests toward positions more congenial to economic resource interests.[58] A somewhat similar evolution of Brazilian maritime policy during the same years from a political sea toward an economic sea suggests that some common basic forces were gradually having an impact within and across national frontiers.

The respective claims in the early 1970s by Brazil to a 200-mile territorial sea and by the United States for a comprehensive guarantee of free navigation through straits and over continental shelves were both viewed as extreme in the global negotiating context preparatory to a third United Nations law of the sea conference. Ironically, insistence of the U.S. military on guarantees for free navigation through straits and beyond narrow territorial waters over continental shelves conflicted with Brazilian insistence on a 200-mile territorial sea. Both the United States and Brazil found it difficult to sustain the extensive political and military interests implicit in their respective ocean policies without suffering diplomatic isolation as preparatory negotiations matured.

International trends favoring an economic zone as a middle ground contributed to more careful Brazilian assessment of the implications of a 200-mile territorial sea and to a more precise, narrow definition of vital U.S. ocean security interests. As both states moved toward more conciliatory policies in the mid-1970s--the United States by accepting a 200-mile economic zone under certain conditions and Brazil by qualifying its sovereignty claim out to 200 miles--their political and military interests became more susceptible to compromise.

Economic realities then helped temper excessive political and military claims. Important economic resources are involved in the definition of ocean space, so that political and military interests, especially when of secondary importance, began to recede before the logic of powerful economic interests. But in the case of Brazil, like the U.S., the decline of military interests was only relative. Brazil made a rather successful drive at the third law of the sea conference to define coastal state rights expansively in an economic zone so as to approximate a territorial sea,[59] and national security interests remained important in the 200 miles.

Other comparisons between domestic ocean policy and international trends may be made. Some common maritime policy problems on the domestic front affect both democratic and authoritarian states, while other problems faced by Brazil are typical of developing states. All such problems condition the way in which domestic politics responds to the international setting.

Bureaucratic politics, with its often parochial tugs and pulls between different organizations, contributed to the tardy emergency of Brazilian maritime policy, just it has complicated policy in developed states. The very diffuseness of maritime affairs and the difficult technical and administrative problems implicit in the transition from underdevelopment to development were indicated as other formidable domestic obstacles to effective policy coordination shared by developing states.

Brazil has responded positively to these typical policy obstacles. In tandem with the general economic progress of the late 1960s and 1970's, progress toward an effective maritime policy was made, if primarily by sectors, by an increasingly qualified maritime community. Just as overall progress of the economy was heavily involved with trends in the international economy, so was progress in maritime affairs.

While domestic-international interaction does exhibit some recurring patterns, the kind of overlap of domestic politics and foreign policy in maritime affairs is often unique. For example, Brazilian aspirations for great power status have influenced both the domestic and foreign policy contexts of maritime affairs. According to naval doctrine, development of national maritime power enhances Brazil's candidacy for great power status and in turn movement toward great power status requires a strong maritime component. To an increasing extent, theory is being translated into reality.

A distinctive foreign policy constellation also complemented domestic forces leading Brazil to extend its territorial sea.[60] Foreign policy problems in subsequently defending a 200-mile territorial sea affected the domestic policy balance as well. Objections to the 200 miles by developed states, for example, contributed to initial primacy of military and foreign policy bodies over civilian, technically-oriented ministries in maritime affairs.[61] With a subsequent return to foreign policy normalcy, technical maritime bodies have reasserted their influence via routine functions and Itamaraty, to repeat, reasserted its traditional moderating influence.

Domestic and international factors, in contrast, at times do exert quite separate influences on maritime policy. Navy enthusiasm after 1970 for an ambitious sovereignty claim out to 200 miles, for example, conflicted with international trends favoring an economic zone. These international trends did stimulate support by other Brazilian groups for a more moderate policy than that espoused by the navy. But the turnabout of the navy in 1970 from opponent to vigorous supporter of the 200 miles resulted from bureaucratic politics, not international politics. The decision to go to 200 miles, based on an army-oriented edict from the top down to cultivate nationalism, was another example of domestic politics functioning quite separately from international politics.

Interaction between, rather than separateness of, international and domestic factors nevertheless tends to be rule in maritime affairs. Such a nexus between foreign policy and domestic politics has not always existed. At one time, mismanagement or neglect of maritime affairs did not have a substantial impact on foreign policy or the domestic economy. As Brazilian ocean policy gained cohesiveness and dynamism in the late 1960s and 1970s, it became complementary to national economic progress and increasingly involved in international economic and political questions. Ocean policy is now so intertwined in domestic and international affairs that effective management requires responses appropriate to each context.

NOTES

1. Alfred Stepan, The Military in Politics: Changing Pat-

<u>terns in Brazil</u> (Princeton, New Jersey: Princeton University
Press, 1974), p. 186. Underlining in original.

2. Chapter 2, "The Brazilian Foreign Policy Elites," especially pages 41-42, of an unpublished 1973 contract study,
<u>Brazil's International Role in the Seventies</u>, of the Foreign
Policy Research Institute of Philadelphia, Pa. The major
author of the original draft of this chapter, Professor Ronald
Schneider, relied primarily on the Almanaque do Exército for
raw data on career patterns. The author coordinated this
Foreign Policy Research Institute project, and subsequently
reconfirmed Schneider's findings with specific reference to
the navy, relying on recent issues of the <u>Boletim de
Oficiais dos Corpos e Quadros da Marinha BOC QM</u>. See also
Stepan and Ronald M. Schneider, <u>The Political System of
Brazil: Emergence of a 'Modernizing' Authoritarian Regime</u>,
1964-1970 (New York: Columbia University Press, 1971).

3. For a synthesis of Brazilian maritime doctrine, see Part
II, "Poder Marítimo," in <u>Panorama do Poder Marítimo Brasileiro</u>,
ed. Mario Cesar Flores (Rio de Janeiro: Biblioteca do
Exército e Serviço de Documentação Geral da Marinha, 1972).
See also the discussion of Brazilian naval doctrine as rela-
ted to interests and missions of the navy in Chapter 6.

4. Hilton Berutti Augusto Moreira, "Transportes Marítimos,
Desenvolvimento e Segurança Nacional," <u>Revista Marítima
Brasileira</u>, 91 (Oct.-Dec. 1971).

5. The Director of the Army Library, for example, has explicitly recognized that classical geopolitical writers such
as Mackinder and Mahan have considered terrestrial and maritime power as antagonistic to one another on a global scale.
On a national scale, however, he adds that land and sea power
complement one another in supporting development and security.
Waldir da Costa Godolphim, "Apresentação," <u>Panorama do Poder
Marítimo Brasileiro</u>, ed. Flores, 5-6.

6. "Homem--O elemento básico do poder marítimo," <u>Panorama
do Poder Marítimo Brasileiro</u>, ed. Flores, 385, 390; and
Gustavo Francisco Feijó Bittencourt, "Mentalidade Marítima
e Dignidade do Trabalhador," <u>Segurança e Desenvolvimento</u>,
20 (1971): 149-153.

7. Rubens Rodrigues dos Santos, "Navegação e Desenvolvimento,"
<u>Digesto Econômico</u>, No. 235 (Jan.-Feb. 1974): 209.

8. During the 1950s, Golbery first was with the Division of
International Affairs and later with the Executive Division of
the Escola Superior de Guerra. After playing a key role in

the 1964 military revolt, in June of that year he was named director of the Brazilian intelligency agency (Serviço Nacional de Informações). During the Geisel government he has been near the pinnacle of power as head of the civilian household of the presidency (Gabinete Civil da Presidência da República), and he will occupy the same position with the Figueiredo government, which is to take office on March 15, 1979. His principal writings, based on his EGS lectures, have been compiled in two books: Planejamento Estratégico (Rio de Janeiro: Cia. ed. americana, 1955); and Geopolítica do Brasil (Rio de Janeiro: José Olympio, 1967).

9. Golbery do Couto e Silva, Geopolítica do Brasil, 62.

10. See footnote 57, Chapter 6. Golbery and Meira Mattos are both discussed briefly in Chapter 6 insofar as their thought relates to Brazilian involvement in the South Atlantic.

11. Carlos de Meira Mattos, Brasil: Geopolítica e Destino (Rio de Janeiro: José Olympio Editora, 1975), pp. 66-67.

12. Carlos de Meira Mattos, A Geopolítica e as Projeções do Poder (Rio de Janeiro: José Olympio Editora, 1977), especially Chapters VIII and IX.

13. Interview with General Carlos de Meira Mattos, Washington, D. C., September 1, 1977. At the time, General Meira Mattos was Vice Director of the Interamerican Defense College.

14. Meira Mattos, A Geopolítica e as Projeções do Poder, pp. 111, 108-109.

15. Unpublished manuscript by John Child, to appear in 1979 in Latin American Research Review, page 21.

16. Wayne Selcher, The National Security Doctrine and Policies of the Brazilian Government (Carlisle Barracks, Pennsylvania: Strategic Studies Institute, Military Issues Research Memorandum), p. 25.

17. "Política: Assuntos internos," Boletim Especial, December 27, 1978, p. 3.

18. Interview with Captain David Blower, Director, Department of Instruction, Escola de Guerra Naval, May 16, 1975, Rio de Janeiro, Brazil.

19. For an elaborate articulation of this navy concern, see Reynalto Zannini Coelho de Souza, "A Criação do Ministério da Defesa," Revista Marítima Brasileira, 85 (1965): 17-55.

20. Maximiano Eduardo da Silva Fonseca, "O Plano Diretor," Revista Marítima Brasileira, 91 (1971): 104. See also Chapter 5, note 54.

21. The National Security Council; the Armed Forces General Staff; the Navy, Agriculture, Mines and Energy, and Planning ministries; the National Research Council; the National Commission of Nuclear Energy; and Petrobrás, the national petroleum monopoly.

22. Strategic Planning division of the Navy General Staff; the Directorate of Hydrography and Navigation of the Navy ministry; and the Foreign Relations, Agriculture, Mines and Energy, and Transportation ministries. For the texts of Decree No. 62, 232 of February 6, 1968 on CIEFMAR and Decree No. 66, 682 of June 10, 1970 on the Interministerial Study Commission, see Mar Territorial, Vol. I (Brasília: Marinha do Brasil, 1971), pp. 111-114.

23. Confidential interview with high-level diplomat at the Ministry of Foreign Relations, Brasília, August 16, 1974.

24. The Navy, Foreign Relations, Agriculture, Mines and Energy, Transportation, Education, Industry and Commerce, and Planning ministries; and the National Research Council. "Prioridades," Jornal do Brasil, September 14, 1974, p. 7.

25. Mario Cesar Flores, "Conceito e situação brasileira," Panorama do Poder Marítimo Brasileiro, ed. Flores, 96. In 1971, Mario Cesar Flores also proposed a comprehensive Maritime Policy Council (Conselho de Política Marítima) to coordinate and oversee all national maritime activities, chaired by the navy, to complement 1967 legislation (Decree-Law 200), which had made the navy formally responsible for national maritime policy. "Formulação de Uma Política Maritime," Revista da Escola de Guerra Naval, No. 2 (1971): 5-19.

26. Subsequent chapters examine the achievements, problems, and foreign policy aspects of the major Brazilian maritime sectors.

27. Edward Wenk, Jr., The Politics of the Ocean (Seattle: University of Washington Press, 1972).

28. Confidential interviews with leading members of the Brazilian maritime community were essential in unraveling domestic forces shaping maritime policy. These included interviews with foreign ministry and navy officials in Brasília, Brazil, August 14-15, 1974, with members of the Brazilian delegation to the Third United Nations Law of the Sea Conference, Caracas, Venezuela, August 22-24, 1974, and subsequent

interviews with Brazilian officials in the United States.
Additional interviews for attribution are cited directly.

29. Admiral Paulo Moreira da Silva, Director of the Navy
Research Institute (Instituto de Pesquisas da Marinha) and
President of the Foundation of Studies of the Sea (Fundação
de Estudos do Mar), as well as a well-known opponent of the
200-mile thesis prior to the 1970 decree, reported that his
views were well received during his frequent lectures at the
Escola Superior de Guerra during the 1960s. Interview with
Paulo Moreira da Silva, Rio de Janeiro, Brazil, March 19, 1975.
      Indeed, the ESG's journal, Segurança e Desenvolvimento,
carried not a single pro-200 mile article during the 1960s.
The first pro-200 mile article in the navy's official journal,
Revista Marítima Brasileira, did not appear until late 1968.

30. Alfred Stepan, "The New Professionalism of Internal
Warfare and Military Role Expansion," Authoritarian Brazil:
Origins, Policies and Future, ed. Alfred Stepan (New Haven:
Yale University Press, 1973), 65.

31. Chapter 3 discusses this and other historical aspects of
Brazilian ocean policy in detail.

32. Senator Vasconcelos Torres has been the most active
legislator of the official ARENA party supporting navy interests and the 200 miles, but he recognized that his initiatives
during the 1960s had largely fallen "in a vacuum, in empty-
ness." Vasconcelos Torres, Mar Territorial e Marinha de
Guerra (Brasília: Serviço Gráfico do Senado Federal, 1970),
p. 90. In the officially-sanctioned opposition MDB party,
Senate minority leader Nelson Carneiro was the most active
in promoting a 200-mile territorial sea before 1970, though
he, too, only dates an increase in support for this measure
from about 1968. Nelson Carneiro, "O Brasil e as Convenções
de Genebra," Revista Brasileira de Política Internacional,
12 (1969): 105, 117-121. This pro-200 mile article was based
on Carneiro's 1968 negative opinion on the Geneva conventions
submitted to the Committee on Constitution and Justice, a
view which the congressional majority rejected, as noted above.

33. Interview with Admiral Paulo Moreira de Silva, December 9, 1974, Rio de Janeiro, Brazil. As an active duty
naval officer, Admiral Moreira da Silva was prohibited from
expressing his anti-200 mile views after the decision was made
to extend the territorial sea.

34. Interview with Professor Élio Monnerat Solon de Pontes,
Niterói, Brazil, November 26, 1974.

35. Ibid.

Professor Monnerat was Secretary-General of the SBDAE, an unofficial organization of air force officers and civilians, whose membership overlaps to a considerable extent with the Brazilian Association of Maritime Law. The deliberations of these two professional organizations received considerable press coverage, but the joint resolution was only approved at the very end of 1969 (December 17, 1969). Monnerat's book covers his activities in favor of the 200 miles in the late 1960s in great detail. Élio Monnerat Solon de Pontes, Brasil, 200 Milhas (Rio de Janeiro: Casa do Homem de Amanhã-- Editora, 1972).

36. Interview with Clóvis Ramalhete, November 6, 1974, Rio de Janeiro, Brazil. Ramalhete was subsequently named to a cabinet-level position as Attorney General (Consultor Geral) de la República) in the Figueiredo administration, which is to take office on March 15, 1979.

37. Carlos Calero Rodrigues, "O Problema do Mar Territorial," Revista Brasileira de Política Internacional, 12 (1969): 125-127.

38. General Figueiredo was later selected to succeed Ernesto Geisel in 1979 as the fifth military president.

39. Interview with Clóvis Ramalhete, November 6, 1974, Rio de Janeiro, Brazil.

40. Documents relevant to the 1970 decision to extend the territorial sea, including opinions of the various congressional committees, may be found in Mar Territorial, Vols. I, II and III (Brasília: Marinha do Brasil, 1971 through 1974).

41. Interview with Clóvis Ramalhete, November 6, 1974, Rio de Janeiro, Brazil.
Interview with Élio Monnerat Solon de Pontes, Niterói, Brazil, November 26, 1974. Monnerat's book also presents examples of grass-roots support for the 200 miles, including popular songs, carnaval themes and soccer terminology ("a 200-mile pass"). Monnerat, Brasil, 200 Milhas, 289, 293-294.

42. Paulo Irineu Roxo de Freitas, "Estudos Sôbre a Ampliação do Mar Territorial para 200 Milhas," Mar Territorial, Vol. I (Brasília: Marinha do Brasil, 1971), 527. Admiral Roxo de Freitas lists newspaper articles and editorials in late 1969 supporting the 200 miles. Part Two of Élio Monnerat's book, Brasil, 200 Milhas, likewise compiles pro-200 mile newspaper articles and editorials prior to 1970. The author also consulted clipping files on maritime affairs at several major daily newspapers and at the documentation division of

the Brazilian Institute of Geography and Statistics in Rio
de Janeiro, Brazil, and interviewed press officers in the
U.S. Consulate in Rio as well as Brazilian journalists.

43. For a more detailed account of Brazilian politics in
this period, see Ronald M. Schneider, The Political System
of Brazil.

44. The outspoken O Estado de São Paulo called attention to
this ulterior motive for the 200 miles: "What prevailed in
the intent of the legislator--that is, of the government--
were reasons of a political order, due to the internal situation." "As 200 milhas e as relações Brasil-EUA," O Estado
de São Paulo, June 10, 1971, p. 3.

45. See Chapters 5 and 6.

46. Admiral Pedro Paulo de Araújo Suzano (Commander-in-Chief
of the Fleet), "Ordem do Dia No. 0061-1960: Incorporação do
NAel Minas Gerais a Esquadra," Revista Maritima Brasileira,
81 (1961): 22.

47. In an interview with the author on July 1, 1975 in Rio
de Janeiro, Captain Max Justo Guedes, a distinguished his-
torian and Vice Director of the navy's General Documentation
Service, acknowledged that there is no satisfactory comprehensive history of the Brazilian Navy. The navy, however, has
commissioned such a study, relying on both foreign and domestic authors, projected for at least 5 volumes. Captain
Guedes allowed this author to peruse the galley proofs for
the first volume of the set, História Naval Brasileira. Two
volumes of the set have now been completed. In a letter of
September 18, 1978 to the author, Captain Guedes added that
the third volume was in press and that only two chapters remained to be completed for the fourth volume.

48. For a lucid account of the transition from military to
civilian rule and army-navy rivalry in the watershed 1889-
1898 period, see June E. Hahner, Civilian-Military Relations
in Brazil, 1889-1898 (Columbia, South Carolina: University
of South Carolina Press, 1969).

49. Stepan, The Military in Politics, 119.

50. Commander Mário dos Reis Pereira recounts the details
of planning by all three armed services for the revolution
prior to March 31, 1964, but does not acknowledge navy hesitancy in following the army lead nor subsequent army displeasure with this. "A Revolução de Março Vista do Mar:
Primeira Fase: 1954-1964," Revista da Adismar, No. 15 (1974):

60-64.

51. Peter Flynn, <u>Brazil: A Political Analysis</u> (Boulder,
Colorado: Westview Press, 1978), pp. 278-280.

52. See Chapter 4.

53. Ibid.

54. Ibid.
    Some former civilian supporters of a 200-mile territorial
sea did avowedly evolve toward patrimonial sea or economic
zone concepts by the mid-1970s. Élio Monnerat, already cited
as an active proponent of a 200-mile territorial sea before
1970, subsequently has argued that a patrimonial sea would not
represent a retreat from the Brazilian position. Interview
with Élio Monnerat Solon de Pontes, November 26, 1974, Niterói,
Brazil. An important segment of the press, during the early
1970s an ardent defender of a 200-mile territorial sea, also
came to regard the patrimonial sea concept favorably by the
mid-1970s. For editorials to this effect paralleling the
Third United Nations Law of the Sea Conference, see, for
example: <u>Jornal do Brasil</u>, "Límites do Mar," May 26, 1974;
"Mar Patrimonial," June 26, 1974; "Mar Econômico," July 13,
1974; "Convergência no Mar," July 20, 1974; "Questões do Mar,"
February 27, 1975; "Consenso Marítimo," March 10, 1975.

55. See Chapter 6.

56. Ibid.

57. See Chapters 5, 6, and 7.

58. Professor H. Gary Knight documents the decisive influence
of the Department of Defense in the formulation of U.S.
draft treaties submitted to the U.N. Seabed Committee in 1970
and 1971. H. Gary Knight, "Special Domestic Interests and
United States Ocean Policy," <u>International Relations and the
Future of Ocean Space</u>, ed. Robert G. Wirsing (Columbia, South
Carolina: University of South Carolina Press, 1974), 10-43.
Professors Ann Hollick and Robert E. Osgood analyze the subsequent trend toward parity between strategic and resource
interests in U.S. ocean policy, but including the expansion
of the conception of security underlying this policy from a
narrow emphasis on military mobility to a major concern with
unhampered commercial navigation as well. Ann L. Hollick and
Robert E. Osgood, <u>New Era of Ocean Politics</u> (Baltimore: The
Johns Hopkins University Press, 1974.

59. See Chapter 4.

60. See Chapters 3 and 4.

61. Clóvis Ramalhete, "Alguns Objectivos das 200 Milhas," Revista Militar Brasileira, 98 (Apr.-Dec. 1971): 77.

3. Brazilian Ocean Policy in Historical Perspective

    Since Brazil has emerged as a leader over the last decade in ocean affairs, an accurate historical interpretation of Brazil's international position and policies in this significant area of international relations is particularly important. Most of the chapters of this study make some reference to the historical background of the particular topic being discussed, such as domestic affairs, naval affairs, and shipping. In this chapter, the historical focus is broader and more systematic. The evolution of national ocean policy up to the 1970s will be examined in relation to relevant international events. A host of unilateral, bilateral, sub-regional, regional and global measures and conferences will need to be surveyed to discern the essential features shaping ocean politics up to the 1970s. Some reference will be made to the Third United Nations Conference on the Law of the Sea, but analysis of the relationship of this crucial ocean affairs conference of the 1970s to Brazil will mostly be dealt with in the next chapter.

    No studies have dealt explicitly with the historical background conditioning the emergence of Brazilian ocean policy, and those which have implicitly addressed some related questions have reached different conclusions than those reached here. By setting the historical record straight, misunderstanding about the contemporary performance of this Latin American leader hopefully can be lessened. First, the historical record of Brazilian ocean policy will be set forth, and its relevance for current policies clarified. Then, interpretations of this record will be developed and implications drawn.

REVISIONISM AND NATIONAL OCEAN POLICIES

Freedom of the seas was generally accepted for
hundreds of years as a satisfactory legal principle
balancing unencumbered use of the high seas by all
with national sovereignty in narrow territorial
seas. Latin American states long adhered to these
traditional rules and practices, but there were latent conflicts with national interests. The old
legal order of the oceans had essentially been formulated in response to the naval, navigational, and
distant-water fishing interests of the major maritime powers. As Latin American states generally became more active and aware in the foreign policy
sphere, recognition grew that the traditional freedom of the seas regime might often be inappropriate
for developing states.

Revisionism may be considered as the response
of states to change the traditional law of the sea.
All Latin American states, Brazil included, essentially have come to favor revision of the traditional law of the sea to one degree or another. Viewed
in historical perspective, Brazilian ocean policy is
an important, if distinctive, component of complex
regional revisionist demands, which together have
had great impact in reshaping the traditional law of
the sea. Due to distinctive historical backgrounds
and interests underlying national ocean policies,
the commitment to revise traditional law has nevertheless differed from state to state. Some states
moved toward revisionism earlier than others and
some have embraced revisionism much more than
others.

While revisionism has become a common element
in Latin American ocean policies, distinctive national interests in each case then tend to shape
specific policy decisions. Revisionism has had a
broad, general impact on all Latin American states,
while distinctive national interests have shaped the
specific directions the drive for change has taken.
The evolution of and interaction between revisionism
and national ocean interests can accordingly indicate, in large part, the general and specific determinants of policy behavior.

The growth of Latin American maritime revisionism nevertheless should not be equated with the
emergence and development of national ocean policies. Numerous Latin American states long rejected
much of revisionism, including Brazil, at a time
when their ocean policies frequently were largely
inactive or inchoate. One can well imagine a

realistic scenario in which the majority of Latin
American states would have continued to reject much
of revisionism, as they began to develop active
ocean policies. For example, the major maritime
powers might have imaginatively consented to the
adaptation or qualification of the traditional ocean
order to the distinctive needs of aspiring, developing states. But concessions to such perceived needs
were not offered, at least in time, to stem the rising tide of revisionism. Instead, from a relatively
early date, the perceived needs of developing states
were coming to include broad national resource zones
in which activities of developed states would be
regulated. Later in time, an international deep
seabed regime, likewise limiting and regulating access of technologically developed states for the
benefit of developing states, was added to the revisionist agenda.

So, if the relationship is not causal, in fact,
the growth of Latin American maritime revisionism
became increasingly associated with the emergence
and development of national ocean policies. Both
events have closely interacted and both have largely
been confined to the postwar period. As revisionism
gradually gained momentum, it provided a powerful
stimulus for the development of national ocean policies to defend and exploit broad offshore zones.
And as emerging national ocean policies began to experience the constraints freedom of the seas placed
on technologically inferior states, revisionism
gained favor.

ORIGINS OF BRAZILIAN OCEAN POLICY

Brazil resisted the revisionist momentum longer
than other major Latin American states, but an early,
if isolated, example of moderate Brazilian revisionism dates back to 1939. In response to the outbreak
of World War II, the Latin American states and the
United States convened the First Consultative Meeting of Foreign Ministers and approved the Declaration of Panama. This document might be considered
revisionist, because it qualified traditional freedom of the seas in establishing a 300-mile security
zone around the continent. Four supplementary documents to the 1939 conference were subsequently singled out as evidence of early revisionism by the Inter-American Juridical Committee (IJC) in 1965, with
a Brazilian as president, in a unanimously approved
report. The 1965 IJC report cited the four 1939

documents as evidence to reconfirm the apparent intention of the Declaration of Panama "to establish a
territorial sea sui generis for the American continent."[1] Two of these four 1939 documents were Brazilian statements, one a "Declaration of the Government of Brazil on the continental sea," and the other a speech by the president of the Brazilian delegation at the final plenary meeting of the conference. In both documents, the Brazilian position
interpreted the 300-mile security zone as a new
"principle of the continental sea" for promoting
peace on the American continent at a time of war in
Europe. The speech spelled out this innovative concept:

> From our point of view, the international
> concept of 'territorial sea' ought to
> have the broadest interpretation possible
> in the American continent in the present
> situation of war in Europe. This was the
> reason why Brazil deemed it advisable for
> the states of this hemisphere to reach
> agreement about a broader limit for the
> territorial sea of America, or to be more
> exact, for the continental one.[2]

Brazil did emphasize later that such a zone was
strictly for purposes of defense and protection in
time of war and that it would be unacceptable in
peacetime.[3]
Because of the special circumstances of such
wartime measures, Latin American states usually
trace the origin of revisionist trends only back to
the Truman Proclamations of September 1945. One
U.S. presidential proclamation asserted "jurisdiction and control" over the natural resources of the
continental shelf out to a 200-meter depth, due to
its alleged character as an extension of the adjoining land mass. The other proclamation asserted the
right of the United States to establish fishing conservation zones in certain areas of the high seas
adjacent to the territorial sea. While Latin American states have generally traced the origins of 200-
mile zones back to these 1945 U.S. documents, the
Truman Proclamations were carefully qualified claims
in areas where the law was ill-defined and were
careful not to interfere with traditional freedoms
of the seas. The continental shelf proclamation was
limited to a resource claim, without making a more
extensive claim of sovereignty over the shelf itself.
Nor did any state protest the U.S. continental shelf

measure, while the established maritime powers all
protested subsequent Latin American attempts to expand the scope of the U.S. continental shelf proclamation in their own national claims. The fishing
conservation zones were never established in any
event, nor was exclusive national jurisdiction
claimed if nations of other countries already fished
in the projected zones.

The Truman Proclamations only constituted an
indirect influence on the 200-mile claims. The origins of the 200-mile offshore zones are instead to
be found in Chilean bureaucratic politics and fear
of foreign fishing competition, and in early Chilean
cooperation with Ecuador and Peru to protect national fishing interests. Other Latin American states
also cited the U.S. shelf proclamation as a precedent for their shelf claims, but again U.S. policy
was generally misunderstood or misinterpreted.[4]

In October 1945, Mexico was the first of many
Latin American states to cite the U.S. shelf proclamation as a precedent in proclaiming control over
its own continental shelf. The Latin American
claims varied in content, but generally tended to
expand the scope of the U.S. continental shelf proclamation, both with respect to the nature of the
claim over the shelf itself and the relationship of
the shelf claim to superjacent waters. Most Latin
American states claimed sovereignty over the shelf,
while the United States, to repeat, had made a more
limited claim to "jurisdiction and control" over
continental shelf natural resources. A number of
Latin American states also attempted to extend national control from the shelf to superjacent waters
as well, again contrasting with the narrowly defined
U.S. claim to shelf resources alone.

In response to the regional trend, Brazil
claimed control over the continental shelf in November 1950, but only in the relatively limited form of
"exclusive jurisdiction" rather than an extreme
claim of sovereignty. Moreover, the limit of the
continental shelf was carefully specified shortly
afterwards in December 1950 as varying between 180
and 200 meters of depth.[5] Brazil was clearly in the
Latin American minority in carefully setting dual
limits, both with respect to depth and jurisdiction,
on its continental shelf claim.[6]

The relatively late date of the Brazilian continental shelf decree also suggests a cautious approach. Between the 1945 Truman Proclamation and
the 1950 Brazilian decree there were 18 continental
shelf claims, 12 of which were in Latin America and

61

the Caribbean, so the Brazilian measure was most
cautious in its revisionism.[7] The decree itself explicitly affirmed the intention to conform to, not
set, a regional precedent: "considering that various states of America, through presidential declarations or decrees have affirmed /continental shelf/
rights that are due them, ... in such conditions it
is incumbent upon the Brazilian government ... to
formulate an identical declaration."[8] Brazil and
several other states in Latin America indeed did not
go beyond the Truman shelf proclamation by limiting
control only to shelf resources and not to the shelf
itself.[9]

Revisionism involving national claims to broad
offshore zones was much slower in gaining general
recognition, including from Brazil, than shelf
claims. Revisionism in this area began when an Argentine decree of October 1946 claimed sovereignty
over both the continental shelf and the superjacent
or "epicontinental" sea covering the shelf. Again,
the Truman Proclamations were cited as a precedent.
The exclusive Argentine claim to superjacent waters
apparently was really limited to fisheries, since
free navigation remained unaffected in the epicontinental sea. In any event, such legislation attempting to link continental shelf rights to rights
over fishing resources in superjacent waters went
beyond the Truman Proclamations, which asserted no
such link.

The 1950 Brazilian shelf decree made no claim
to superjacent waters, but did reserve a right to
promulgate subsequent fisheries legislation in that
area ("rules governing navigation in the waters
covering the aforesaid continental shelf shall continue in force without prejudice to any further
rules ... especially as regards fishing in that
area"). One commentator has seen an important revisionist implication in this provision.

> Because it /the 1950 Brazilian shelf claim/
> reserved a right relative to the fisheries
> in the superjacent waters, it emphasized
> the significance of a 'Shelf' plus super-
> jacent waters connexion, ... /and/ pointed
> in the direction of a maritime zone.[10]

If this perhaps reads more revisionism into the historical record than was really there, at least this
example indicates that Brazilian policy-makers,
while unwilling to take such a revisionist step with
respect to superjacent waters at the time, did want

to reserve such an option for the future.

Eight Latin American states did make a link between shelf rights and rights in superjacent waters in their legislation between 1945 and 1950 (Argentina, Chile, Costa Rica, Ecuador, El Salvador, Honduras, Panama and Peru).[11] But such an approach to control offshore fisheries through linkage with shelf rights never achieved a majority position in the region, so most of these types of claims were eventually superseded by other kinds of claims to the same superjacent waters.[12]

Unilateral claims of Chile and Peru in 1947 and Ecuador in 1950, if ostensibly resembling some other Latin American claims to the shelf and superjacent waters, were really more ambitious and led to protracted difficulties with the United States. The CEP states (Chile, Ecuador, Peru) suffer from very narrow continental shelves which drop off quickly into the Pacific, so that they could not benefit from literal application of previous continental shelf proclamations. The precedent of coastal state control over resources of the adjacent continental shelf was accordingly expanded once again, this time without reference to the physical characteristics of the continental shelf. A broad national zone for exploitation of living and non-living resources was declared, covering both the seabed and superjacent waters regardless of depth. Claims of sovereignty (Chile) or "sovereignty and jurisdiction" (Peru) were asserted over both the seabed and superjacent waters out to a distance of 200 miles (Chile and Peru) or to a depth of 200 meters (Ecuador). The Declaration of Santiago on the Maritime Zone of August 18, 1952 reconciled some differences in these CEP claims and provided for a common policy on the basis of "sovereignty and jurisdiction" over the seabed, subsoil and superjacent waters out to 200 miles from their coasts, in which only the restrictive legal regime of innocent passage of vessels, not free navigation, would be permitted.

The legal language of the Santiago Declaration was ambiguous. The terms "sovereignty and jurisdiction" in a "maritime zone" suggested that a relatively limited claim to jurisdiction over resources was intended, but "sovereignty" and "innocent passage" were characteristics of a territorial sea. So it was uncertain just how ambitious the CEP claims really were, whether to full, unqualified sovereignty out to 200 miles or to more limited jurisdiction over resources. Whatever the exact mix of sovereignty and jurisdiction intended in the original CEP claims, the United States consistently opposed them on grounds of "creeping jurisdiction." Extensive assertions of sovereignty over the continental shelf by some other Latin American states had been disturbing to the United States and the other established maritime powers as well. But they perceived a much more serious challenge in the CEP claims, which allegedly distorted the continental shelf doctrine even more by first ignoring the depth of superjacent waters and then using the doctrine as a springboard for making broad fishing or territorial sea claims.

Most Latin American states responded ambivalently to the recurring controversy between the CEP states and the United States. They were often attracted to the extensive offshore claims and calls for equity of revisionism, but generally were more cautious in their maritime claims than the CEP states. Brazil, too, pursued a cautious course on this issue. In this initial stage of Latin American revisionism, Brazil did not link or follow up its restrained 1950 continental shelf claim with any claim to superjacent waters. Brazil's self-imposed shelf limitations of depth and jurisdiction contrasted with Peru's 1947 claim to 200 miles of seabed and superjacent waters regardless of depth and with Argentina's 1946 epicontinental sea claim, which did not specify the distance limit of sovereignty asserted over the continental shelf and superjacent waters. At this early juncture, Brazilian interests, in any event, did not require firm support of revisionism. Since east coast South American states have broad continental shelves, Brazil did not need to rely on radical revision of existing practice, as the narrow shelf, west coast CEP states had felt compelled to do by omitting reference to depth of superjacent waters. Nor did Brazil harbor greater shelf ambitions at the time, while Argentina, Brazil's southern neighbor, aspired to control its extremely broad shelf which extends at some points over 400 miles into the South Atlantic. Fishing likewise bulked much larger in the CEP economies than in that of Brazil, and foreign fishing still had not posed a challenge.

The Brazilian approach to the territorial sea and related issues was likewise cautious in endorsing revisionism. The 1930 Conference on the Progressive Codification of International Law at the Hague, sponsored by the League of Nations, was the first world conference to deal at least in part with the breadth of the territorial sea. With most Third

World states still in colonial status, only 48 delegations attended the Hague Conference, of which 32
took a stand on the territorial sea breadth issue.
Of these 32 states, 16 supported a 3-mile territorial sea, sometimes with an additional contiguous
zone, while the remainder favored a broader limit.
With positions split so evenly, no voting took place
nor was any convention elaborated. The established
maritime states all took a 3-mile territorial sea
stand, with no additional contiguous zone, which reflected their interest in maintaining the traditional freedom of the seas regime with narrow coastal
state offshore sovereign powers. In contrast, a
group of weaker, coastal states, mostly from Europe
and Latin America, made revisionist claims, mostly
moderate but a few more radical in the context of
the time, to broader coastal state zones of control
more commensurate with their interests.

Radical Latin American claims were not prominent at the 1930 Conference, nor were the Latin
American states "as outstandingly active as some of
them were later in the Geneva conferences /1958 and
1960/."13 Of the 9 Latin American participants at
the 1930 Conference, only four responded to the invitation of the President to put forward proposals
they supported. Brazil, Chile and Uruguay proposed
a 6-mile territorial sea with no contiguous zone,
which was cautiously revisionist in the context of
the time. The instructions for the Brazilian delegation "advocated the enlargement of the territorial
sea so that the needs of administrative law would
coincide with the provisions of international
law."14 Of the Latin American states, Cuba alone
made a somewhat more ambitious proposal for a 6-mile
territorial sea with an additional contiguous zone.

The failure of the Hague Conference to establish a commonly agreed breadth for the territorial
sea did not lead Brazil unilaterally to revise national legislation along the lines of its mildly revisionist 6-mile territorial sea proposal. A less
revisionist approach was relied upon by establishing
a contiguous zone out to 12 miles in 1932 and by
setting fishing regulations in the same area several
years later. Brazil was reluctant to revise territorial sea legislation without clear multilateral
approval, and continued to adhere to a 3-mile territorial sea for more than three decades, until 1966,
when it claimed a six-mile territorial sea with an
additional six-mile contiguous zone. Brazil's cautious, legalistic position on this issue is particularly significant, since the major area of conflict

at the 1958 and 1960 global law of the sea conferences, as in 1930, was just this area of the limit
of the territorial sea and the related problem of
limits of jurisdiction over coastal fisheries.

Brazil's cautious approach to the question of
the breadth of the territorial sea, if compatible
with a mildly revisionist proposal in 1930, became a
more traditional stand in the context of increasing
Latin American revisionist claims of the 1950s and
1960s. Brazilian behavior in the Inter-American
Juridical Committee of the Organization of American
States illustrates the evolving ocean policy context. In 1952, Brazil, Colombia and the United
States filed a joint protest against the Committee's
"Draft Convention on Territorial Waters and Related
Questions," which essentially endorsed views of the
more radical Latin American group voting as the majority (Argentina, Chile, Mexico and Peru). A 200-
mile territorial sea is not part of accepted international law, the three dissenting states jointly
argued, since most states endorse no more than a 3
or 6 mile territorial sea and an additional contiguous zone up to a total of 12 miles. Nor is it correct, they added, that international law endorses
sovereign claims over the continental shelf, and indeed, the joint dissent explicitly noted that Brazil
and the United States had made no such claim themselves.[15]

The three dissenting states, a minority of the
representatives in the Inter-American Juridical Committee at the time, demonstrated less than a year
later that they really were part of a regional majority rejecting the most radical claims. In 1953,
in what was then the parent body, the Inter-American
Council of Jurists, in which all OAS members were
represented, 18 states implicitly endorsed the position of the three dissenters in remanding the Draft
Convention to the Inter-American Juridical Committee
for further study.[16]

The more revisionist Latin American states,
still a regional minority, continued their drive to
reshape the law through regional conferences in 1956,
when their views were largely reflected in the Principles of Mexico on the Juridical Regime of the Sea.
These principles, adopted in Resolution XIII of the
Third Meeting of the Inter-American Council of Jurists, have been called "perhaps the most important
of the contributions realized by the inter-American
system to the progressive development of Latin American international maritime law."[17] But, in fact,
Latin American states remained divided on the law of

66

the sea, with eleven states making reservations and statements to the resolution. The Brazilian reservations were among the most insistent in supporting traditional law. In different reservations, Brazil indicated that it is not true that a three-mile territorial sea is insufficient in all cases, but where this is the case, a contiguous zone could supplement it in a satisfactory way; that each state does not have unqualified unilateral competence to set the breadth of its territorial sea; and that Brazil concurs in the principle of coastal state resource control over the continental shelf, but Brazil's claim is limited to exclusive jurisdiction.[18]

The Inter-American Specialized Conference on Conservation of Natural Resources convened several months after the Mexico City meeting in March 1956. The resulting Ciudad Trujillo Resolution reflected similar differences among Latin American states, save an agreement reached on the definition of the continental shelf. This continental shelf definition later received global endorsement at the First United Nations Conference on the Law of the Sea. A Brazilian reservation to the resolution still cautiously added that conclusions reached at the Ciudad Trujillo conference would not prejudice subsequent regional and global agreements that might be reached.[19]

INTERNATIONAL LAW COMMISSION PREPARATORY DISCUSSIONS

Latin American efforts to revise the law through unilateral claims and regional conferences, persistent if often thwarted even within the region, ran parallel with global law of the sea discussions. Global law of the sea negotiations eventually came to occupy center stage. The International Law Commission (ILC), a technical group functioning within the United Nations framework, had chosen the law of the sea at its first session in 1949 as one of three areas in which to undertake codification and progressive development of international law. Draft conventions were to be prepared and then submitted to an international conference for approval. By 1956, after discussion in seven subsequent annual sessions and several revisions in response to comments from governments, ILC draft articles on the law of the sea were indeed submitted to the United Nations General Assembly as working documents for an international conference on the subject. But this did not stem the tide of revisionism. "The work of

the ILC led directly to the First United Nations
Conference on the Law of the Sea in 1958, but in the
years between 1951 and that conference 28 more
states unilaterally extended their maritime jurisdiction ... (with) Latin American states ... prominent in the list of claimants."[20]

While revisionism continued to gather strength,
it still was not a decisive force at the global level. The ILC draft articles broadly reflected compromises between moderate revisionists and more traditional states. This included existing law and
some elements of generally acceptable new law, but
excluded the more extreme revisionist demands.
Since the draft articles served as working papers
for the law of the sea conference, they had an extremely important impact on subsequent global negotiations at Geneva.

As a moderate revisionist or perhaps even a
moderately traditional state in law of the sea matters at the time, Brazil was in an advantageous position to influence the important preparatory stage
of the First United Nations Conference on the Law of
the Sea. Brazil participated directly in the ILC
debates during the 1950s as one of only 15 members,
and unlike some of the other Latin American states,
made no extreme unilateral maritime claim in the
period. Representatives from Brazil and Mexico were
the only two from Latin America on the ILC during
the entire 1949-1956 period of preparatory work for
the law of the sea conference. The other Latin
American members were Panama and Colombia from 1949
to 1953 and Cuba and Bolivia from 1954 to 1956. The
Latin American ILC members were mostly moderates at
the time and helped influence the outcome in that
direction. Six traditional maritime states (the
U.K., the U.S., the Netherlands, Sweden, France, and
Greece) rounded out most of the rest of the 15-mem-
ber ILC, and helped assure that revisionism would be
limited in the ILC draft articles.

The structure of the ILC was also compatible
with the projection of Brazilian influence. The ILC
was a legal, technical body made up of leading jurists, in contrast to the more political bargaining
and negotiations at the subsequent law of the sea
conference. Influence in the preparatory period
consequently was exerted mainly through technical
comments, opinions and proposals of individual jurists. This kind of influence exerted by Brazil's
distinguished representative, Gilberto Amado, was
considerable. For example, at the ILC's first meeting in 1949, Amado was unanimously elected

Rapporteur of the Commission and was responsible for drafting the first ILC report to the United Nations General Assembly later that year. Georges Scelle, the eminent French delegate, subsequently "paid a special tribute to the Commission's Rapporteur who had fulfilled his task to perfection."[21] Diplomatic etiquette perhaps, but the close personal relationship between Scelle and Amado nevertheless helped reconcile interests between developing and developed regions. Amado was later elected Second Vice-Chairman of the ILC in 1952 with 7 out of 8 votes, and was elected First Vice-Chairman in 1953 by acclamation, serving as Acting Chairman during nearly all the law of the sea discussions that year. Amado's selection to three ILC offices during the 1949-1956 preparatory years constituted a considerable proportion of total Latin American representation in official capacities.[22] Amado was also the only Latin American jurist serving continuously during all eight of the ILC 1949-1956 preparatory sessions. Amado brought his deep experience and influence to bear again in support of Brazilian ocean policy as Chairman of the Brazilian delegation at the 1958 and 1960 law of the sea conferences.

Individual participation on such international legal bodies is therefore a good indicator both of the nature of evolving national ocean policy and of influence exerted by that policy. Even when representatives serve in a personal capacity, as in the International Law Commission and the Inter-American Juridical Committee, with very few exceptions they accurately reflect national policy.[23] For example, Amado occupied key national law of the sea positions for over a decade, so that he both influenced and was deeply influenced by national ocean policy. Members have been known to act in variance with national policy, but when in 1971 the U.S. member of the Inter-American Juridical Committee came to favor a compromise with the Latin American members on an extensive economic zone, the Department of State successfully insisted that he cease any effort to reach such a compromise.[24]

Brazil's moderate ocean policy, moreover, was basically compatible with the ILC middle-of-the-road approach to the codification and development of the law of the sea. For example, the ILC draft articles endorsed jurisdictional continental shelf claims, as in the U.S. and Brazilian legislation, and rejected more radical sovereign shelf claims (Argentina and others). The ILC majority, including Brazil, also rejected alleged links between shelf rights and rights in superjacent waters (the CEP states and others) and territorial sea claims greater than 12 miles (El Salvador and others). These avowedly revisionist Latin American states, to repeat, were not included in ILC membership during the years of preparatory work for the law of the sea conference.

Brazil's advantageous position was reinforced by the relative continuity of national ocean policy before, during, and after the ILC preparatory sessions. Moderation characterized policy throughout. Yet, policy did not conform blindly with tradition. While Brazil's ILC participation on law of the sea matters was generally compatible with tradition, Amado stressed that revisions should be pragmatically incorporated into the law where appropriate.

> ... there was no need for the Commission
> to restrict itself to the formulation of
> universally accepted traditional rules.
> Its main duty was to fill the many gaps
> in existing law, to settle dubious in-
> terpretations wherever they arose and
> even to amend existing law in the light
> of new developments, having particular
> regard to the principles of the Charter
> ... The work could not, of course, be
> purely theoretical. It would have to
> take into account political contingen-
> cies and the opinion of governments.[25]

The Brazilian approach was nevertheless cautious in searching for mutually acceptable compromises. The continental shelf issue illustrates these inter-twined themes of tradition, revisionism, caution, and pragmatic compromise.

In exploratory discussions at the 1950 mid-year session, Amado favored deferring ILC consideration of the continental shelf issue, since many governments' positions on the matter, including that of Brazil, were still uncertain.[26] Brazilian caution, it will be recalled, was likewise evident in delaying a continental shelf decree until late 1950, although numerous other states already had made such a claim. The following year at the 1951 ILC session, after the Brazilian shelf decree had been promulgated, Brazil remained on its cautious, moderate path. A Brazilian shelf proposal set a moderate 200-meter depth limit with jurisdictional rights only, in accord with national legislation, in order to safeguard freedom of the seas and avoid giving "States control over much too large an area."[27] An expansive shelf definition based solely on ability to exploit seawards was nevertheless included in the 1951 version of the draft articles. Brazil was influential in subsequently excising this expansive shelf definition from the draft articles and substituting a 200-meter depth limit for it. In 1953, Brazil reaffirmed support for two important limitations on the shelf definition, "sovereign rights" of the coastal state over the shelf (rather than "sovereignty") and a fixed limit for the shelf (rather than ability to exploit).[28] Both limitations gained ILC approval in 1953, with Amado as the active ILC First Vice-Chairman and Acting Chairman on law of the sea matters that year.

The "sovereign rights" formula Brazil supported was eventually included in the final draft articles, but the issue of the outer limit of the continental shelf was reopened in the final ILC session devoted to the law of the sea. Here, the pragmatic evolution of Brazilian policy was evident. By 1956, in the Ciudad Trujillo Resolution, Brazil had given qualified support to a compromise continental shelf definition depending both on depth and ability to exploit seawards. This dual depth-exploitability shelf formula represented a compromise in limiting shelf claims on the basis of depth but allowing for some progressive expansion on the basis of exploitability. Later that year Brazil supported the same compromise definition at the ILC. All Latin American ILC members, including Brazil, successfully supported the initiative of the 1956 ILC Chairman, García Amador of Cuba, in reinserting the expansive exploitability formula into the final version of the draft articles. Reasonable revisionist shelf demands should be recognized, Amado stressed, including special provisions for the CEP states.

> Jurists from the American continent appreciated the problems of those countries which had no continental shelf, and he /Amado/ felt that the Commission could not prevent such countries exploiting the natural resources of the sea-bed at a greater depth than 200 meters if exploitation were possible.[29]

The complex amalgan of tradition, revisionism, caution, and pragmatic compromise evident in the evolution of Brazilian policy toward the continental shelf was evident in other key issues as well. The high seas and related issues constitute a case in

point. Principles proposed by Brazil in 1950 for
the high seas stressed the traditional principle of
freedom of the seas and generated extended discussion. The traditional emphasis of this Brazilian
proposal was qualified by mildly revisionist provisions for a contiguous zone and for fisheries conservation zones in the high seas.[30] The contiguous
zone provided for in the Brazilian proposal would
have been adjacent to the territorial sea yet part
of the high seas, with a breadth not more than twice
that of the territorial sea up to a combined maximum
of 12 miles. The contiguous zone draft article
eventually adopted by the ILC did embody some features of the Brazilian proposal.[31]

A much more revisionist feature for coastal
state control for security purposes in a contiguous
zone, subsequently supported by Brazil and Mexico,
was excluded from the same ILC draft article.[32]
Brazilian support for this revisionist plank indicates that national emphasis on freedom of the high
seas and consequently on narrow territorial seas as
well was less emphatic than separate analysis of
each issue might suggest. Traditional maritime
states have regarded security control as akin to a
territorial sea, in spite of the additional legal
ramifications of a territorial sea, hence their opposition to the Brazilian-Mexican proposal. A related U.S. concern about "creeping jurisdiction" has
expressed opposition to just such piecemeal extension of state competence into previously unregulated
ocean space. So Brazilian willingness to explore
various kinds of proposals and compromises for more
extensive coastal state jurisdictions beyond the
territorial sea and into the high seas did distinguish it from this traditional group.

The Brazilian approach to fisheries conservation zones in the high seas likewise balanced tradition and innovation. In the 1951 ILC session, a
U.S. fisheries conservation proposal provided for
management solely by states engaged in high seas
fisheries in zones determined by them. This proposal, Amado argued, "coldly envisaged that a powerful and rich State might establish itself in any
area of the high seas and take possession of it." A
competing and moderately revisionist fisheries conservation proposal was described by Amado, in contrast, as following "the slow and natural evolution
of law." This moderately revisionist proposal provided for joint fisheries management by the coastal
state and other interested states in a 200-mile zone
adjacent to the coastal state. "An endeavor should

be made to reconcile these two formulae," Amado added, and accordingly he voted with the ILC majority for a composite proposal for fisheries conservation zones. This composite proposal provided for joint management if the zone were adjacent to the coastal state and management solely by states engaged in high seas fisheries if the zone were not adjacent to a coastal state.[33] Part of the compromise in Brazilian eyes, to be sure, was that fisheries conservation zones not unnecessarily limit traditional freedoms of the seas, including freedom of fishing. So Brazil opposed 1955 Cuban amendments to the Commission's draft articles on fisheries, because of "the undue latitude given to the coastal State" and the failure to specify the "maximum distance from the coast to which the powers of the coastal State would be restricted."[34]

Brazil's middle-of-the-road policy nevertheless leaned toward moderate revisionism on the fisheries issue. Besides giving continuous support during ILC discussions to the principle of shared responsibility of the coastal state and other concerned states in fisheries conservation zones in adjacent high seas, late in 1955 a Brazilian government note verbale to the ILC expressed willingness to accept exclusive coastal state fishing rights out to 12 miles.[35] That is, the coastal state would have exclusive fishing rights out to 12 miles and still would share in management of adjacent fisheries conservation zones beyond 12 miles.

Amado supported a related revisionist plank in 1956, in urging recognition of the special position of the coastal state in the conservation of living resources in any area of the high seas adjacent to its territorial sea. To emphasize the point, revisionist Peru was cited in his statement as an example of the need for such a coastal state right for conservation. In cooperation with Latin American ILC members and others, Brazilian support helped pass an amendment to the relevant draft article on fisheries to that effect over the opposition of the traditional maritime states.[36] On Amado's initiative, a supplementary commentary was also added to the same draft article to reinforce its innovative nature: "The 'special' character of the interest of the coastal State should be interpreted in the sense that the interest exists by reason of the sole fact of the geographical situation." The traditional maritime states insisted, in turn, that this sentence of commentary be immediately followed by another, stipulating that: "However, the Commission did not wish to imply that the 'special' interest of the coastal State would take precedence per se over the interests of the other States concerned."[37]

The breadth of the territorial sea was a final major issue in which Brazil tried to balance traditional and more revisionist approaches. The traditional maritime states continued to argue that a three mile limit was a binding rule of international law, while more revisionist states supported broader limits. Brazil still maintained a three-mile territorial sea, Amado noted in the 1952 ILC session, but did not recognize any traditional rule governing the breadth of the territorial sea. Accordingly, he added that Brazil would accept a six-mile proposal then before the ILC if a majority supported it.[38] As a compromise, Amado later proposed substituting the six-mile proposal still before the Commission with a proposal rejecting three miles as a binding rule, yet setting twelve miles as the maximum permissible breadth of the territorial sea. This 1952 Brazilian proposal received mixed responses from traditional maritime states and more reform-minded states, so that a decision on territorial sea breadth was deferred to a subsequent session.[39]

When the ILC returned to consider the territorial sea breadth issue in 1955 at its 7th session, Amado introduced the same proposal again with great success. After extensive discussion of the Brazilian proposal, an amended version was adopted by a 7 to 6 vote:

> 1. The Commission recognizes that international practice is not uniform as regards traditional limitation of the territorial sea to three miles.
> 2. The Commission considers that international law does not justify the extension of the territorial sea beyond twelve miles.
> 3. The Commission, without taking any decisions as to the breadth of the territorial sea within that limit, considers that international law does not require States to recognize a breadth beyond three miles.[40]

The draft article based on the 1955 Brazilian proposal was a masterpiece in the art of compromise. This conciliatory description of the legal situation was all that could be achieved, since underlying disagreement prevented precise formulation of rules of law in this area. The traditional maritime states were displeased with the failure of the draft article to recognize three miles as a binding rule, yet they could only be pleased that any limit beyond 12 miles was explicitly rejected and that claims between 3 and 12 miles were not specifically endorsed. As a carrot for this traditional group of states, Amado emphasized that the proposal "would serve to restrain the more extensive claims being made by some States," particularly when coupled with the draft articles on fisheries conservation zones.[41] With these reassurances, Great Britain, the traditional champion of the three-mile limit, declared its support for the Brazilian proposal, although the United States remained opposed. There were advantages for the revisionists, too. The revisionists had heretofore been accused of violating law in extending the territorial sea beyond 3 miles, so they welcomed recognition that territorial sea breadth was unsettled in law between 3 and 12 miles. In support of this group, Amado said that "he could not accept the thesis that international law laid down a three-mile limit." Accordingly, he added, "the Commission would do well to bear in mind the relative size of, for example, the Pacific Ocean and the Mediterranean Sea, and approach the issue in a more realistic spirit."[42] In response, the Soviet Union and those Latin American ILC members of a mildly revisionist stripe also supported the Brazilian proposal.

The Soviet ILC member, in opening the eighth ILC session in 1956 as Vice-Chairman, subsequently paid "a tribute to Mr. Amado for his outstanding contribution, which had led to some measure of agreement on the subject of the breadth of the territorial sea."[43] Because comments were received from governments on the draft article corresponding to Amado's proposal in the interim between the 7th and 8th sessions, the territorial sea breadth issue was reopened a final time by the ILC in 1956. Explicitly relying on the 1955 Brazilian proposal, Mr. Spiropolous of Greece proposed several amendments to the wording in Amado's three paragraphs. A fourth paragraph also was added recommending that an international conference fix the breadth of the territorial sea. This amended proposal was subsequently adopted by 9 votes to 2, with 4 abstentions, and was incorporated in exactly the same form in the final version of the draft articles prepared for the law of the sea conference as Article 3:

1. The Commission recognizes that international practice is not uniform as regards the delimitation of the territorial sea.
2. The Commission considers that international law does not permit an extension of the territorial sea beyond twelve miles.
3. The Commission, without taking any decision as to the breadth of the territorial sea within that limit, notes, on the one hand, that many States have fixed a breadth greater than three miles and, on the other hand, that many States do not recognize such a breadth when that of their own territorial sea is less.
4. The Commission considers that the breadth of the territorial sea should be fixed by an international conference.[44]

The draft article went further in promoting compromise between diverging groups on the key issue of territorial sea breadth than any other global law of the sea conference before or since. The 1930 Hague Conference had foundered on the issue; the First United Nations Conference on the Law of the Sea did not follow up on the ILC recommendation to fix the breadth of the territorial sea and even failed to approve the ILC draft article corresponding to Amado's proposal; the second law of the sea conference ended in failure because of its inability to resolve the issue; and the third law of the sea conference still continues to wrestle with the issue. If a master treaty is eventually produced at the third law of the sea conference, it will certainly support a 12-mile territorial sea, but if the conference fails, state practice could remain fluid in this area.

FIRST UNITED NATIONS CONFERENCE ON THE LAW OF THE SEA

Although there were basic disagreements among Latin American states, the years of regional and ILC law of the sea discussions had prepared many of them well for the First and Second United Nations Conferences on the Law of the Sea (UNCLOS I and II) at Geneva. The general Latin American contribution to UNCLOS I and II has been generally recognized,[45] but

Brazil's low-key, yet important role has been over-looked.

UNCLOS I assembled over 86 states in 1958 to discuss the entire law of the sea field, in contrast to the 1930 Hague Conference, with little more than half as many participants debating only one maritime issue, the breadth of the territorial sea. In spite of a comprehensive agenda and numerous participants at Geneva, the law of the sea was codified and developed through four conventions (the territorial sea and the contiguous zone, the high seas, fishing and conservation of the living resources of the high seas, and the continental shelf). The conventions included a 12-mile overall limit on a contiguous zone adjacent to the territorial sea for the specific purposes of customs, fiscal, immigration and sanitary regulations. Territorial sea claims greater than 12 miles consequently did not seem permitted, but the draft article based on Amado's ILC proposal, which had clearly set a maximum 12-mile territorial sea limit, was not approved at UNCLOS I. Also recognized at Geneva was a narrowly defined, yet special, coastal state interest in fisheries' conservation in the high seas adjacent to the territorial sea. Finally, the Convention on the Continental Shelf codified the law on the subject, although not recognizing the more ambitious versions of shelf rights.

So there was qualified recognition by the world community of a need for more extensive zones for coastal state sovereignty (the territorial sea) and especially for jurisdiction (the contiguous zone, the fisheries' conservation zones, and the continental shelf). But the revisionist group obviously favored moving further and faster in this direction than the more traditional group. UNCLOS I did not resolve this fundamental conflict over acceptable limits of coastal state jurisdiction and sovereignty, nor did UNCLOS II. UNCLOS II was convened in 1960 to resolve two such questions left unresolved at UNCLOS I, the breadth of the territorial sea and the limits of coastal state jurisdiction over fisheries, yet the conference ended in a deadlock.

On the one side at UNCLOS I and II were the revisionists, some radical and others more moderate, with some Latin American states playing a prominent role in this grouping. On the other side were the traditional maritime powers, a group in which the United States emerged as a particularly prominent actor. Also prominent was an East-West Cold War cleavage, in contrast to considerable overlapping of superpower interests as détente matured during the years of the Third United Nations Conference on the Law of the Sea (UNCLOS III).

Overlaps in coalitions there still were at Geneva. Latin American states, revisionists and moderates alike, generally rallied around U.S. leadership on Cold War issues. The more moderate revisionists and the more pragmatic traditional maritime powers also shared some interests and approaches. It is in this gray area that Brazilian policies evolved, sometimes endorsing traditional freedoms of the seas and at other times cautiously endorsing some revisionist planks, or at least exploring possibilities for compromise. This cautious, compromising posture has obscured Brazilian influence at the Geneva conferences, because both radical revisionists and traditional maritime powers gained prominence, but not necessarily influence, in pushing their respective positions vigorously. It has already been demonstrated that Brazil was active and influential at the ILC preparatory discussions, which in turn shaped the subsequent Geneva negotiations. Yet, accounts of Latin American participation at the ILC and at the subsequent Geneva conferences do not even mention Brazil, while noting the relative prominence of moderately revisionist Mexico and of the more radical revisionist CEP states.[46] None of these commentaries discuss Brazilian participation at the ILC preparatory meetings, at UNCLOS I and II, or any other circumstances conditioning Brazilian ocean policy.

A recent tabulation of Latin American proposals at UNCLOS I implicitly reached a similar conclusion that states making few proposals, including Brazil, had a very low level of influence and activity in the Geneva debates. Thirteen proposals were introduced by two or more Latin American states, five of which were adopted. The only proposal Brazil co-sponsored, which was one of the five adopted, merely dealt with a procedural matter relating to the number of Vice-Presidents of the Conference. Taking into account both sponsored and co-sponsored proposals at UNCLOS I which were adopted, Mexico led with 12, Argentina, Chile and Uruguay had 4, Venezuela 3, Peru 2, and Brazil only 1 (the co-sponsored procedural proposal mentioned above).[47] The writer has calculated that Brazil itself only sponsored two proposals at UNCLOS I, one on flags of convenience and the other on the high seas, neither of which was adopted.[48] In contrast, "Mexico, which undeniably was the most active Latin American State at the

Conference, and the one which made a substantial contribution, ... sponsored 18 proposals of its own, and co-sponsored another 14."[49]

This tabulation of UNCLOS proposals does reconfirm the finding of other studies that Latin American states have been very influential members of the revisionist group. However, tabulation of proposals is an inappropriate indicator of Brazilian influence. While tabulation of UNCLOS I proposals may be useful in gauging influential members of the revisionist group, Brazil did not belong to the revisionist group at the time. For moderate states, such as Brazil, UNCLOS I proposals were not the only route to influence.

Prior to UNCLOS I, Brazil had been active and influential at the ILC preparatory sessions, so that a number of provisions important to Brazil had already been included in the ILC draft articles through its own proposals or through support of others' proposals. Since Brazil was largely satisfied with the draft articles, it obviously had no incentive to submit a large number of proposals at UNCLOS I to alter these very draft articles. Yet, like the other studies cited previously, no mention whatsoever is made in the tabulation study of Brazilian participation at the ILC preparatory sessions. UNCLOS I revisionist proposals, in contrast, were largely designed to alter the ILC draft articles and thereby reorient the course of the Geneva negotiations. Influence was accordingly just as real at UNCLOS I through support for the draft articles or through encouragement of constructive compromises as through revisionist proposals. In terms of final results, after all, the ILC draft articles were carried over in large part into the four 1958 Geneva conventions. Consequently, Brazil's influence was greater and its relationship to Latin American and other states was different than that usually implied.

By and large, Brazilian performance at UNCLOS I and II, as at the ILC preparatory sessions, balanced traditional and moderately revisionist approaches. But UNCLOS I and II were not merely a replay for Brazil of the technically-oriented ILC discussions between a limited number of jurists. In a dynamic, complex global setting, political interaction and adjustment with major actors and forces was required.

Moderation, for example, characterized the Brazilian approach to continental shelf issues. Latin American states took a leading role at UNCLOS I in promoting the compromise ILC definition of the breadth of the continental shelf, which was eventually adopted at Geneva. The compromise shelf definition included a 200-meter depth limit, also present in the 1945 U.S. shelf definition, and added an exploitability provision: "the seabed and subsoil of the submarine areas adjacent to the coast but outside the area of the territorial sea, to a depth of 200 meters, or, beyond that limit, to where the depth of the superjacent waters admits of the exploitation of the natural resources of the said areas." The first element of the Geneva continental shelf definition, the 200-meter depth limit, represented an exact measurement, but the second element, shelf breadth depending on ability to exploit seawards, varied according to the state of technology at the particular time and presumably allowed for progressively broader national claims beyond 200 meters. Brazil, like other Latin American states, came to support the two-fold continental shelf definition of depth of superjacent waters (200 meters) and ability to exploit, which was more extensive than the 180 to 200-meter limit set in its own national legislation. The cautious evolution of Brazilian policy toward this moderately revisionist position, first in the 1956 Ciudad Trujillo Resolution and then in ILC discussions, has already been noted.

While Latin American consensus then emerged around a compromise definition for the breadth of the continental shelf, a debate about the extent of coastal state rights on the shelf split Latin America at UNCLOS I. Brazil again adopted a moderate approach, this time in conformity with its own national legislation. Brazil favored limiting coastal state continental shelf powers to jurisdictional resource rights, not unqualified sovereignty, just as the Truman shelf proclamation and the Brazilian continental shelf decree had done. Such restrictive coastal state rights were indeed eventually included in the Geneva Convention on the Continental Shelf: "The coastal State exercises over the continental shelf sovereign rights for the purpose of exploring it and exploiting its natural resources."

The moderate stance led Brazil explicitly to criticize ambitious Argentine and Mexican claims to continental shelf sovereignty, as well as an Argentine proposal giving coastal states special rights in the superjacent waters of the shelf as a consequence of rights over the shelf.[50] Brazil similarly stressed limits which should be put on shelf claims in criticizing a Venezuelan proposal for an

unqualified coastal state right to make regulations
concerning routes to be followed by submarine cables
and pipelines.[51] Brazilian moderation on the same
issue was also evident in lending support to a
French proposal to restrict the ability of coastal
states to withhold consent for scientific research
on the continental shelf.[52] Brazil was on the
winning side each time against the revisionists.

Revisionists were active at UNCLOS I and II as
well in pushing for greater breadth of the territorial sea. Between the 1930 Hague Conference and
1960, for example, "36 states had made territorial
sea claims beyond three miles, and 48 states had
made some sort of claim to the continental shelf."[53]
As at previous regional fora, Peru vigorously advocated unilateral competency in determining the
breadth of the territorial sea "within reasonable
limits." While Peru's vague, expansive formula was
decisively rejected at UNCLOS I, Mexico was much
more influential, if also ultimately unsuccessful,
in proposing a solution to this thorny problem. A
Mexican-Indian proposal at UNCLOS I would have permitted territorial seas up to 12 miles, and did
manage to achieve a tie vote (35 in favor, 35
against and 12 abstentions). However, Latin America
again was badly divided, with only 7 Latin American
states voting in favor, 6 against (including Brazil)
and 7 abstaining.

In view of the considerable overall support
attracted by the Mexican-Indian proposal, several
additional attempts were unsuccessfully made to have
a modified version reconsidered. The generally more
extreme CEP states lent their support to these attempts to reconsider the proposal, but otherwise the
divisions continued, with Brazil and many others,
including the traditional maritime powers, still opposing the 12-mile approach.

In a new historical context, with revisionists
supporting 12-mile territorial sea proposals, 6-mile
proposals, at one time themselves revisionist in nature, had become cautious. Brazil's relatively consistent 6-mile territorial sea stance at the 1930
Hague Conference, at the ILC sessions, and at UNCLOS
I and II was affected accordingly. The Brazilian 6-
mile territorial sea proposal at the 1930 Hague Conference and even the Brazilian six-mile offer at the
1952 ILC session had been moderately revisionist,
but in the Geneva context Brazil's support of a similar "six-plus-six" formula had become cautious.
The "six-plus-six" formula referred to a maximum
six-mile territorial sea plus an adjacent exclusive

fishing zone up to 12 miles from the territorial sea baseline.

By 1958, the six-plus-six formula was proposed as a compromise by traditional maritime powers to head off revisionism. National legislation of the traditional maritime powers continued to limit the territorial sea to three miles, but they had failed to gain general recognition of the three-mile limit either in the ILC sessions or in the early phase of the UNCLOS I negotiations. In response, the six-plus-six proposals essentially made a rather limited concession on the territorial sea issue (up to six miles), while offering special coastal state juris-diction rights between six and twelve miles as an enticement for the revisionists. The hope was that revisionists would accommodate themselves to a rela-tively narrow zone of sovereignty in exchange for recognition of special jurisdictional rights beyond the territorial sea. The carrot of special juris-dictional rights beyond a 6-mile territorial sea would include a contiguous zone and an exclusive fishing zone, both of which would extend to a maxi-mum of 12 miles from the territorial sea baseline.

The six-plus-six proposals, with still greater concessions on details, might have provided the basis for an overall conference compromise, but the mari-time powers, and Brazil as well, tended to put ex-cessive stress on traditional elements of the mix. A case in point was Brazilian support for the six-plus-six proposal of the United States since it re-spected historic fishing rights of foreign states in the projected fishing zone and criticism by Brazil of the Canadian six-plus-six proposal for omitting mention of these historic rights.[54] In revisionist eyes, such a qualification gravely diluted the ex-clusive nature of the fishing zone (to repeat, with a maximum 12-mile limit), and compounded the failure of six-plus-six proposals to allow for coastal state fishing jurisdiction beyond twelve miles. When the conference failed to resolve the territorial sea breadth question clearly, Brazil still remained cautious in delaying a transition in national legis-lation from three miles to a six-plus-six formula until 1966.

The U.S. six-plus-six proposal eventually did receive an absolute majority (45 affirmative, 33 negative and 7 abstentions), but this fell short of the two-thirds majority necessary for approval in the Plenary. While concessions implicit in the proposal did not suffice to attract support of the more revisionist states, it did attract more support

than any other territorial sea proposal at UNCLOS I.
For its part, Brazil, in supporting the six-plus-six
proposal, did go beyond 3-mile territorial sea national legislation, and supported compromise.

> Although Brazil had a very long coastline,
> it could not support the various proposals
> put forward by the other Latin American
> States. He /the Brazilian delegate/
> hoped very much that conciliatory efforts
> would be made in the plenary Conference
> and that the Conference would terminate
> in a spirit of harmony.[55]

A recent tally of all national positions on the
territorial sea issue at the two Geneva conferences
permits systematic comparison of Brazilian participation with that of other states.[56] Strong support
for narrow territorial sea limits and strong opposition to wide limits was correlated with negative
votes on 12-mile proposals and affirmative votes on
six-plus-six proposals. On this basis, fourteen
Latin American states were relatively moderate. Of
these fourteen, six Latin American states, including
Brazil, were the most committed to tradition in supporting a six-plus-six formula. Two Latin American
states voted no or abstained on twelve miles and abstained or voted yes on the six-plus-six formula,
therefore reflecting support for, but less commitment to, narrow limits. Six Latin American states
voted affirmatively on both proposals, therefore not
expressing strong preference for either alternative.
Joining these 14 relatively moderate Latin American
states were almost all members of the Western states'
group (28 out of 29 states, with Iceland being a
special case), which included the established maritime powers, but only a few African and Asian states.
A final group of six Latin American states was
clearly revisionist, voting affirmatively on twelve
miles and negatively on six-plus-six proposals and
therefore demonstrating strong support for wide limits and strong opposition to narrow limits. Joining
this avowedly revisionist Latin American group on
the territorial sea issue were many Arab and Asian
states, as well as the East European group.
A more ambitious quantitative study has reconfirmed and extended these findings about national
positions.[57] Factor analysis of all votes taken at
UNCLOS I and II by all participants demonstrated
that territorial sea/contiguous zone breadth was the
most conflictual issue at the conferences, followed

by the issue of fisheries rights of coastal states. The Latin American states were polarized on the territorial sea breadth issue, according to the study. Brazil was confirmed as one of the more traditional Latin American states on the territorial sea issue, while a majority of Latin American states (11) was either traditional, moderate or ambivalent about the issue. Only 8 Latin American states were clearly revisionist on the territorial sea issue, according to the factor analysis method. On the fisheries jurisdiction issue, the bulk of Latin American states was revisionist to one degree or another, with Brazil indicated as one of the less committed states of the group. The Latin American states split on this issue as well in reacting to compromise fisheries proposals at UNCLOS II, which a subsequent section of this paper will examine in some detail.

So the Latin American line-up on key law of the sea issues was complex indeed. While Brazil was no doubt slow in endorsing revisionism, so were most other Latin American states. Moderates of one variety or another, from more traditionally-oriented Brazil to those ambivalent about revisionist proposals, constituted a majority in Latin America, most dramatically on the territorial sea breadth issue. This moderate majority was by no means unified or often even very active, and its degree of opposition to revisionism varied a great deal according to the issue and the specific context. Analysis of a variety of ocean issues over several decades in shifting contexts has shown that Brazilian ocean policy was both more influential and not as traditional as appearances might suggest.

Just as Brazilian opposition to revisionism should not be exaggerated, neither should innovative aspects of policy be ignored. Early in the negotiations at UNCLOS I, for example, when the traditional maritime powers still were hoping to gain recognition of a three-mile territorial sea as the norm, Ambassador Gilberto Amado, Chairman of the Brazilian delegation, warned that their intransigence on the territorial sea and fisheries issues would block conference success. Avid supporters of a three-mile territorial sea were criticized by the Brazilian representative, since intensive fishing that close to coasts of other states "could result in the depletion of fish stocks, and even threaten the well-being of the population of coastal States, as had been recognized in Iceland and also in Peru and the other countries of South America bordering on the

84

Pacific Ocean."[58] In these circumstances, the only
course that would enable the conference to make
progress was that "of separating the question of the
territorial sea from that of fisheries and conservation."[59] Such a course could be pursued, Amado believed, by following up on the innovative Brazilian
approach to fisheries developed at the ILC sessions.
He explicitly called attention to the "new legal
principle" establishing a special coastal state position in management of adjacent fisheries conservation zones in the high seas, which had been endorsed
in the ILC preparatory work for UNCLOS I. This special coastal state right existed "by virtue solely
of its geographical position," Amado added, thereby
reinforcing the same formula he had introduced into
the ILC draft article. "In a sense, therefore, the
rights vested in the coastal State were actually
more extensive than the claims made by certain
States to jurisdiction over large sea areas."[60]
While Amado then disapproved of unnecessarily ambitious maritime claims, he clearly recognized that
such claims often were prompted by concern over
fishing so that progressive fishing provisions were
required for the success of the conference.
    A related Brazilian proposal on the high seas
at UNCLOS I suggests as well that policy was not as
rigid as it might appear and that it contained elements around which much support could be mustered.
In explaining the proposal, which stated that "The
waters of the high seas are for the joint use of all
States," the legal adviser to the Brazilian delegation, Mr. Bulhões Pedeira, argued that the nature of
traditional areas of ocean space was evolving.

> Recent technological and economic develop-
> ment has given rise to discussions about
> the sea-bed, the living resources of the
> sea and the air space above the sea. The
> sea was thus coming to be regarded from a
> three-dimensional aspect, the demarcation
> line of the territorial sea was losing its
> traditional value as the sole frontier with-
> in which a coastal state could exercise its
> authority, and the traditional concept of
> the freedom of the high seas was at the
> same time undergoing some modification.
> The former idea of the high seas as an area
> in which freedom was not subject to any
> restrictions at all was gradually being
> replaced by the concept of the high seas
> as an asset for joint exploitation by all

states.[61]

Here were the seeds of revisionist concepts that
were to reappear with greater vigor at UNCLOS II and
III.

SECOND UNITED NATIONS CONFERENCE ON THE LAW OF THE SEA

Brazil made a more successful attempt to forge
a viable compromise between the traditional and revisionist factions at UNCLOS II than at UNCLOS I.
Brazil's performance at UNCLOS II was still consistent with its positions at UNCLOS I, but at the 1960
Geneva conference Brazil played a more prominent
role. Positions of most of the 88 states at UNCLOS
II likewise remained roughly the same as at the
first Geneva conference, held just two years previously. The 1960 debates did polarize around variations of six-plus-six and 12-mile territorial sea
proposals even more than in 1958, but a plurality
of positions remained within each camp. UNCLOS II,
to repeat, focused on two problems directly related
to these proposals, the breadth of the territorial
sea and the limits of coastal state jurisdiction
over fisheries.
Latin American unity again proved elusive at
UNCLOS II. Peru once again defended the distinctive
CEP policy of offshore jurisdiction to an unspecified, yet very broad limit, to be determined unilaterally by the coastal state. The proposal was
withdrawn when it became obvious that opinion had
coalesced around the six-plus-six and 12-mile territorial sea proposals. Mexico also played a prominent role at UNCLOS II as at UNCLOS I, at first proposing an unusual compensatory system in which the
breadth of an exclusive fishing zone would be fixed
in inverse proportion to the breadth of the territorial sea. When the maritime powers came out
against this compensatory proposal, Mexico returned
to a 12-mile territorial sea proposal, which was
eventually integrated into an "18 Power Proposal"
co-sponsored by 16 Afro-Asian states and one other
Latin American state, Venezuela. The large support
this 12-mile proposal received at UNCLOS II, like
the similar Mexican-Indian proposal at UNCLOS I,
"undoubtedly contributed to the future greater
acceptance of the 12-mile limit."[62] The Mexican-
originated 18 Power Proposal nevertheless did not
even attain the simple majority required in the

Committee of the Whole for sending proposals on to the Plenary (39 votes against, 36 for, and 13 abstentions). The proposal only received active support of 5 out of the 20 Latin American states, with 8 voting against, including Brazil, and 7 abstentions.

A U.S.-Canadian proposal providing for a 6-mile territorial sea and an adjacent 6-mile fishing zone resulted from a compromise merging earlier, separate U.S. and Canadian six-plus-six proposals at UNCLOS II. This proposal was the only one at the 1960 conference approaching the required 2/3 majority at the Plenary. In the early weeks of UNCLOS II at the Committee of the Whole, the U.S.-Canadian six-plus-six proposal had been in direct competition with the Mexican 12-mile approach, and indeed contributed to its eventual rejection by offering a viable, more conventional alternative. At the final meeting of the Committee of the Whole on April 13, 1960, the same day the 12-mile 18 Power Proposal was rejected, the U.S.-Canadian six-plus-six proposal was approved (43 for, 33 against, 12 abstentions), including Brazil's affirmative vote.

While the winning six-plus-six coalition in the Committee of the Whole attained the required simple majority, it still fell short of the 2/3 majority that would be required in the Plenary. A continuing deadlock between 12-mile and six-plus-six supporters appeared likely at the Plenary of UNCLOS II as long as both positions continued to be defined in mutually exclusive, rigid ways. State positions, after all, had not changed much since UNCLOS I and similar six-plus-six proposals had fallen short of the necessary number of votes then. Moreover, with the 12-mile group now in the position of a substantial, but disgruntled, minority, compromise had to come from the six-plus-six camp. Twelve-mile supporters, unless accommodated further, would not be likely to rally around the very six-plus-six proposal that had just prevented their national policies from receiving approval of an international conference.

Brazil played a decisive role in the search during the waning days of UNCLOS II for a compromise six-plus-six formula acceptable to 12-mile supporters. The search culminated in April 22 amendments to the U.S.-Canadian six-plus-six proposal, jointly sponsored by Brazil, Cuba, and Uruguay. In a session lasting from March 17 until April 26, 1960, Ambassador Amado called these "three Power amendments" "a last attempt ... to obtain a substantial majority and achieve the result generally expected

of the Conference."[63] Previous amendments in early
April sponsored by Argentina to the same U.S.-Cana-
dian proposal had been hastily drafted on the basis
of inadequate consultation and had been rejected.
This time, lengthy behind-the-scenes negotiations
between the opposing groups by the three Latin American co-sponsors produced amendments which appeared
to constitute a viable overall compromise.

The general context of the "three Power amendments" of Brazil, Cuba, and Uruguay warrants close
attention. It was noted that the ILC draft articles
and the 1958 Geneva fishing convention both recognized special coastal state interest in the maintenance of productivity of living resources in any
area of the high seas adjacent to its territorial
sea. Recognition of this special interest had generally been welcomed by revisionists, but only as
an initial step toward more comprehensive, exclusive
coastal state jurisdiction over offshore fisheries.
Coastal state fisheries control beyond the territorial sea had been authorized only for purposes of
conservation, not for exclusive management of resources, and several Geneva qualifications had severely limited even this authority. Any unilateral
conservation measures taken could not discriminate
against foreign fisherman and had to rely on appropriate scientific findings about conservation of
fisheries. In instances where other concerned
states opposed such unilateral measures, disputes
would be resolved by a special commission established by the 1958 fishing convention. With international, rather than national, discretion in event
of controversies, there was no guarantee for the
coastal state that even limited conservation measures could be applied. Such tentative recognition
of special coastal state interest in fisheries fell
far short of revisionist demands, so the fisheries
issue was reopened at UNCLOS II.

The 1958 U.S. six-plus-six proposal at UNCLOS I
had not met revisionist fishing demands either.
Historic fishing rights would have been recognized
in perpetuity in the outer 6-mile fishing zone and
no provision was made for coastal state jurisdiction
over fisheries beyond 12 miles. The 1960 U.S.-Cana-
dian six-plus-six proposal did make a concession
about historic fishing rights. Historic fishing
rights would continue to be recognized in the outer
6-mile fishing zone, but only for 10 years. At the
end of the 10 year period, coastal states in effect
would gain exclusive fishing rights out to 12 miles.
Still separating the six-plus-six and 12-mile groups

in 1960 were the issues of the breadth of the territorial sea (6 or 12 miles), historic fishing rights
(the rejection in principle by some revisionists of
even qualified historic fishing rights), and the
status of preferential coastal state fishing rights
beyond 12 miles.

In this context, the three Power amendments of
Brazil, Cuba, and Uruguay attempted to bridge the
gap between the two contending groups. The central
element of the compromise provided that "the coastal
State has the faculty of claiming preferential fishing rights in any area of the high seas adjacent to
its exclusive fishing zone when it is scientifically
established that a special situation or condition
make the exploitation of the living resources of the
high seas in that area of fundamental importance to
the economic development of the coastal State or the
feeding of its population."[64]

The amendments went beyond previous six-plus-
six proposals, as well as the 1958 Geneva fishing
convention, in several important ways. Coastal
state fisheries jurisdiction now was to be clearly
recognized beyond 12 miles. This would occur
through preferential fishing rights in any area of
the high seas adjacent to the outer 6-mile exclusive
fishing zone, and would be linked directly to the
coastal state through the degree of importance of
fisheries for its economy, not indirectly to the
coastal state through the general need for conservation as in 1958. This proposed fisheries jurisdiction beyond 12 miles was only preferential, not exclusive, but it was nevertheless a marked improvement over previous six-plus-six proposals from the
revisionist point of view.

The amendments responded to yet another revisionist demand by further limiting historic fishing
rights in the outer 6-mile exclusive fishing zone.
These rights, the amendments stated, "shall not
apply or may be varied as between States which enter
into bilateral, multilateral or regional agreements
to that effect."[65]

Through such concessions and compromises promising more extensive coastal state jurisdictional
rights over fishing, the amendments essentially
attempted to entice 12-mile territorial sea supporters to accept a less ambitious sovereign claim to a
6-mile territorial sea. A more limited sovereign
claim would be traded for more extensive fisheries
jurisdiction.

The three Power amendments therefore amounted
to a package approach toward simultaneous resolution

of the two issues facing UNCLOS II, the breadth of the territorial sea and the limits of coastal state jurisdiction over fisheries. The package approach later predominated at UNCLOS III, but it will be recalled that at UNCLOS I Brazil had favored separate resolution of these and other issues. At UNCLOS I, Brazil had expected that separate resolution of issues would limit extensive territorial sea claims while permitting sufficient coastal state regulation of fisheries in adjacent high seas. Neither Brazilian expectation proved correct--revisionist demands for both a 12-mile territorial sea and for extensive coastal state jurisdictional rights over fishing remained strong, while the traditional group only made limited concessions. So in the two years from 1958 to 1960 Brazilian strategy and procedure shifted. This shift was pragmatic, not ideological in nature. Brazil's moderate policy continued as the characteristics of flexibility and compromise observed at UNCLOS I asserted themselves in the final days of UNCLOS II.

The amendments still fell short of revisionist demands. The added restrictions placed by the amendments on historic fishing rights in the outer 6-mile exclusive fishing zone were an improvement, but did not go far enough. In revisionist eyes, this concession did not provide the necessary sovereign guarantees of a 12-mile territorial sea and still unfairly rewarded established maritime states. Many revisionists also wanted more extensive jurisdictional fishing rights beyond 12 miles than the preferential status provided by the amendments. The preferential status was not as generous as it might appear. The amendments provided that any dispute about preferential fishing claims in adjacent high seas would be decided by the special commission established by the 1958 fisheries convention. The commission was explicitly given power to judge any claim to preferential fishing beyond 12 miles on the basis of scientific criteria. So the power of coastal states to regulate fishing beyond 12 miles was ultimately contingent on the commission. This stands in contrast to a revisionist demand for unilateral control. The USSR was a special case in supporting a 12-mile territorial sea and opposing any coastal state fishing jurisdiction beyond 12 miles.

The amendments nevertheless represented "the minimum demands of the revisionist states and the maximum concession acceptable by the Europeans who had already been adversely affected by the time limit set on historic fishing rights," according to a contemporary observer.[66] On the very last day of the conference, April 26, 1960, the amendments were put to a vote in the Plenary, separate from the six-plus-six proposal they amended, and received a strong 2/3 majority (58 affirmative, 19 negative and 10 abstentions). Revisionists such as the CEP group and Mexico supported the amendments as a viable compromise. Not a single Latin American state voted against the amendments, and only three Latin American states abstained in the voting (Guatemala, Haiti, and Venezuela).[67] The U.S.-Canadian six-plus-six proposal, of which the three Power amendments were now a part, was then put to a vote in the Plenary. Since opposition to a six-mile territorial sea within the 12-mile group remained strong, the proposal itself fell one vote short of the necessary 2/3 majority (54 affirmative, 28 against and 5 abstentions), so the amendments were struck down as well. After having voted for the amendments alone, the CEP group, Mexico and two other Latin American states subsequently voted against the proposal to express opposition to a six-mile territorial sea. Two other states from the region abstained in the voting.[68] At least the compromises in the closing days of UNCLOS II helped muster much additional support for the proposal in the Plenary, so that the six-plus-six approach fared substantially better than at UNCLOS I.

THE ROAD TO REVISIONISM

While the gap between revisionists and traditional maritime powers appeared to be narrowing in the closing days of UNCLOS II, the final stalemate led the traditional maritime powers to retract their negotiating concessions and reaffirm support for narrow territorial sea limits and limited coastal state fisheries jurisdiction. At the end of the conference, the United States explicitly emphasized the conditional nature of its 1958 and 1960 six-plus-six proposals and reaffirmed the continued validity of its traditional policy of a 3-mile territorial sea in international law.[69] In a similar vein, the Chairman of the U.S. delegation emphasized that "his delegation had supported those /Brazilian co-sponsored three Power/ amendments only within the context of the joint proposal (A/CONF.19/L.11) and in an effort to reach agreement" and "had not supported the terms of the amendments as an independent position."[70]

The UNCLOS II three Power amendments co-sponsored by Brazil nevertheless influenced the course
of subsequent revisionism, including that of Brazil
and of other states. One contemporary actor, for
example, concluded that:

> First, the adoption of the three Power
> amendment by a large majority constitutes
> a vital encouragement for the defense of
> preferential fishing rights /beyond 12
> miles/. One can be sure that, benefiting
> from such large support, this will in-
> evitably be introduced in all subsequent
> law of the sea conferences and will not
> cease to gain adherents. On the other
> hand, if the 6-mile system formulated
> by the joint /U.S.-Canadian/ proposal
> was so near defeating the 12-mile pro-
> posal, it was due to the amendment which
> gave it a new element of progressivism.[71]

Indeed, preferential fishing rights were incorporated into a 1965 resolution of the Inter-American
Juridical Committee, with a Brazilian as president
(to be noted subsequently). The distinguished Latin
American jurist, García Amador, has likewise attributed Latin American UNCLOS II proposals on fisheries
jurisdiction beyond the territorial sea as the in-
spiration for a new round of regional claims, and
cited Brazil's own 1966 six-plus-six legislation as
an example.[72] The prediction that preferential
fishing rights beyond 12 miles would reemerge
strongly at any future law of the sea conference
has also proved accurate. By UNCLOS III the economic zone/patrimonialist approach had received general
approval, and was indeed considerably broader in
scope than one of its apparent antecedents, the 1960
Brazilian-Cuban-Uruguayan amendments. The patrimonialist position in turn was less revisionist than
the extreme 200-mile territorial sea position, since
it was limited to a 12-mile territorial sea and selected coastal state jurisdictions out to 200 miles.
Even though the UNCLOS II three Power amendments marked a subsequent parting of the ways between traditional maritime states and revisionists,
the Geneva effort to codify and develop the law in
1958 and 1960 did help provide a pause in maritime
controversies between the United Sates and Latin
America. By the mid-1960s a new round of disagreements began. In this round Brazil assumed a more

revisionist role.

In a new context, revisionism tended to occur in different ways. Restrictive features of the 1958 Convention on the Continental Shelf did discourage further Latin American attempts to use continental shelf claims as the basis for additional claims to superjacent waters, as in the 1940s and 1950s. UNCLOS I and II, however, had not clearly set a limit on territorial sea breadth nor reached consensus about the limits of fisheries jurisdiction, so it was in these areas of unsettled law that a new Latin American assault on traditional narrow limits began.

Four additional South American states, including Brazil, declared 200-mile maritime zones or territorial seas in the latter half of the 1960s (Ecuador and Argentina in 1966, Uruguay in December 1969, and Brazil in March 1970), and in Central America, Panama claimed a 200-mile territorial sea in 1967. Brazil's measure completed a ring of 200-mile states in South America south of the equator and heightened the concern of the United States about extensive territorial sea claims.

> In 1970 this problem in our relations with Latin America suddenly acquired a new dimension, when Brazil, the largest country of South America and a country with which the U.S. has long enjoyed close and friendly relations, joined the regional trend towards extended jurisdiction in its most extreme form by claiming a territorial sea of 200 miles.[73]

Brazil's conversion to the extreme 200-mile territorial sea formula occurred rapidly, since only in 1966 had it extended the territorial sea from three miles to a six-plus-six formula and again in April 1969 to twelve miles. The 1966 and 1969 measures were not regarded at the time as radical nor as a prelude to a 200-mile territorial sea, since there was no domestic 200-mile movement of any consequence until late 1969. Domestic politics, especially nationalism, set Brazil on a 200-mile course in 1970. Other factors than revisionism were likewise responsible for failure to ratify the Geneva conventions during the 1960s, especially bureacratic inertia and turbulent internal politics.[74] Failure to follow up on previous support for the ILC draft articles and for the Geneva conventions consequently did not signal a policy change.

On the international front as well, Brazil held to a relatively moderate policy until a late date. In 1965, the Inter-American Juridical Committee, with representatives from five Latin American states including a Brazilian as president, Raul Fernandes, reached unanimous agreement on a territorial sea resolution. The IJC resolution included draft articles for a recommended convention that went cautiously beyond the 1958 Geneva conventions, and resembled previous Brazilian compromise proposals. The right of states to extend their territorial sea up to a limit of twelve miles was explicitly recognized, just as it had been in the ILC draft article based on Amado's proposal. The IJC resolution added that in cases where the territorial sea is narrower than twelve miles the coastal state can establish an exclusive fishing zone up to that limit. Then, clearly reflecting the 1960 Brazilian jointly-sponsored amendments at UNCLOS II, the IJC resolution approved coastal state preferential fishing rights in areas adjacent to the exclusive fishing zone beyond the 12-mile limit.

The Colombian and Argentine jurists who signed the recommendation nevertheless went beyond its compromises in respectively supporting a 200-mile resource zone and an epicontinental sea in separate statements.[75] With such underlying divisions still within Latin American ranks, the 1965 recommended convention was never adopted. But Brazil had again staked out a relatively moderate compromise position which offered promise, even if revisionists, like traditional maritime powers, were reluctant to endorse it fully.

The course of revisionism in the 1960s and 1970s may be summed up, so that the historical record can be interpreted in light of recent events in a final section. Failure to resolve crucial issues at UNCLOS II contributed to the generally ineffective application of the conventions adopted at UNCLOS I. As the crisis of traditional law deepened, revisionism gained momentum and the long road toward UNCLOS III commenced. If traditional law tended to dominate in the 1940s and 1950s, with some exceptions such as the introduction of the principle of the continental shelf, the tide of change grew stronger in the 1960s, with Latin America at the forefront. By 1967, the deep seabed emerged as an important, unresolved issue in the law of the sea and was placed on the agenda of the United Nations. By 1970 the deep seabed debate had broadened into a debate over revision of the entire law of the sea and a Third United Nations Conference on the Law of the Sea was called. The developing states were definitely on the offensive at UNCLOS III in the 1970s, particularly through the Group of 77 in which Brazil emerged as a leader.[76]

INTERPRETATIONS AND IMPLICATIONS

The 1970 decision to extend the territorial sea to 200 miles was a watershed in the evolution of Brazilian ocean policy, both because of the great expansion of national ocean space and the rapidity of the movement from a narrow territorial sea to a broad one. Because of the importance of the 200-mile territorial sea for ocean policy, analysis of the 1970 decision can provide a vantage point for assessing the historical record and its relationship to recent events.

Interpretations of the 1970 decision essentially concur that the territorial sea extension amounted to a repudiation of the historical record. Up to 1970, Brazilian ocean policy had been quite cautious and moderate, while from 1970 on Brazil emerged as a leader of the territorialists, the group supporting the most extreme or ambitious territorial sea claim of 200 miles. This conclusion that the 1970 territorial sea extension represented a sharp break with past ocean policy underlies both complementary and uncomplementary interpretations. Both interpretations also agree that international factors were decisive in the decision. The complementary interpretation, espoused mostly by Brazilian policy-makers and commentators, holds that ocean policy had been excessively conservative until an extensive territorial sea claim propelled it on a progressive path.[77] The uncomplementary version, articulated mostly by U.S. policy-makers and publicists, essentially maintains that an extensive territorial sea claim was made for opportunistic gains at the expense of the long-term yield and good-will generated by traditional Brazilian ocean policy.[78]

International factors allegedly influencing the 1970 territorial sea decision will now be surveyed briefly both to test their real importance and their relationship to the historical record. This survey indicates that both interpretations are in error in regarding the 1970 decision as a repudiation of the historical record taken primarily for international reasons. Implications for the

95

historical record will then be drawn.

Regional economic and political considerations were factors influencing the territorial sea extension, but certainly were not decisive ones, as both Brazilian apologists and U.S. critics of the 1970 measure have argued. Regional pressures to go to 200 miles did intensify somewhat with the 1966 and 1969 decrees of Brazil's east coast South American neighbors, Argentina and Uruguay, since coordination of fisheries was difficult with neighbors with claims of 200 miles. While Argentina and Uruguay asserted fisheries jurisdiction out to 200 miles, foreign ships still could fish at will beyond Brazil's 12-mile limit. This relatively limited fishing jurisdiction allegedly made Brazil vulnerable to a shift northwards in foreign fishing operations from Argentine and Uruguayan waters to those of southern Brazil. Increasing attention was drawn as well to alleged foreign fishing abuses off Brazil's north and northeastern coasts, where destructive fishing practices by sophisticated foreign factory ships were believed to be decimating local stocks, especially shrimp. From 1969, domestic proponents of the 200 miles repeatedly painted a picture of foreign depredation of the national patrimony, which found ready nationalistic appeal.

With increasing attention being paid to alleged foreign fishing depredations, west coast South American fishing policies for controlling foreign abuses came to be seen more favorably.[79] Another similarity asserted between CEP ocean policies and that of Brazil from 1970 on was the common need to protect living marine resources because of the social and economic needs of their domestic populations. In the case of Brazil, related military justifications were made as well for extending the territorial sea, particularly the need to curb alleged use of foreign fishing ships for spying. But such security considerations were explicitly subordinated to economic ones.[80]

Such foreign policy considerations undoubtedly contributed in some degree to the 200-mile decision. Yet, fishing, which was at the root of these arguments, has only had secondary importance for the Brazilian economy, both before and after 1970. Nor did Brazil's eventual assimilation with the regional trend toward broad offshore claims signal that new importance had been placed on Brazilian fisheries. Fishing, for the narrow shelf CEP states on the west coast of South America, has been an extremely important industry, while it has not been for Brazil, on the east coast with a broad continental shelf.

> Comparing the development of coastal
> jurisdiction on the East Coast to that
> on the West Coast, it is evident that
> control over the continental shelf was
> and still is the most important concern
> of the East Coast while the main inter-
> est on the West Coast was and still is
> protection of fishing resources.[81]

Any Brazilian economic hardships which may be resulted from foreign fishing would have negotiable
in any event at the upcoming law of the sea conference.

Had fishing abuses really been the central concern, the 1970 claim would have been limited to a
fisheries or resource zone, as Argentina and Uruguay
had done, rather than an extreme 200-mile territorial
sea. Fishing and especially alleged foreign fishing
abuses had more impact on the Brazilian 200-mile decision in terms of nationalistic fervor generated
than of intrinsic economic importance. At a politically difficult moment at home, the Brazilian government essentially took advantage of growing nationalistic agitation against alleged foreign fishing abuses by cultivating and guiding nationalism in
this and other areas for some time.[82]

Nationalism in the CEP states, in contrast, had
long been associated with the 200-mile claim, primarily due to recurring foreign challenges, especially from the United States, to the vital national
fishing industry.[83] So to a considerable extent, up
to the late 1960s, distinctive west coast South
American maritime interests had been expressed
through different kinds of ocean policies than those
of east coast states. Since distinctive, concrete
national interests guided ocean policies differently
in each case, it follows that abstract regional interests, such as regional solidarity, were subordinate to national interests. This appears just as
true for Brazil, before as well as after 1970, as
for other states in the region.

But a final regional political consideration,
promotion of regional solidarity, was stressed as a
key factor in extending the Brazilian territorial
sea to 200 miles. Failure to become associated with
an apparent regional trend toward broad offshore
claims, it was argued, would increase the isolation
and perpetuate resentment of the alleged aloofness
of the only Portuguese-speaking state in the area.

97

Regional interests did benefit from greater overlap with national interests by the 1970s, as Latin American ocean policies came to rely more on borad offshore claims. But national interests remained distinctive and dominant. A recent study demonstrated, for example, that important law of the sea differences have separated and continue to seperate Latin American states.[84] Indeed, Brazil's extreme 1970 territorialist claim, by tending to seperate it from the more moderate patrimonialist group, did not particularly enhance overall Latin American solidarity. As in the area of regional economic integration, Brazil has been willing to cooperate regionally on law of the sea matters, but only selectively to promote national interests.

If all regional foreign policy considerations had a much different relationship to Brazilian ocean policy than that claimed, the very concept of regional solidarity being invoked may be distorted. The image of regional solidarity on law of the sea matters indeed appears to have been given a revisionist bias. Revisionism has been regarded as the norm by many Latin American analysts, and more traditional policies consequently have been regarded as deviations from the norm. For example, on the basis of analysis of voting patterns at UNCLOS I and II, a recent study by Szekely categorized Brazil as a "regional dissenter" in 1958 and 1960 and presumably up to 1970 as well. Brazil was placed with Cuba, the Dominican Republic, Haiti, and Nicaragua in a group of "regional dissenters," since their voting pattern at UNCLOS I and II generally opposed proposals sponsored or co-sponsored by countries of the region. "They cast their votes against such proposals in several instances while many countries of the region would vote in favor or abstain, simply for the sake of regional solidarity."[85]

Instead, most Latin American UNCLOS I and II proposals originated from a relatively small, if very active, revisionist group. Analysis of Latin American ocean trends and policies, including voting patterns and coalitions, has revealed that it was the revisionist group that historically was in the minority in Latin America. Szekely's own count reconfirms this finding. Out of a total of twenty Latin American states at UNCLOS I, most were not revisionist. There were five "regional dissenters," as well as another "'passive' group ... composed of 9 States, that is almost half of all Latin American States." Also Bolivia and Paraguay, largely preoccupied with their land-locked status and inactive

98

on most other issues, were put in yet another group
separate from the coastal state revisionist group.
Szekely adds that Latin American behavior at UNCLOS
II "did not substantially vary from the one observed
in 1958," when "Only 8 States of the region sponsored or co-sponsored proposals at the Conference,
whereas the remaining majority were 'passive' or
'regional dissenters.'"[86]

Since Brazil clearly belonged to a Latin American moderate majority at UNCLOS I and II, even by
Szekely's own count, its characterization as a regional dissenter only was possible by regarding
regional solidarity as interpreted by the minority
revisionist group as the norm. Brazil, besides being associated with the large, if generally passive,
Latin American moderate majority at UNCLOS I and II,
was also closely related to the most powerful, numerous group at the conferences, the supporters of
traditional law.

So Brazil was not isolated by a revisionist
majority that propelled it toward revisionism. Regionally and globally, Brazil was associated with
majority groups favoring moderation. Any Brazilian
isolation on law of the sea matters only occurred
by the late 1960s, and even then only in South America, not in the Latin American region as a whole nor
globally at the Seabed Committee, as will be shown.
The revisionist group did gradually acquire additional adherents in the region over the years,
but the revisionists did not clearly emerge as the
majority in the region until the 1970s. In any
event, by then Brazil itself had converted to revisionism and had moved into the forefront of the revisionist camp.

The revisionist bias of the literature on Latin
America and the law of the sea then has led to a
number of historical inaccuracies. Wishful thinking
in regarding revisionism as the norm has led to in-
accurate dating of the rise of revisionism. The
origins of revisionism can be traced at least as far
back as the early postwar era, but the revisionist
chronology has attributed a majority position to the
group in Latin America at a much earlier date than
is warranted. Similarly, the influence of the revisionists has been exaggerated through reliance on
indicators which stress change, while evidence which
suggests the persistence of tradition has been minimized as deviation from the norm. Since revisionism
has long been regarded as the wave of the future by
most writers on Latin America and the law of the
sea, the bulk of the literature refers to

revisionist states, not moderate ones, with the consequent implication that their ocean policies are particularly important.

The revisionist bias of the literature on Latin America and the law of the sea has consequently overlooked or minimized the influence of regional moderates and their position as the majority group in Latin America until a fairly late date. Such an error is perhaps not so serious in the case of most regional moderates, since they were not particularly active nor influential in law of the sea affairs. But as a group, they were able to thwart revisionist ambitions time and again.

Neglect of Brazilian ocean policy before the 1970 turn to revisionism is particularly serious, since Brazil was traditionally influential and has become more so in recent years. Moreover, Brazil's traditionally moderate policy was not devoted simply to devising hindrances to block the progress of revisionism, as the revisionist bias would have it. Its emphasis on both tradition and innovation repeatedly played a constructive role in searching for compromises between the opposing camps. Such slighting of the conciliatory role of an influential moderate does not even seem to have served the cause of revisionism.

If regional factors were not decisive in the abrupt change in Brazilian ocean policy in 1970, what about global law of the sea politics? The Third United Nations Conference on the Law of the Sea has stretched over nearly a decade, from preliminary discussions in the late 1960s in the Seabed Committee, to the call to hold the conference in 1970, and later through preparatory discussions and the various sessions of formal negotiation. With widespread support building up for a 200-mile zone in Spanish America, regional solidarity at the upcoming Third United Nations Conference on the Law of the Sea still would not be possible, it was argued, without Brazil's conversion to revisionism.[87] Promotion of regional solidarity at the upcoming law of the sea conference as a motive for the extension of the territorial sea is essentially another version of the same view that relatively abstract considerations dictated policy. Evidence instead again indicates primacy of national interests. The perception of national interest evolved with time, to be sure, but the causes of this evolution were primarily national, not regional or global in character.

A less complementary, but related, interpretation is that Brazil intentionally adopted a hard-

line territorial sea policy at an early date in the
global negotiations as a temporary bargaining ploy
to elicit concessions from other states. This interpretation is likewise refuted by the historical
record and by current Brazilian behavior. At all
international conferences in which the territorial
sea was negotiated during this century, from the
Hague Conference to the Geneva Conferences and then
at the Inter-American Juridical Committee, Brazil
upheld distinctive positions and made conciliatory
initiatives to reconcile opposing camps. While this
policy had mixed results, it certainly was anything
but opportunistic. Brazilian law of the sea behavior during the 1970s cannot be characterized as
opportunistic either. Had the territorial sea decision merely been opportunistic, nationalism surely
would not have been permitted to lock policy into an
extreme position as it did, which tended to slow cooperation within the Latin American group. Since a
less extreme measure would have facilitated greater
Latin American cooperation, opportunism might have
led policy in that direction. And to be opportunistic, even critics acknowledged that a hard-line territorial sea policy would only be a temporary posture. Brazil did make some concessions in this area
later, but held to the policy throughout the negotiations. Accordingly, many of those who deemed Brazilian policy opportunistic in the early stages of
UNCLOS III later expressed uncertainty about Brazilian objectives.

Review of the separate elements of Brazilian
ocean policy helps clarify cause and effect with respect to UNCLOS III. By 1970, in the Seabed Committee, Brazil had emerged as an important, influential
actor in encouraging extension and revision of the
law relating to the deep seabed.[88] In contrast,
questions of national jurisdiction were only reopened for negotiation at the global level in the
1970s. In the late 1960s, Brazil maintained its
basically moderate position while moving from a
three to six and then a twelve mile territorial sea,
and then it moved abruptly to an extreme revisionist
200-mile territorial sea in March 1970. Cause and
effect between Brazilian ocean policy, regional
solidarity, and the global negotiations in each of
these issue-areas, the deep seabed and questions of
national jurisdiction, were consequently different.

Brazil's deep seabed approach did encourage the
eventual emergence of a unified Latin American position on the issue at UNCLOS III, but its roots are
separate from and earlier than the March 1970

territorial sea decision. Brazilian deep seabed policy was oriented toward UNCLOS III, but then so were all other national policies in this area, so this did not constitute opportunism. As for the territorial sea, national policies and needs were naturally the determining factors affecting such an issue of territoriality and frontiers, as with other Latin American states. Moreover, Brazilian coopera- tion with the revisionist group, especially with the territorialists for development of a unified region- al position for UNCLOS III, can only be dated to the May and August 1970 Montevideo and Lima Declarations. This subsequent limited cooperation was the result, not the cause, of the earlier March 1970 Brazilian territorial sea decision. Because distinctive na- tional interests and historical backgrounds shaped territorial sea policies, overall Latin American co- operation on the issue in both regional and global fora proved difficult after 1970 just as before.

No global or regional motive was then decisive in the 1970 200-mile Brazilian decree. By process of elimination of all international motives attri- buted to Brazil, it may be deduced that the abrupt policy change in 1970 primarily resulted from domes- tic, political considerations. This reconfirms the conclusion of Chapter 2 that domestic policies, es- pecially nationalism, set Brazil on a 200-mile course in 1970.

Another implication that may be drawn from the historical record is that there has been more con- tinuity in Brazilian ocean policy than has been generally recognized. Since largely fortuitous do- mestic factors led Brazil to extend its territorial sea, the decision was not, as alleged, a conscious repudiation of the historical record. Since the key domestic factors influencing the 1970 decision were essentially extraneous to ocean policy, they receded in time and tradition was subsequently reconciled with the policy change. Accordingly, there have been important elements of continuity in ocean poli- cy. Caution, compromise, and pragmatism character- ized Brazilian ocean policy both before and after 1970. Although the 200-mile decree was extreme and did reorient the course of Brazilian ocean affairs, it was implemented cautiously. Absent were the con- frontation tactics which a few other Latin American states have apparently pursued at times. After the nationalistic fervor surrounding the 1970 decree died down, Brazil concluded pragmatic fishing agree- ments with foreign states and bargained shrewdly at UNCLOS III.[89]

Even during the nationalistic period, 1970-1971, inordinate stress on revisionism conformed to the Brazilian tradition of legalism and respect for law. Traditional law of the sea, it was argued at that time by Brazil, was so outdated and inequitable that a new law of the sea was emerging through Latin American consensus. Tradition was equated with failure to adapt to an emerging regional norm and revisionism was correlated with respect for new law. Presentation of new Brazilian policy as adapting to new law, even if not really motivating the 200-mile decree, was useful in mustering domestic support. Shrewd revisionist politics, perhaps, but certainly not radicalism or commitment to ideology.

If recent Brazilian revisionism has not been radical, neither did Brazilian tradition reject revisionism outright. Numerous important examples have been cited of moderate revisionism up to 1970 including: vigorous Brazilian support in 1939 for the Declaration of Panama; Brazilian endorsement of the continental shelf doctrine and ambivalence toward related claims to superjacent waters; Amado's ILC territorial sea proposal; the UNCLOS II three Power amendments; and seabed policy in the late 1960s. These and other early examples of Brazilian moderate revisionism reinforce the conclusion that historically policy combined traditional and innovative elements and was not as conservative as it might seem.

Moreover, the evolution of Brazil's national development, including maritime development, was moving ocean policy toward a revisionist course. Brazil's emergence as a major power, evident in the late 1960s and more pronounced in the 1970s, had a maritime counterpart. From the late 1960s, more active, innovative Brazilian approaches began to emerge in uncoordinated fashion in a number of separate maritime sectors--naval policy, merchant marine policy, fishing policy, and minerals policy. Emergence as a maritime power in a world of established maritime powers, Brazil was discovering, required reformulation of established rules. Similar conclusions were reached about numerous constraints in many fields hindering Brazil's emergence as a major power, and were summed up in a protest against the "freezing of world power."[90]

Brazil's policy evolution in the late 1960s from a three-mile territorial sea to a six-plus-six formula and then to a 12-mile territorial sea also reflected pressure to claim more maritime space as national capabilities and needs escalated. These claims were still all compatible with established law as set out in the Geneva conventions and were certainly not precedents for an extreme 200-mile territorial sea like that claimed in 1970. But these quick, successive expansions of national maritime space up to the conventional maximum limit of twelve miles by 1969 did reflect pressures from Brazil's rapid growth and escalating aspirations that only with difficulty might have remained contained by established rules. And as early as UNCLOS II, Brazil had favored preferential coastal state fishing rights beyond twelve miles.

Brazilian ocean policy therefore seemed to be evolving in a moderately revisionist direction up to 1970, although the particular kind of revisionism Brazil eventually adopted that year was largely fortuitous. Had the domestic context been different in 1970, there is little reason to conclude that an extreme 200-mile territorialist decree would have been promulgated then or later. The evolution of policy was instead pointing in the direction of a more moderately revisionist patrimonialist or economic zone-type formula. So a projection of the main characteristics of Brazilian ocean policy and maritime affairs from the 1940s, 1950s and 1960s into the 1970s suggests that revisionism would have been embraced in any event, if not so abruptly or in so extreme a form. In this sense, current policy is not as discontinuous with tradition as it might seem. Just as policy historically combined tradition and innovation, so has current policy.

A final implication that may be drawn from the historical record is that interpretations must take account of the entire historical sweep of Brazilian ocean policy, because of the close association of tradition and innovation. Interpretations about recent Brazilian ocean policy have been misleading because they have focused on the 1970 decision at the expense of the historical record. The oversimplistic description of Brazilian ocean policy as reactionary before 1970 and as progressive since 1970 (the complementary interpretation) therefore must be rejected. Similarly, Brazilian ocean policy cannot accurately be described as predominantly opportunistic (the uncomplementary interpretation).

Instead, Brazilian ocean policy has been described here as an evolving, complex amalgam of tradition, revisionism, caution, and pragmatic compromise. History does take strange, if comprehensible, turns, and in 1970 Brazilian ocean policy abruptly embarked on an extreme, yet cautious, course. As this new phase adds yet another layer of innovation to tradition, the web of historical distinctiveness will become yet more complex. Ocean policy may be a relatively new facet of national development in developing states, but its historical record is already considerable and necessarily conditions policy initiatives. These policy initiatives may acquire considerable importance in the case of emerging great powers, such as Brazil.

NOTES

1. "Comité jurídico interamericano: Dictamen sobre la anchura del mar territorial," Derecho de mar, 2 vols. (Washington, D.C., 1971), 1:98-100. (OEA/Ser. Q II.4, CJI-7) This report was a background study for the Inter-American Juridical Committee resolution cited in footnote 75. Translation of the writer.

2. Ibid., 1:99-100. Translation of the writer. Underlining in the original.

3. United Nations, Yearbook of the International Law Commission: 1950 (A/CN.4/Ser. A/1950), 1:204. Hereafter cited as ICL, with appropriate year also underlined.

4. Ann L. Hollick, "The Origins of 200-Mile Offshore Zones," American Journal of International Law 71 (July 1977): 494-500. Ann L. Hollick, "The Roots of U.S. Fisheries Policy," Ocean Development and International Law Journal 5 (1978): 61-105.

5. Barry Auguste, The Continental Shelf: The Practice and Policy of the Latin American States with Special Reference to Chile, Ecuador and Peru (Geneva, 1960), p. 110 (footnote 19). Auguste does note that there is some uncertainty about the legal status of the December 1950 proclamation of the political division of the Ministry of Foreign Affairs of Brazil.

6. F.V. García Amador, "La contribución de América Latina al desarrollo del derecho del mar," Primer curso de derecho internacional organizado por el comité jurídico interamericano: Conferencias pronunciadas (Washington, D.C., 1975), p. 95 (footnote 6). (OEA/Ser. Q/V. C-1, CJI-26). This article is a revised edition of an English version which appeared in American Journal of International Law 68 (January 1974).

7. Tito Mondin, "Plataforma Continental," Mar territorial, 3 vols. (Brasília, n.d.), 2: 480-481.

8. "Decreto 28.840--de 8 de novembro de 1950," Revista Brasileira de Política Internacional, 12 (Set/Dez. de 1969): 143-144. Translation of the writer.

9. García Amador, "La contribución ...," p. 96 (footnote 7).

10. Auguste, pp. 110-111, 170.

11. Barry Buzan, Seabed Politics (New York, 1976), p. 9.

12. García Amador, "La contribución ...," p. 114.

13. Alberto Szekely, Latin America and the Development of the Law of the Sea: Regional Documents and National Legislation, 2 vols. (Dobbs Ferry, New York, 1976), 1: 22-23, 30.

14. Vicente Marotta Rangel, "Brazil," The Changing Law of the Sea: Western Hemisphere Perspectives, ed. Ralph Zacklin (Leiden, 1974), p. 137.

15. "Opinión disidente de los delegados del Brasil, Colombia y Estados Unidos de América," Derecho del mar, 1: 27-28.

16. Ibid., pp. 29-32.

17. Edmundo Vargas Carreño, América latina y los problemas contemporáneos del derecho del mar (Santiago, Chile, 1973), p. 38. Translation of the writer.

18. "Declaración del Brasil," Derecho del mar, 1: 56-57.

19. "Declaraciones," Derecho del mar, 1: 64, 68-69.

20. Buzan, p. 12.

21. Interview with Dr. Renato Ribeiro, Secretario-Adjunto of the Inter-American Juridical Committee, Rio de Janeiro, Brazil, January 30, 1975.

22. Clarence A. Hill, Jr., "U.S. Law of the Sea Position and Its Effect on the Operating Navy: A Naval Officer's View," Ocean Development and International Law Journal 3 (1976): 347-348, 353-354.

23. ILC, 1949, pp. 14, 221-226, 270, 278.

24. On the basis of a survey of ILC Yearbooks, the writer has compiled a list of ILC officers from Latin America, excluding Brazil which is mentioned in the text, from 1949 to 1956. 1950: Ricardo Alfaro of Panama, Rapporteur. 1951: J.M. Yepes of Colombia, Second Vice-Chairman; Roberto Córdova of Mexico,

Rapporteur. 1952: Ricardo J. Alfaro of Panama, Chairman.
1954: Roberto Córdova of Mexico, First Vice-Chairman. 1955:
García Amador of Cuba, Second Vice-Chairman. 1956: García
Amador of Cuba, Chairman of ILC.

25. ILC, 1949, p. 18.

26. ICL, 1950, 1: 180, 182-183, 215.

27. ICL, 1951, 1: 271-273.

28. ILC, 1953, 2: 6. ILC, 1953, 1: 202. About the same
time, a Brazilian jurist wrote a treatise in French on the continental shelf, which was well received at the time. In one of
only several references in the book to Brazil, the author did
criticize the Brazilian emphasis on jurisdiction and called for
sovereignty over the continental shelf. Gastão Nascimento
Ceccato, L'Evolution Juridique de la Doctrine du Plateau Continental (Paris, 1955), pp. 107, 114, 132-133.

29. ILC, 1956, 1: 135.

30. ILC, 1950, 1: 188.

31. ILC, 1951, 1: 325-327.

32. Ibid., 1: 417-418.

33. ILC, 1951, 1: 305, 311, 314, 414.

34. ILC, 1955, 1: 86, 91-92, 103.

35. ILC, 1956, 2: 40.

36. ILC, 1956, 1: 27, 92-93.

37. ILC, 1956, 1: 268. ILC, 1956, 2: 262, 288.

38. ILC, 1952, 1: 154.

39. Ibid., 1: 167-170.

40. ILC, 1955, 1: 194. Discussion of the proposal from pages
157-195.

41. Ibid., 1: 164, 180.

42. Ibid., 1: 193, 169.

43. ILC, 1956, 1: 1.

44. Ibid., 1: 173, 182. Amado's own amendment to his 1955 proposal was rejected by 8 votes to 7. Ibid., 1: 174, 18. Article 3 of the final version of the draft articles appears at ILC, 1956, 2: 256.

45. Emilio N. Oribe, "The Geneva Convention--Ten Years Later," The Law of the Sea: International Rules and Organization for the Sea, ed. Lewis M. Alexander (Kingston, Rhode Island, 1969), p. 65.

46. F. V. García Amador, The Exploitation and Conservation of the Resources of the Sea: A Study of Contemporary International Law (Leyden, 1959). Alfonso Garcia Robles, La Anchura del Mar Territorial (Mexico, 1966). See especially Chapters V, VI and pages 120-122, which deal explicitly with the Latin American states at the Geneva conferences. Jan H. Samet and Robert L. Fuerst, The Latin American Approach to the Law of the Sea (Chapel Hill, North Carolina, 1973). Sea Grant Publication UNC-SC-73-08. Robert A. Friedheim, "The 'Satisfied' and 'Dissatisfied' States Negotiate International Law: A Case Study," World Politics, 18 (October, 1965): 20-41. Oliver J. Lissitzyn, "International Law in a Divided World," International Conciliation, No. 542 (March 1963), especially 49-52.

47. Szekely, 1: 291, 295 and 309 (footnote 34).

48. United Nations Conference on the Law of the Sea, Official Records, 7 vols. (A/CONF. 14/40), 4: 118, 133. Hereafter cited as UNCLOS I Official Records.

49. Szekely, 1: 295. This tabulation refers to total Mexican sponsored and co-sponsored proposals, whether or not adopted. A number of Mexico's co-sponsored proposals had no other regional co-sponsor, and hence are in addition to the regionally co-sponsored proposals mentioned above.

50. UNCLOS I Official Records, 6: 55, 78.

51. Ibid., 6: 79.

52. Ibid., 6: 88.

53. Buzan, p. 30.

54. UNCLOS I Official Records, 3: 183.

55. Ibid.

56. Buzan, pp. 46-47.

57. Robert L. Friedheim, "Factor Analysis as a Tool in Studying the Law of the Sea," The Law of the Sea: Offshore Boundaries and Zones, ed. Lewis M. Alexander (Columbus, Ohio, 1967), pp. 56-58, 60-61.

58. UNCLOS I Official Records, 3: 4.

59. Ibid. For similar Brazilian stress on separation of issues in the negotiations, see UNCLOS I Official Records, 4: 42.

60. Ibid., 3: 4.

61. Ibid., 4: 42, 133.

62. Szekely, 1: 306, 300.

63. Second United Nations Conference on the Law of the Sea, Official Records (A/CONF. 19/8), p. 15. Hereafter cited as UNCLOS II Official Records.

64. Ibid., p. 173.

65. Ibid.

66. Nguyen Quoc Dinh, "La Revendication des Droits Préférentiels de Pêche en Haute Mer Devant Les Conférences des Nations Unies sur le Droit de la Mer de 1958 et 1960," Annuaire Français de Droit International 6 (1960): 108. Translation of the writer.

67. UNCLOS II Official Records, pp. 29-30.

68. Ibid., p. 30.

69. Ibid., p. 34.

70. Ibid., p. 35.

71. Dinh, p. 109. Dinh was the Chairman of the Delegation of South Vietnam at UNCLOS I and was Vice-Chairman at UNCLOS II. Translation of the writer.

72. Garcia Amador, "La contribución ...," pp. 115-116.

73. Statement by Ambassador Donald L. McKernan, Coordinator of Ocean Affairs, before the Committee on Foreign Relations, September 28, 1972, p. 6. (Mimeographed.)

74. See Chapter 2. Ten Latin American states, all in the Caribbean basin area, either went on to ratify or adhere to

some or all of the four Geneva conventions--Colombia, Cuba, the Dominican Republic, Guatemala, Guyana, Haiti, Jamaica, Mexico, Trinidad and Tobago, and Venezuela. Vargas Carreño, pp. 157-158.

75. "Voto razonado ..., " Derecho del mar, 1: 160-161.

76. See Chapter 4.

77. Confidential interview with high-level diplomat at the Ministry of Foreign Relations, Brasília, Brazil, August 16, 1974. Also see footnotes 79, 80 and 87.

78. See footnote 73. Also see Leigh S. Ratiner, "United States Ocean Policy: An Analysis," Journal of Maritime Law and Commerce 2 (1971), 234-235; and Wolfgang Friedmann, "Selden Redivivus--Towards a Partition of the Seas," American Journal of International Law 65 (October 1971), 764.

79. Múcio Piragibe Ribeiro de Bakker, "Comentários sôbre a soberania marítima: fundamentos da posição peruana," Revista Marítima Brasileira 91 (Jan.-March 1971): 113. Revista Marítima Brasileira is the official journal of the Brazilian Navy.

80. Ibid. Also see, Clovis Ramalhete, "Alguns objectivos das 200 milhas," Revista Militar Brasileira 97 (April-Dec. 1971): 73. Another important Brazilian figure, Calmon Filho, lists the two central reasons for the 1970 Brazilian measure as prevention of indiscriminate foreign fishing and the exclusion of Soviet spy ships possibly used for research of military value or spying. O Estado de São Paulo, April 3, 1970, p. 7.

81. Karin Hjertonsson, The New Law of the Sea: Influence of the Latin American States on Recent Developments of the Law of the Sea (Leiden, 1973), p. 60.

82. See Chapter 2.

83. Bobbie B. Smetherman and Robert M. Smetherman, Territorial Seas and Inter-American Relations with Case Studies of the Peruvian and U.S. Fishing Industries (New York, 1974), pp. 6, 14-15, 42, 119-120.

84. Szekely, especially Chapter V, "The Regional and Sub-Regional Approaches."

85. Ibid., pp. 295, 305.

86. Ibid., p. 295.

87. Clovis Ramalhete included almost all of the regional and global economic-political considerations listed above in his December 1969 opinion, which served as the legal basis for the 200-mile territorial sea. "Parecer," Mar territorial, 2: 511-522.

88. See Chapter 4.

89. See Chapters 4 and 7.

90. J.A. de Araújo Castro, "O congelamento do poder mundial," Revista Brasileira de Estudos Políticos 33 (1972).

4. Brazil at the Third United Nations Conference on the Law of the Sea

INTERNATIONAL SYSTEM, NATIONAL POLICY, AND THE LAW OF THE SEA CONFERENCE

Brazil affects and is affected by on-going global law of the sea negotiations in distinctive, significant ways. As for the impact of national ocean policy, the potential for significant Brazilian influence in global and regional law of the sea fora long existed. Brazilian influence during the 1940s, 1950s, and early 1960s in regional and global law of the sea discussions was not great, although more extensive than generally presumed. For example, as noted in the last chapter, at the First and Second United National Conferences on the Law of the Sea (UNCLOS I and II), Brazil played a significant role in encouraging viable compromises. Yet, it was only as Brazil began to emerge as a major power in the years leading up to the Third United Nations Conference on the Law of the Sea (UNCLOS III) that national ocean policy came to have a quite continuous, distinctive impact on global law of the sea negotiations.

Brazil's participation at UNCLOS III offers a particularly good vantage point from which to analyze its more prominent international role as an emerging major power, its related growth as a maritime power, and its significant contribution to international organization. UNCLOS III has been protracted, the conference has dealt with a multiplicity of issues with broad implications, and Brazil has interacted with a large number of states and groups.

UNCLOS III, in turn, affects Brazil. Three kinds of effects of UNCLOS III on the international system were noted in a recent study.

> First, it [UNCLOS III OR LOS III] has been
> the means whereby a comprehensive revolution
> in the Law of the Sea has been effected, the
> consequences of which will touch to varying
> degrees all dimensions of marine use. Second-
> ly, the transition period from the old to the
> new regime is likely to be fraught with con-
> flict. New confrontations are likely to be
> generated and old ones exacerbated. Since the
> salience of the oceans as an issue in the in-
> ternational system has increased substantially
> in recent times, the ramifications of this
> increase in conflict will be global and may
> combine with other unrelated issues in dif-
> ferent places and at different times. Thirdly,
> LOS III has been the most developed example
> to date of the structure and dynamics of the
> North-South confrontation now occurring in the
> UN General Assembly, other intergovernmental
> organizations, and ad hoc global conferences.[1]

These three kinds of effects of UNCLOS III on the
international system have influenced Brazilian ocean
policy as well. At the same time, Brazil's impact
on the negotiations as an emerging major power has
interacted with these three global trends in distinctive ways.
First, the conference is concerned with establishing a revised global regime for the oceans within which Brazil must operate, as well as with some
specific legal rules which will affect the major
Brazilian maritime sectors. This chapter will focus
on the broad implications of the emerging ocean
order for both national and international zone
issues within which Brazilian ocean policy must
operate. More specific implications of UNCLOS III
for the major maritime sectors--naval affairs, ocean
resources, and shipping--will also be given some
attention, in order to complement more detailed
discussions of these sectors in later chapters.
Because Brazilian ocean policy has tended to become
more autonomous and national maritime sectors have
been growing in importance, if in uncoordinated
fashion, national policy has not simply been dependent on this first global trend, change in the
law of the sea. In fact, Brazil evolved from a
position as a supporter of the traditional ocean
regime to a revisionist position, just as ocean

114

affairs were acquiring greater national prominence
and its international contacts were proliferating
with new regions and groups. So, with respect to
the second global trend, likelihood of conflict in
the transition period, Brazil has contributed to
the transition. Brazil has nevertheless tended to
promote compromise at UNCLOS III and elsewhere.
Brazil's proclivity toward compromise and its distinctive position as an emerging power between the
First and Third Worlds have conditioned its involvement in the North-South conflict at UNCLOS III,
the third global trend. A recent survey of
Brazilian participation in major international organizations concluded that "Brazil is among the most
active states in a wide range of IGOs [international
organizations]," and "one of Brazil's most active
and influential IGO roles is in the law of the sea."
But still, Brazil "... is alert to guard against
multilateral measures which may threaten its own
freedom of action or access to resources, whether by
developed countries seen as trying to freeze international relationships or by LDC majorities seeking
to impose unacceptable standards of political conduct."[2]
    Analysis of Brazil's distinctive position in
the international negotiations will proceed as
follows. A chronology will first be developed relating Brazil's emergence as a major power to the
various stages in the development of UNCLOS III.
Then Brazilian participation during each of the
major stages of UNCLOS III will be discussed.

BRAZIL'S EMERGENCE AS A MAJOR POWER AND UNCLOS III

    Brazil's prominent role at UNCLOS III has been
generally recognized. Several attempts have been
made to select the most influential states at UNCLOS
III, and Brazil has figured prominently in each list.
For example, Professor Edward Miles included Brazil
among the 25 most influential states at UNCLOS III
among nearly 150 states participating. Six other
Latin American and Caribbean states were included in
the list (Bahamas, Chile, Jamaica, Mexico, Peru,
and Trinidad-Tobago), giving the region the largest
number of influential states of any region. Brazil's Thompson-Flores likewise appears on Miles'
list of the 36 most influential individuals among
hundreds at UNCLOS III, along with 10 others from
the Latin American/Caribbean region, thereby also
giving the region the largest number of influential

delegates of any region.[3] Relying on advice from
Professor Miles, Professor J. S. Nye similarly in-
cluded Brazil on a shorter list of the most impor-
tant 20 states at UNCLOS III. This short list in-
cluded three other Latin American states (Argentina,
Chile, and Peru), tying the region with Asia and
Western Europe as the most represented.[4] Among
Latin American states, too, Brazil has been recognized as a leader. For example, Professor Alberto
Szekely included Brazil as part of an "active"
Latin American group of 13 states in the Seabed
Committee (through 1973), and ranked Brazil third in
order of importance (Peru, Chile, Brazil, Mexico,
Ecuador, Colombia, Argentina, Uruguay, Jamaica,
Trinidad-Tobago, Venezuela, Bolivia and El Salvador).[5] Interviews conducted by this author with
numerous delegates from Latin America and other
regions at UNCLOS III corroborated the impression
of Brazil as an extremely influential law of the
sea actor and of Brazilian diplomats as skilled
negotiators.[6]

However, Brazil's role at UNCLOS III has not
been the focus of these or of other studies, nor
has its relationship to other Latin American states
or to other major regions and groups been explored
in depth. In this chapter, the evolution of
Brazilian policy at UNCLOS III will first be traced
during the period of preparations for the conference, as well as during the conference itself.
During each of these stages in the development of
global negotiations, prominent relationships between Brazil and major regions and groups will also
be explored.

A comprehensive profile of this influential
country's participation at UNCLOS III must also
take into account the impact of Brazilian development on national ocean policy during the decade of
conference-related activities (1967-present). A
difficult period of economic and political consolidation and stabilization (1964-1967) followed the
1964 military overthrow of a civilian government. A
period of rapid economic growth followed (1968-1973),
during which Brazil effectively began to mobilize
latent national resources and emerge as a major
power. Brazil was particularly hard-hit by rising
oil prices in 1974, since it imports approximately
80 percent of the crude petroleum it uses. Brazil
also had to cope with rising international protec-
tionist tendencies and world recession. The period
since 1974 has not demonstrated the economic buoy-

ancy of the 1968-73 boom years, but it has shown that Brazil's rapid development was no fluke and could be sustained. Economic stresses emerged and difficult readjustments were required, yet long-term growth appeared probable if political stability could be maintained.

Distinct phases of conference-related activities parallel Brazil's emergence as a major power. A first period included steps leading to the convening of UNCLOS III (1967-1970), and roughly coincided with the initial phase of Brazil's emergence as a major power. In 1967, the deep seabed was introduced in the General Assembly by Malta as a new subject of international concern and possible regulation, and a 35-member Ad Hoc Committee was established to study the peaceful uses of the seabed beyond the limits of national jurisdiction. The Ad Hoc Committee was transformed into the Seabed Committee in 1968 and by 1971 had grown to 91 members. Discussion likewise expanded from the seabed issue to encompass nearly all law of the sea matters. By 1970, sufficient interest had been awakened, particularly among developing states, to obtain the adoption of a UN resolution calling for a moratorium on deep seabed exploitation, a Declaration of Principles establishing the seabed beyond national jurisdiction as the common heritage of mankind, and a resolution calling for a Third Conference of the United Nations on the Law of the Sea.[7]

From 1971 to 1973, the Seabed Committee worked as a preparatory body for the conference and prepared several alternative versions of draft articles. These years coincided with the completion of the initial phase of Brazil's emergence as a great power.

From late 1973 until the present, UNCLOS III has convened periodically to discuss and negotiate law of the sea issues. Seven sessions had been held through 1978, as well as a number of intersessional meetings. A first session on organizational matters was held in New York City in late 1973. At a first substantive session of UNCLOS III at Caracas in the summer of 1974, states expressed their views on key issues and discussed the alternative texts submitted by the Seabed Committee. A third session (or second substantive session), held at Geneva in the spring of 1975, produced a three-part "Informal Single Negotiating Text" as a basis for negotiations. This text was prepared by the chairmen of the three main committees, and later was supplemented by a fourth part on dispute settlement prepared by the Conference President. A fourth session in New York City during the spring of 1976 led to a "Revised Single Negotiating Text" based on the Geneva text. A fifth session, also in New York City, in late summer of 1976 was not able to resolve a continuing impasse on the question of how deep seabed mining should be organized and regulated. A sixth session held in New York City in the summer of 1977 led to yet another draft of the basic text for negotiation in the form of an "Informal Composite Negotiating Text," when some additional deep seabed changes unacceptable to developed states were introduced. Two rounds of a seventh session were held in Geneva and New York City during mid-1978, when the conference moved nearer consensus on a number of disputed articles of the Informal Composite Negotiating Text. While changes introduced in the seventh session essentially amended a number of the disputed articles in the Informal Composite Negotiating Text, they were not sufficiently numerous to lead to the issuance of an entirely new negotiating text. So general agreement emerged on most of the draft articles by the end of the seventh session, although the negotiating text still contained a number of disputed articles, especially relating to deep seabed matters. An eighth session is projected for the spring of 1979 in Geneva to discuss remaining problems. It is the hope of numerous delegations that the current negotiating text can be revised and perhaps be formally converted into a draft treaty for subsequent modification and eventual signing, but very real problems still remain to be resolved, especially deep seabed questions.

By the time the first substantive round of UNCLOS III commenced in June 1974 in Caracas, Brazil already had gone through a prolonged period of boom projecting it as an emerging major power. As the conference experienced difficult problems over the next few years, so did Brazil face serious domestic and international challenges. But Brazil demonstrated that it could sustain its emergence as a major power and its position as an influential law of the sea actor.

Subsequent sections of this paper will deal in turn with the evolution of the influential Brazilian role during each of the main periods of conference-related activities. First, the prelude to UNCLOS III will be analyzed (1967-1970). Then the prepara-

tions for UNCLOS III will be assessed (1971-1973).
The conference sessions (late 1973-present) will be
analyzed in a final section.

PRELUDE TO UNCLOS III, 1967-1970

Four conventions at UNCLOS I in 1958 had codified the existing customary law of the sea and incorporated the principle of the continental shelf.
But the Geneva conventions had not definitively
settled a number of important national jurisdiction
issues (especially the breadth of the territorial
sea, extension of the continental shelf, and coastal
state resource rights). The Geneva deliberations
also did not deal with deep seabed issues (possible
international control of the deep seabed and the
division between national the international seabed
areas).

Some Latin American states had demanded revisions in the law of the sea before, during, and
after Geneva, particularly with respect to more
traditional national jurisdiction issues. Their
revisionist drive gradually gained momentum in the
Latin American region and beyond after Geneva. This
included demands for extensive territorial seas and/
or expansive coastal state resource rights. On the
relatively new deep seabed issue, revisionist Latin
American states responded more ambivalently.

In 1967, Ambassador Arvid Pardo of Malta had
called for a seabed treaty to prevent unilateral
appropriation of the deep seabed and to promote
development of seabed resources for the primary
benefit of developing countries through creation of
an international seabed authority (or the Authority).
Latin American revisionists, that is, those with
extensive offshore national claims, welcomed the
possibility of an international seabed regime insofar as it might lead to significant benefits for
developing states, but they were suspicious of any
innovation in the law which might limit their
claims. For example, they feared that a precise
limit between national and international seabed
areas might put their extensive claims to waters
superjacent to the shelf in jeopardy. Since the
Seabed Committee worked on the consensus principle,
these 200-mile states were able to block efforts to
define a boundary for the international area during
these early years of the negotiations.

Many other states, including the maritime
powers, responded cautiously as well to the 1967

Maltese initiative for a study of the peaceful uses of the seabed and ocean floor beyond national jurisdiction. Deep seabed mining, after all, was being proposed as a fitting subject for international regulation for the first time, and, to many, mining appeared neither immediately feasible, nor were its implications clear. The concern of the maritime powers, especially the United States, was that internationalization of the deep seabed would discourage development of seabed mining.[8]

Brazil's response to the introduction of the seabed issue was different from that of either group, since it was neither an established maritime power nor a revisionist state. Brazil was not a revisionist, since it did not support extensive offshore national claims of the kind associated with the revisionist camp. That is, Brazil did not support contentious revisionist claims over waters superjacent to the shelf out to 200 miles, although it did endorse the expansive Geneva shelf definition, which had gained considerable recognition in the international community. Brazil eventually did extend its territorial sea to 200 miles in 1970, and soon afterwards became a leader of the territorialist group. But it has been shown that this change was abrupt and largely unrelated to seabed policy. Failure to understand the complexity and distinctiveness of the Brazilian situation has led to much confusion and will be clarified here.

Up to 1970, Brazil's only extensive offshore claim was to its broad continental shelf. A 1950 Brazilian shelf claim had specified a limit varying between 180 and 200 meters in depth, but by 1958 national policy-makers came to support the more expansive shelf definition provided in the Geneva Convention on the Continental Shelf. This expansive shelf definition provided for national control out "to where the depth of the superjacent waters admits of the exploitation of the natural resources of the said [seabed] areas," in addition to the more restrictive 200-meter depth limit. The Brazilian delegate at UNCLOS I favored such dual criteria (depth and exploitability) in order to assure national control of the continental shelf:

He was in favor of keeping the double criterion of depth of water and possible exploitation. Even if it were true that the seabed and subsoil could at present be exploited in places where the sea was more than

200 metres deep, he was in favour of retaining the provision of the 200-meters
limit, because it would make clear that no
State had the right to exploit the natural
resources of the sedbed and subsoil less
than 200 metres below the surface of the high
seas off the coast of another State. There
would be a great ado if one State started
exploiting the submarine resources within
a very short distance of the coast of another
State without first obtaining its agreement.[9]

The open-ended nature of the Geneva shelf
definition, while compatible with Brazilian interests, would lead to subsequent problems in deline-
ating between national and international seabed
areas. The "exploitability" clause of the Geneva
definition appeared to legitimize national resource
control over the seabed progressively out to the
outer edge of the continental margin, where the
ocean basin or abyssal floor begins, as seabed
mining capabilities advanced. The Geneva exploitability criterion therefore permitted increasingly
extensive coastal state claims over three geological
areas extending successively seawards at greater
depths--the physical continental shelf, the continental slope, and the continental rise. Together,
these areas comprise the continental margin.
Brazil did not ratify the Geneva continental
shelf convention, with its expansive definition of
the shelf, primarily for reasons of internal political instability and bureaucritic inertia.[10] In
practice, Brazil simply accepted the expansive
Geneva shelf definition as an apparently widely
accepted legal norm. When a 200-mile school finally
did appear in Brazil, it, too, favored ratification
of the Geneva Convention on the Continental Shelf,
with its expansive definition of the shelf, while
opposing ratification of the Geneva Convention on
the Territorial Sea and Continguous Zone, with its
apparent 12-mile limit on the territorial sea. The
200-mile supporters argued that extension of the
territorial sea would largely resolve the problem
of consolidating national control over the shelf,
since this sovereign claim to both shelf and superjacent waters would include most of the Brazilian
continental margin.[11] Where the continental margin
extended beyond 200 miles, the Geneva exploitability
clause would be the basis for national control.
Brazil's only immediate concern in the emerging

deep seabed debate, before and after 1970, consequently was limited to maintenance of national control over the continental margin. Waters superjacent to the shelf or margin were recognized as high seas belonging to no state until 1970 and as under national sovereignty after 1970.

Brazil was also interested in longer-term benefits that internationalization of the deep seabed appeared to hold out for developing states. So Brazil emerged as an early supporter of an international seabed regime for the particular benefit of developing states. Brazil invited the Ad Hoc Committee for discussions in Rio de Janeiro in August 1968, and took a decisive role in transforming it into the permanent Seabed Committee. Brazil and Chile also took the initiative at the Rio de Janeiro session to propose the concept of the "common heritage of mankind" for the deep seabed and its resources, which later received general approval in the Declaration of Principles.[12] Other early examples of active support for an international seabed regime benefiting developing states were Brazilian/Chilean leadership during 1969 in insisting that any international machinery must be linked inseparably with the Declaration of Principles and a 1969 resolution, led by Brazil, India, and Kenya, for machinery with power to exploit.[13]

While Brazil favored an international seabed regime with power to exploit the seabed itself, especially for the benefit of developing states, pragmatism and compromise conditioned the Brazilian position. In 1969, for example, one of the leading figures of the Brazilian maritime community, Ambassador Ramiro Elysio Saraiva Guerreiro, spelled out a careful compromise between the needs and demands of the poorer states and the power and technological expertise of the industrialized states. Negotiations would be necessary to create new law for the seabed, he began, but this political process would tend to favor the more powerful states at the expense of weaker states, such as Brazil, especially if the matter were resolved by unilateral action. The maritime powers would try to extend the freedom of the seas regime to the deep seabed, in order to enjoy freedom of action in applying their advantages of capital and technology fo seabed mining. In turn, less advanced states, such as Brazil, supported the common heritage of mankind principle through the United Nations to offset these advantages of a few developed states and to assure

122

that seabed mining would benefit and be supervised
by the entire international community. These diverging interests were not incompatible, added
Saraiva Guerreiro, in quoting from Brazilian Foreign
Minister Magalhaes Pinto's introductory speech at
the 1968 Rio de Janeiro session of the Seabed Committee. Interests of both developed and developing
states were legitimate, argued Magalhaes Pinto, so
that a balance should be sought between access to
deep seabed mining and supervision by the international community. Saraiva Guerreiro then went on
to elaborate the elements of a seabed compromise
acceptable to Brazil. An international seabed
authority having direct and exclusive responsibility
for seabed mining would only be viable as an initial
bargaining position. The authority would also need
to issue licenses for exploration and exploitation
to states, or through states to corporations,
which could carry on mining directly as well.
Royalties for mining would be paid to the Authority,
which would exercise supervision without a great
power veto through control of licenses.[14]

While the proposed Brazilian compromise made
concessions to the developed states, it still emphasized a relatively strong international authority
to assure that developing states' interests were
promoted. For example, a study of major positions
in the debate on international machinery, 1968-
1970, included Brazil with nearly all other developing states in a strong machinery group (those who
"Favor Establishing Strong Machinery Along Exploit-
ing/ Strong Licensing Lines") in contrast to two
groups of developed states favoring weak machinery
(those "opposed to Establishing International
Machinery" and those who "Favor Establishing Weak
Machinery Along Registry/ Weak Licensing Lines").[15]

This moderate Brazilian approach was in conformity with national diplomatic tradition and past behavior at international maritime fora, and contrasted with those Third World states that interpreted the common heritage of mankind of rigid,
ideological terms. This contrast would continue
throughout the negotiations.

In another way, the seabed debate tended to
unify the Third World. Support grew among developing states for a Declaration of Principles including the concept of the deep seabed as the common
heritage of mankind, meaning that proceeds from deep
seabed exploitation would be particularly for their
benefit. Yet, unanswered questions about how the

international area would benefit developing states continued to provoke differences with developed states. The question of limits proved particularly troublesome and affected the kind of international conference that might be called.

The scope and orientation of a conference was consequently a major source of disagreement between revisionists and traditional states favoring main- tenance of as much of the settled law as possible. Coastal developing states were increasingly inclined toward extensive, revisionist claims over ocean resources off their shores. Traditional states, especially the great maritime powers, tried to curb such revisionist demands in 1969 by calling for a law of the sea conference narrow in scope and, there- fore, unsympathetic to extensive coastal state claims. A 1969 joint U.S.-Soviet proposal called for limiting the scope of a new law of the sea con- ference to consideration of navigation rights through international straits and the breadth of the ter- ritorial sea, and included draft articles for a 12- mile limit for the territorial sea. Revisionists rejected this superpower proposal, as well as a related 1969 Maltese draft resolution for a new conference.

The 1969 Maltese proposal stressed the need to arrive at a precise and internationally acceptable limit of the deep seabed through a new law of the sea conference before a regime for such an area was agreed upon. A restrictive 200-meter depth mark would be the sole dividing line between national and international seabed areas. So both 1969 pro- posals presented the probability of restricting coastal state rights, at least as expansively inter- preted by revisionists. The U.S.-USSR proposal would have limited the territorial sea to 12 miles, and the Maltese resolution threatened to limit coastal state rights over the continental margin, possible restricting rights over superjacent waters as well.

Brazil played a key role in shifting and ex- panding the orientation of these proposals. As a result of amendments which Brazil co-sponsored, the Maltese draft resolution was expanded into a pro- posal which absorbed the two superpowers' original proposal and called for a new conference to deal with all aspects of the law of the sea. The amended draft resolution, which was eventually approved, also favored establishment of an international regime before the limits of the international area

would be defined. While the thrust of this resolution leaned toward the developing states, something
was offered to the developed states as well. The
inadequacies of the flexible limit of the Geneva
continental shelf definition were acknowledged as a
concession to the developed states. At the same
time a compromise acceptable to developing states
was fashioned, since a strong regime would be
established first before settling the delicate question of limits at a subsequent date, and all aspects
of the law of the sea would be negotiated.

Only a few Latin American states joined Brazil
in its leadership role, none of which were 200-mile
states at the time. Most 200-mile states did eventually vote for the amended draft resolution, but
many had felt that it would have been better if no
conference took place or if it could have been delayed as long as possible.[16] Revisionists did
eventually lend their support to the Brazilian
approach, since of the available alternatives, a new
law of the sea conference covering all questions,
with determination of limits deferred still further,
at least headed off attempts to curb extensive offshore claims. But the Brazilian approach rested on
different grounds than that of the revisionists.

The 1969 12-mile territorial sea proposal of
the two superpowers had directly challenged revisionist 200-mile claims, but did not adversely affect
Brazil which only claimed 12 miles at the time.
Similarly, proposed conference negotiations about an
international regime for the deep seabed, such as
the 1969 Maltese draft resolution, did not pose
problems for Brazil, which already had emerged as
an early supporter of a strong international seabed
regime. Instead, other aspects of the 1969 Maltese
proposal alarmed Brazilian policy-makers.[17] Proposals, like those of Malta, which supported a precise, restrictive definition or demarcation line
between the national and international areas
threatened to limit expansive continental shelf
claims. The 1969 Malta proposal would have elimi-
nated the expansive Geneva exploitability clause,
leaving the more precise yet more restrictive 200-
meter depth mark as the sole dividing line between
national and international seabed areas. Exclusive
national control only out to the 200-meter depth
limit would roughly cover just the first stage of
the continental margin, that is, the continental
shelf. So a law of the sea conference that would
endorse such a precise, yet restrictive, shelf

definition threatened to undercut extensive off-shore mineral rights which Brazil had come to regard as secure in international law. For Brazil, the 200-meter depth criterion alone would have been tantamount to renouncing existing rights guaranteed through the Geneva exploitability clause, of Latin American origin. A 200-meter depth criterion or some similar restrictive formula limiting continental shelf claims, if generally accepted, would have severely damaged interests of states like Brazil, with broad and apparently resource-rich continental margins.

So several basic interests oriented Brazilian ocean policy up to 1970. These included support for a strong international seabed regime, insistence on national control of the continental margin, and support for a relatively narrow 12-mile territorial sea. The first two elements of this policy tended to function separately from the third element, narrow territorial sea limits, up to 1970. When Brazil moved from the moderate to the revisionist camp in 1970 with respect to the third issue by declaring a 200-mile territorial sea, all three policy stances tended to become entangled. The 200-mile territorial sea claim represented a unified approach to all national jurisdiction issues, with national control over shelf, superjacent waters, and territorial sea all defined in terms of the same distance from shore. In turn, this expansive, categorical national claim defined the preferred relationship between national and international areas more exactly. Brazil continued to support a strong international seabed regime and to insist on national control of its extensive continental margin, but in the context of its new territorialist position. Only that limited portion of the continental margin beyond 200 miles remained in somewhat uncertain status in national policy.

The 1970 200-mile territorial sea decision consequently changed some aspects of Brazil's negotiating aims while continuing others. Issues of national ocean jurisdiction have been of most immediate interest to Brazil and other coastal developing states throughout the negotiations, even when the deep seabed issue was the focus of negotiations from 1967 to 1970. Pay-offs from areas under national contol were certain, while benefits from deep seabed mining remained problematical, especially for developing states which would have to rely on the technology of the industrialized states. Yet, this

did not mean that deep seabed policy was literally a
function of issues of national ocean jurisdiction,
either before or after 1970. Cause and effect was
much more complex than this. As the scope of the
UNCLOS negotiations expanded from 1970 to encompass
all law of the sea issues, a package deal involving
both national and international zone issues appeared
to present the only viable solution. Both national
and international zone issues therefore tended to
become entangled, yet each issue also developed its
own dynamics in a protracted, complex negotiating
context.

In the case of Brazil, national and international zone issues were therefore becoming entangled
in national policy, just as a parallel trend linking
national and international area issues was occurring in the global UNCLOS III negotiations. The
complexity of this policy context has led to much
confusion about the relationship between Brazil's
1970 200-mile territorial sea extension and UNCLOS
III. A number of interpretations of Brazil's 1970
shift in territorial sea policy and its relationship
to the law of the sea negotiations have been presented, but all have been oversimplistic. Essentially, U.S. interpretations have focused too much
on the law of the sea negotiations, while Brazilian
interpretations have concentrated excessively on
national policy. A more complete explanation, which
takes both perspectives into account, will be offered here.

By 1970, a number of factors were converging to
push Brazil from a 12-mile to a 200-mile territorial
sea, and law of the sea developments, as perceived
by Brazil, reinforced these other factors. One such
law of the sea development, already examined, was
the 1969 Maltese proposal. Another was the adverse
reaction of the developed states to the 1969 moratorium resolution.

Brazil was one of the most active sponsors of
UN resolution 2574D (XXIV), which declared a moratorium on the exploitation of seabed areas beyond
national jurisdiction pending establishment of an
international regime not subject to great power veto.
This "moratorium resolution" was eventually approved
on December 15, 1969 over the intense opposition of
the developed world. Since the moratorium resolution involved the first sharp cleavage between
developed and developing states in the seabed negotiations, the North-South division attracted attention and variations within each camp have tended to

be glossed over. Western criticisms of Brazil's prominent role in co-sponsoring the moratorium resolution accordingly have assimilated it with an alleged Third World aim to preserve or encourage expansive coastal state claims at the expense of developed states.

One recent study noted, for example, that Brazil "was on the brink of making its own 200-mile claim" when it sponsored the moratorium resolution, and was joined by three "long-time exponents of large national claims"--Chile, Ecuador, and Peru. On this basis, it was concluded that the moratorium resolution "was clearly aimed at restricting nodule exploitation by a handful of developed states, and not at restricting claims to coastal jurisdiction by the developing countries."[18] Bernard Oxman, at the time Assistant Legal Adviser for Ocean Affairs of the Department of State and a member of the U.S. delegation to the Seabed Committee, likewise linked Brazil's sponsorship of the moratorium resolution directly to its subsequent 200-mile decree:

> . . . there is a critical flaw in the Moratorium Resolution in that it doesn't put a moratorium on exploitation, but simply puts a moratorium on exploitation beyond what someone will regard as national jurisdiction. We all know of one case [Brazil] in which one of the staunchest supporters of the Moratorium Resolution turned around a bare few months later and extended its national jurisdiction by a very substantial amount.[19]

Leigh Ratiner, another member of the U.S. delegation and at the time Chairman of the Department of Defense Advisory Group on the Law of the Sea, reached a very similar interpretation. Brazil supported the 1969 moratorium resolution, Ratiner noted, which tends to encourage expansive national claims, and indeed shortly afterwards made a 200-mile territorial sea claim. This extreme, inflexible claim, Ratiner asserts, was well-timed to stake out a strong negotiating posture at the upcoming global negotiations.[20]

The U.S., while concerned about restraints being placed on deep seabed mining, was more immediately concerned with discouraging "creeping jurisdiction," whereby national claims would gradually extend further seawards and expand into full claims of sovereignty. While the moratorium resolution intended to delay deep seabed mining, it set no limit

on national jurisdiction. So Brazilian policy was
regarded as a particularly opportunistic example of
creeping jurisdiction, since it began by trying to
prevent unilateral deep seabed claims by others and
then itself made a sweeping unilateral claim to
sovereignty. But the U.S. interpretations of the
relationship between Brazilian co-sponsorship of the
moratorium resolution and the Brazilian 200-mile
territorial sea claim rely entirely on quite selective circumstantial evidence.

Intense U.S. feelings, in essence, led to guilt
by association. Brazil was associated with exponents of large national claims on the moratorium
resolution, so it was assumed that Brazilian deep
seabed policy was opportunistic. This has overlooked
the distinctive aims of Brazilian ocean policy and
has exaggerated the solidarity of Third World motives and objectives. Such a vague document as the
moratorium resolution, which did not define the
limit between national and international areas, en-
compassed divergent motives.

As for the states which already had made broad
jurisdictional claims, the moratorium resolution was
not particularly important insofar as promotion of
their national claims were concerned. The resolution did not prevent creeping jurisdiction, it is
true, but neither was a moratorium on deep seabed
mining particularly useful in promoting extensive
national claims. So such states merely went along
with the resolution:

> The Latin American states, given their
> "expansionist" policy, had no particular in-
> terests to defend by supporting the moratorium
> resolution. However, to maintain the soli-
> darity of the group of developing states with-
> in the Sea-Bed Committee, practically all Latin
> American states joined with the rest of the
> developing world and outvoted the developed
> states.[21]

Developing states, such as Brazil, which still
had not made 200-mile claims, tended to have a different perspective.[22] The moratorium resolution,
Brazilian diplomats reasoned, provided the basis for
a global law of the sea compromise. Developed
states would merely be postponing, not renouncing,
deep seabed mining through a moratorium until mutually satisfactory arrangements could be negotiated.
A moratorium on mining the deep seabed, including a

ban on mining of the continental margins of other
states, would avoid unnecessary friction, it was argued. The United States would be able "to exploit
all of its continental margins," but "as pointed out
by . . . the representative of Brazil," "what it
[the moratorium] probably did preclude the United
States from doing was exploiting the continental
margin of any other state."[23] This same Brazilian
concern had been expressed as early as UNCLOS I,
it will be recalled. Brazil feared that developed
states, through their giant corporations, could
encroach into the continental margins of other
states with mining operations, were there no moratorium or were a restrictive 200-meter continental
shelf definition approved. Indeed, existing technology at the time did permit seabed exploitation
beyond 200 meters, if not yet out to the deep seabed.
So the Brazilian concern--that large private companies from developed states would be able to control exploitation activities in the deep seabed and
encroach or "creep" inwards to exploit less developed states' continental margins--was opposite from
the outward creeping jurisdiction concern of the
United States.

As matters turned out, the moratorium resolution provoked confrontation, rather than the compromise Brazil had hoped for. The generally unsettled legal status of the continental margin, as
had been most recently reflected in the Maltese
proposal and the opposition of the developed states
to the moratorium resolution, helped galvanize
Brazilian policy-makers to take a revisionist approach to the territorial sea and related issues.
Interpretations differ here, too, in emphasis.

One recent study of the moratorium resolution
suggested that oil was the underlying motivation of
Brazilian policy: "Both Brazil and Argentina are
engaged in extensive oil exploration so that the
interest of east coast Latin nations in broad shelf
claims may be reinforced by actual interest in oil
recovery as well as by the value of jurisdictional
claims as a negotiating tactic for the Latin bloc
as a whole."[24] Brazil's heavy dependence on imported oil did made it anxious to explore offshore
oil possibilities and to prevent multinational oil
companies from any exploitation activities on the
continental margin without Brazilian permission.
Some have argued on this basis that oil was a decisive consideration in the 200-mile decision. For
example, Brazilian Admiral Sylvio Heck has stated

that "In the case of Brazil, oil was the main reason for the 200 mile decree."[25]

Oil and the apparent reluctance of the developed states to respect the moratorium resolution did help tip the scales, but this was by no means the decisive consideration. A leading Brazilian petroleum expert has concluded that problems with foreign fishermen were "much more important than petroleum problems in influencing the 1970 territorial sea decision."[26] Other findings, previously cited, showed that domestic political considerations, not foreign fishing or foreign threats to shelf rights, were the decisive factors in propelling Brazil to an extreme 200-mile territorial sea claim.[27]

Since the territorial sea was extended primarily due to domestic political considerations, deep seabed and continental margin positions remained quite consistent throughout. Oil did play a role in the 1970 territorial sea extension, but this did not reflect weakening of traditional Brazilian support for a strong international seabed regime. Accordingly, relationships between the different elements of Brazilian ocean policy have been quite different than generally posited. Many Latin American diplomats, like U.S. critics, have erroneously interpreted Brazil's 200-mile territorial sea claim as a shrewd technique for establishing a strong bargaining position at UNCLOS III.[28] While territorial sea, deep seabed, and continental margin positions became more interrelated after 1970, there is little evidence, other than of a tenuous circumstantial nature, supporting the view that Brazilian policy-makers diabolically manipulated domestic policy in 1969-1970 to maximize benefits from international negotiations. If Brazilian ocean policy has been less purposeful than both U.S. critics and Latin American supporters argue, so has it been less conspiratorial and more constructive in nature. Comparison with the ocean policies of other east coast South American states reconfirms these conclusions.

Brazil's concern about threats to broadly defined shelf rights, in particular from the 1969 Maltese proposal, was shared by Uruguay, its immediate southern neighbor with an equally broad shelf. Both these east coast South American states only claimed 12-mile territorial seas at the time, yet moved in quick succession to make 200-mile claims. The perceived threat from the Maltese proposal was a factor in leading both Uruguay to make a

200-mile resource claim in December 1969, and Brazil to make a more extreme 200-mile territorial sea claim in March 1970.[29] But here the similarities end.

Brazil's eventual response was more extreme than that of Uruguay, but Brazil had first searched for another viable alternative through the Seabed Committee by co-sponsoring the moratorium resolution, while Uruguay did not. The First Committee approved the moratorium resolution on December 2, 1969, and passed it on to the General Assembly for a final vote. Uruguay rushed through its 200-mile legislation on December 3, 1969, in order to be able both to benefit from an extensive national resource zone and to vote for the moratorium resolution "without being forced to disregard it obviously,"[30] The Brazilian 200-mile decision, in contrast, was not definitively made until late December 1969,[31] only after heavy opposition by the developed states to the December 15, 1969 moratorium resolution had been expressed. Public approval of the 200-mile decision was given by the executive on March 25, 1970, and confirmation from the legislature was given in May 1970.

U.N. seabed politics then influenced both the Uruguayan and Brazilian decisions, but in very different ways. Uruguay, like many other developing states with aspirations to extensive offshore coastal rights, including control of waters superjacent to the shelf, only lent pro forma support to the moratorium resolution and quickly moved to consolidate an extensive national claim prior to the U.N. vote. Brazil, in contrast, actively supported the moratorium resolution throughout as a possible alternative to extensive offshore claims through a compromise involving national control of the continental margin and continued freedom of the seas status for waters superjacent to the shelf. The 200-mile Brazilian claim only came after intense opposition to the moratorium resolution by developed states had questioned the viability of this approach. The majority of the Brazilian maritime community still appeared committed to a 12-mile territorial sea well into 1970, until the Médici administration silenced critics and began an active nationalistic campaign in favor of the 200 miles.[32]

Seabed politics was still but one factor involved in the Brazilian territorial sea extension, so UNCLOS III only relates tangentially to the kind of claim that was made. Brazil made an extreme

132

200-mile territorial sea claim in 1970, while her
neighbors, Argentina and Uruguay, in roughly similar
geographical circumstances, made much more qualified
200-mile resource claims, in 1966 and late 1969
respectively. So the question has been asked:

> Why did Brazil's claims on jurisdiction
> differ so sharply from those of Argentina and
> Uruguay, considering the fact that all three
> states faced the same international political
> circumstances, possessed the 'same' geological
> and geographical characteristics and shared
> identical interests in the exploitation of
> adjacent sea and sea-bed?[33]

The answer, the same study suggested, must lie in
one of two alternative explanations.

> The answer must be that Brazil's position
> either was the result of a more intensely
> nationalistic policy of the military regime in
> Brazil, or it was adopted as a 'bargaining
> chip' for future international negotations on
> the law of the sea.[34]

Factors related to the first explanation constituted, as shown, the decisive considerations leading
Brazil to take a hard-line territorial sea posture.
The second explanation, bargaining chip advantages
for UNCLOS III, was not a decisive consideration.
The need for Brazil to go to 200 miles for reasons
of regional solidarity at the upcoming law of the
sea negotiations was mentioned in both the Brazilian
National Security Council "Statement of Motives"
supporting the 200-mile legislation and in the relevant legislative documents.[35] But regional solidarity could have been achieved as well through a more
moderate 200-mile resource claim, similar to the
prior claims of Argentina and Uruguay, and without
the risk of isolation, from which Brazil later indeed did suffer.
    Yet another variation of bargaining advantages
as a consideration was expressed by Clóvis Ramalhete,
the so-called "father of the 200 miles." This related the extreme character of the 200-mile territorial sea claim explicitly to Brazil's emergence
as a great power. At a time when Brazil's rapid
growth was projecting it more actively into international political and economic affairs,

> . . . the act gave notice to the world of
> a power of decision that projected Brazil into
> certain spheres of interest, with projection
> [already] into other spheres (for example,
> UNCTAD; the 'battle of the liner conferences';
> coffee policy; the dispute over the prices of
> raw materials), and presented the country in a
> positive way. . .[36]

Yet, in an interview with this writer, Ramalhete
recognized that domestic factors still dominated
Brazilian thinking, including Brazilian attention on
westward expansion and limited interest or problems
in international affairs, and had been responsible
for the long delay in claiming 200 miles of sea.[37]
   While global ocean politics did not play a decisive role in the 200-mile Brazilian decision, the
measure did have important implications for the
international negotations. Brazil's 200-mile claim
did complete a ring of 200-mile states in South
America south of the equator, and led to efforts to
build regional unity for the global negotiations.
Twice in 1970 Brazil joined other regional states in
declarations supporting broad coastal state jurisdiction. It was Uruguay, with its more moderate
200-mile resource claim, that took the first important initiative to increase regional solidarity at
the upcoming law of the sea conference. The
Montevideo Conference, called by Uruguay, did unite
the nine Latin American states at the time claiming
200-mile zones or territorial seas, including
Brazil, around the principle of unilateral coastal
state competence to fix claims of "sovereignty and
jurisdiction." But since national versions of the
200 miles differed so much, the resulting Declaration of Montevideo of May 8, 1970 had to rely on
this ambiguous formula of "sovereignty and jurisdiction," and the 200-mile limit was not even
explicitly endorsed. So it was not clear if coastal
states' rights, as endorsed by the declaration,
were limited to exploitation of economic resources
or were all-encompassing, as territorialists like
Brazil advocated. For example, traditional rights
of free navigation and overflight were reaffirmed
in the declaration within the area of maritime
sovereignty or jurisdiction. Five territorialist
states, including Brazil, felt that such a compromise was not compatible with their hard-line position (Brazil, Ecuador, Nicaragua, Panama, and Peru),
so they issued separate reservations to the effect

that their 200-mile territorial seas only permitted
a limited right of innocent passage, not more extensive rights of free navigation and overflight.

In spite of these disagreements at Montevideo,
the nine 200-mile states did agree to convoke a subsequent broader conference of all Latin American
states later in the same year to coordinate regional
policies of national marine jurisdiction. This resulted in the Lima Declaration of August 8, 1970,
which again endorsed the traditional regime of freedom of navigation and overflight in national areas
of "maritime sovereignty or jurisdiction." Again
the same five territorialist states, including
Brazil, issued reservations recognizing only the
more limited right of innocent passage. A price
was paid as well for the Lima attempt to recruit
non-200 mile states to an expansive coastal states'
rights position. Twenty states participated in the
meeting, but the two South American landlocked
states and four Caribbean states opposed the declaration. Five other moderate Latin American states
did sign the Lima Declaration, along with the original nine Montevideo states, but two of these moderates felt compelled to issue reservations.

While the 1967-1970 United Nations discussions
focused on the deep seabed issue, the two Latin
American declarations of 1970 signaled that more
basic coastal state interests were being reasserted
as all law of the sea questions were being reopened
for negotiation. Both 1970 regional declarations
stressed broad coastal states' rights and neither
mentioned the deep seabed issue. Their common
emphasis on unilaterally determined "reasonable"
limits on national jurisdiction even seemed to be
at the expense of the "common heritage of mankind."
To the extent that national jurisdiction zones expanded, the international seabed area would necessarily become more restricted.

Brazil's new territorialist position shaped
its participation at the two regional meetings, but
its interest in a strong international deep seabed
regime continued. Resolution I of the Lima Conference did refer to the deep seabed and has even
been called a precedent for the 1970 Declaration of
Principles and for the 13-power Latin American deep
seabed Working Paper of August 4, 1971.[38]

Paralleling these developments within the Latin
American camp, the United States was attempting to
forge a unified seabed policy from disparate domestic interests. President Nixon first presented a

seabed proposal on May 23, 1970, which was later submitted to the Seabed Committee as a more elaborate working paper on August 3, 1970. The working paper posited a 200-meter limit of exclusive shelf control, a trusteeship zone from that limit to the far edge of the continental margin in which revenue would be shared, and a weak international authority for the deep seabed. In a separate draft treaty, the U.S. proposed 12 miles as the limit of exclusive national claims over superjacent waters. These measures both qualified national rights over the continental margin and threatened 200-mile claims, so Latin American expansionist states, led by recently converted Brazil, consequently opposed the U.S. approach.[39]

Brazil's position in these developments was unique in being an early and continuous supporter of a strong international regime for the deep seabed, while also shifting later from a moderate to an extreme territorial sea position. This involved elements of both nationalism and internationalism. On the one hand, Brazil's internationalist influence was considerable throughout the early stage of the seabed discussions up to 1970, when it was described as one "of the 13 most active developing countries in the law of the sea negotiations."[40] Nationalism, on the other hand, enveloped the 1970 territorial sea decision, but was not an important influence on Brazilian ocean policy before then and tended to recede after the decision was made. Consistent Brazilian support for national control over the entire continental margin resulted from self-interest, not nationalism or internationalism.

Latin American states active in the UN seabed debates, including the prominent CEP states and Brazil, have been ranked on a more simplistic national-international continuum in a well-known study. On this basis, these states were categorized as extremely nationalistic throughout the seabed debates because of their opposition to any international effort to delimit the continental shelf. Discussions of continental shelf delimitation were regarded as a threat to their extensive claims to offshore rights, according to the study. Such a group of states, which allegedly included Brazil, was held to have isolated itself through its highly nationalistic position.[41] The findings here indicate that Brazilian ocean policy has been much more complex and less obsessed with nationalism than suggested, but do confirm the enduring importance of nationalism for most of the Latin American revisionists.

PREPARATIONS FOR UNCLOS III, 1971-1973

As the preparations for UNCLOS III began, Brazil found itself in the anomalous position of a recently converted hardline territorialist with a tradition of compromise and internationalism in multilateral negotiations. This distinctive historical legacy lent complexity to Brazilian ocean policy and made prediction difficult. Ratiner, in his critique of Brazilian policy, did predict correctly that a hard-line territorialist position would gain bargaining advantages in the early stages of the negotiations with a risk of isolation later on.[42] The 1970 200-mile territorial sea extension did tend to isolate Brazil for a time. Yet, the complexity of Brazilian ocean policy qualified this isolation, thereby rendering such a prediction oversimplistic.

Brazil occupied a strong bargaining position as preparations for UNCLOS III began. Policy toward the deep seabed had been planned and Brazilian leadership on the issue continued. But territorial sea policy had grown like Topsy, with the 1970 territorial sea extension having largely resulted from fortuitous domestic circumstances. Yet the policy change suddenly projected the country toward a position of leadership as well of what would become the territorialist group. Brazil stood out among 200-mile states as an emerging power, as an established leader on the deep seabed issue, and now as a vigorous supporter of a territorialist position.

On all major ocean issues, Brazil had therefore come to favor change, whether the formation of new law in the case of the deep seabed or approval of expansive coastal state rights on national jurisdiction matters. This concern with comprehensive change was evident in Brazil's active role in the 1971-1973 Seabed Committee debates. Much attention was given to development of a consensus on a list of subjects and issues for the upcoming conference. Revisionist-oriented states favored reconsideration of all major law of the sea issues, and hence backed a list equally comprehensive in scope. Brazil, along with thirteen other Latin American states, including the CEP group, plus Spain, accordingly proposed a comprehensive, broadly defined list of items in 1971. A 32-power Afro-Asian proposal (including Yugoslavia) was likewise comprehensive and broadly defined to include all issues relevant to revisionist demands.[43] In 1972, the Afro-Asian and Latin American groups, Brazil included, managed to merge their lists into a 56-power list, which exerted such an impact that all other proposals took the form of amendments to this document. At this session, a compromise list resembling that of the developing states was eventually approved.[44]

Efforts to coordinate Latin American policies at UNCLOS III still faced important obstacles. The Latin American group had not been active in the first stage of discussion leading to UNCLOS III, 1967-1970, in contrast to previous international negotiations. At UNCLOS I and II, the small Latin American revisionist group had been active in supporting extensive offshore claims, but the 1967-1970 discussions leading to UNCLOS III had focused on the deep seabed. Much uncertainty resulted. As the negotiations matured and expanded in scope to include both national and international jurisdiction questions, more intensive efforts were made to coordinate maritime policies in the region.

The 200-mile movement had grown erratically, but was becoming more organized. The Montevideo and Lima Declarations of 1970 reflected an initial effort by the 200-mile states to forge a coordinated regional movement. Shortcomings of this effort have been noted. Latin American cooperation was more successful on the deep seabed issue.

Initial Latin American efforts in 1971 in the Seabed Committee to coordinate positions revealed that differences on national jurisdiction matters continued, but that a consensus might be fashioned on the deep seabed issue. The Brazilian delegate was designated as one of five special rapporteurs to draft a common working paper, and, with Trinidad-Tobago, was in charge of the question of the structure of the authority. Throughout these informal consultations within the Latin American group, the seabed authority was envisaged as the primary entity in charge of all activities in the international area. But Brazil had a more flexible interpretation of this principle of control by the international seabed authority than many other Latin American states. This Brazilian pragmatism or willingness to compromise on the deep seabed issue was also evident in the earlier 1967-1970 stage of the negotiations, it will be recalled.

Negotiations among the Latin American states to develop a common seabed position at first gave some support to an informal document prepared by the rep-

resentative of Brazil, which provided for a system
of licenses for exploration and exploitation to be
issued by the international seabed authority directly to states. As the negotiations evolved within the
Latin American group, the difference in emphasis
between Brazil and most others became more marked.
Step by step the majority position became more hard-
line while Brazil continued to stress compromise.
Licenses were subsequently limited to exploration
only, while for exploitation the proposed powers of
the international authority were extended still
further to limit possible abuses of a licensing system by providing instead for "service contracts"
and "joint ventures." Decisive international control over both exploration and exploitation of resources in the area was assured in a final stage of
the negotiations by restricting the role of states
to that of service contractor or joint venture partner with the authority. This proposed scheme of
service contracts was at first to have been a transitional regime until the authority could gain momentum and more liberal participation arrangements
could be negotiated. This might have been palatable
to the developed states, but as Latin American positions hardened an interim formula became the basis
for a permanent system and thereby antagonized the
developed countries.[45]

Thirteen Latin American states sponsored a
working paper on this regime for the deep seabed on
August 14, 1971 (A/AC. 138/49). The co-sponsors included all influential Latin American coastal states,
save Brazil. The proposal did unity most coastal
states of a major region in the developing world on
deep seabed provisions that elaborated the 1970
Declaration of Principles. Of the 11 seabed proposals made during 1971-73, the Latin American one
advocated the strongest powers for an international
authority and devised a formula that would later be
endorsed in large part by the entire Group of 77.
While the Latin American seabed position then obviously exerted substantial influence on other
developing states, Brazil declined to associate itself formally with an uncompromising proposal.
Latin American consensus on the deep seabed issue
has frequently been assumed, but Brazilian preference for compromise on this key issue was evident
here and would resurface dramatically later in the
negotiations.

The extent of seabed differences within the
Latin American group still should not be exaggerated.

Brazil, after all, had been one of the earliest supporters of a relatively strong international seabed
regime and had contributed in numerous ways toward
a regime that would benefit developing states.
Brazilian dissent from the 1971 proposal, moreover,
had been low-key, and there was much in the proposal
that Brazil accepted. The comprehensive 1971 document included a list of fundamental principles, a
detailed description of the functions and powers of
the authority, and a detailed presentation of the
institutional structure of the authority. Brazilian
disagreement focused on the issue of the degree of
control which the seabed authority should exercise
in the international area, while Brazil was pleased
that the Latin American seabed proposal did not
define the limit between the national and international areas. So on a related deep seabed issue,
unilateral mining claims by developed states, Brazil
again played a leading role shortly afterwards in
the Group of 77. Brazil co-sponsored a draft decision in August 1972 critical of a proposed U.S.
Hard Minerals Bill as a breach of the moratorium and
the Declaration of Principles.[46]

But the issue of the degree of control of the
Authority did set Brazil apart from many other Latin
American states. The Latin American seabed proposal
essentially involved a unitary regime, in which the
Authority would directly control all activities in
the deep seabed and would carry out mining itself,
while Brazil was inclined toward a parallel or mixed
regime permitting seabed mining both by the Authority
and by private or state-backed enterprises. In mid-
1972, for example, a leading Brazilian diplomat and
participant in the law of the sea negotiations expressed doubt that a unitary seabed regime could be
accepted, and that if it were, that it could function efficiently. A leading naval figure in the law
of the sea negotiations and the navy's representative
on the Brazilian delegation to UNCLOS III likewise
recognized in mid-1973 that a parallel system, if
favoring developing states, could be particularly
advantageous for Brazil, since its own state-owned
corporations could thereby be assisted in undertaking seabed mining. Relevant technology and know-
how would be transferred by developed states to the
Authority, which would then also advise and help
finance potential developing state seabed miners.[47]

While Brazil's willingness to compromise on the
control issue set it apart in that portion of the
seabed debate from most other Latin American states,

its uncompromising territorialist position ironically tended to isolate it as well from many Latin
American states. Brazil firmly supported its 1970
200-mile territorial sea claim for several years.
The hard-line Brazilian reservations at the Montevideo and Lima conferences in 1970 in favor of a
restrictive regime of innocent passage in the entire 200-mile territorial sea have been previously
analyzed. Other Brazilian statements in 1971 and
1972 repeat the same theme in the same rigid terms.[48]
Brazil alone also sponsored a territorial sea proposal on July 13, 1973 (A/AC. 138/SC II/L. 25), which
emphasized the right of every state to establish the
breadth of its territorial sea within reasonable limits up to 200 miles. This territorialist proposal
and another related proposal co-sponsored by Ecuador,
Panama, and Peru were the most extreme territorial
sea proposals submitted to the Seabed Committee. On
the matter of innocent passage, the Brazilian proposal was the least compromising of all: "Among
those few proposals that do not contemplate a 12-
mile limit, only the articles submitted by Brazil
would establish a full territorial sea with control
over navigation and overflight out to 200 nautical
miles."[49]

The 1973 Brazilian territorial sea proposal was
still somewhat flexible in providing for different
legal regimes according to the specific circumstances
of the coastal state. Accordingly, an explanatory
statement stressed Brazil's own need for a 200-mile
territorial sea, but also recognized that the patrimonial sea is an "important, constructive effort"
and a "firm step in the right direction." Other
states would have the right to establish a patrimonial sea with a 12-mile territorial sea and a 188-
mile economic zone, as advocated in the Santo Domingo Declaration of June 1972, but Brazil itself
required sovereignty over a full 200-mile territorial
sea.[50]

Ten Caribbean states had signed the Santo Domingo Declaration, whose patriomonial sea concept
was presented as more moderate and conciliatory than
the territorialist approach. The patrimonialist
approach indeed did attract much support on its own
and in association with economic zone proposals. So
during this period the territorialist group began to
coalesce, but still contrasted with the patrimonialist group, which in turn began to attract economic
zone (or "zonist") allies. A moderate coastal state
group also began to emerge, which would be active

at later stages in the negotiations. Members included some developed states and representatives
from the major regions of the developing world, but
no territorialists until later stages of the negotiations.

While Brazil maintained the hard-line territorialist doctrine throughout the preparatory period
for UNCLOS III, 1971-1973, pressure built up to
modify this extreme position. Some pressures were
domestic, stemming from service rivalries and their
consequences.[51] Internationally, the opposition of
the maritime powers to the territorialist position
continued and the influence of the more moderate
patrimonialist/economic zone position increased.
This led Brazilian policy-makers to reformulate some
of the more extreme legal implications of a 200-mile
sovereignty claim. For example, the United States
and Brazil were able to conclude a shrimp agreement
on May 9, 1972, through compromises on both sides.[52]

Somewhat greater Brazilian willingness to compromise was evident on the regional level as well.
In early 1973 the Inter-American Juridical Committee
approved a resolution on the law of the sea after
two years of deliberations. This attempted to
reconcile the territorialist and patrimonialist
positions prior to UNCLOS III, in order to present
a united Latin American front. A compromise formula
was adopted to describe the nature of coastal state
control out to a maximum of 200 miles ("sovereignty
or jurisdiction"). There was also agreement in
principle between patrimonialists and territorialists
on coastal state control over the entire continental
margin, although their legal regimes for this control differed. In another area the patrimonialist
formula rather than the territorialist one was clearly endorsed, that of innocent passage in a 12-mile
zone and free navigation and overflight in a 188-
mile economic zone beyond this. The Brazilian delegate, Vincente Rao, signed the document with the
reservation that Brazil exercises sovereignty in the
entire 200 miles and that the right of free navigation and overflight in the 188-mile zone should be
"subject to the pertinent regulations of the coastal
state with regard to the protection of its security."[53] Brazil therefore reasserted its territorialist
position, but it did not reject the possibility of
compromise. Brazilian association, albeit with
reservations, with a document which merged elements
of the patrimonialist and territorialist positions
was significant. In a background paper for the IJC

law of the sea study, Ambassador Rao similarly combined a rigid restatement of territorialist policy with a suggestion of compromise. In the event the Committee recommended the patrimonial sea thesis as then proposed, it would not alter Brazilian policy, but he added that free navigation and innocent passage are the same in practice since both respect the needs of national security, public health and fiscal laws.[54]

Many Latin American coastal states, whether of an economic zone or territorialist stripe, also coincided in favoring minimal access by land-locked states to resources in the 200 miles. Considerable support did build up for a Caribbean regional regime, but no South American counterpart proposal was seriously considered. South American coastal states were generally reluctant to allow meaningful participation by the two regional land-locked states, Bolivia and Paraguay, in the exploitation of their 200-mile zones. But the Declaration of Principles had stated that deep seabed mining should particularly benefit developing states, whether coastal or landlocked. Throughout the course of the negotiations, land-locked states have tried, with limited success, to extend this obligation to share resources of the deep seabed to a similar obligation to share resources of national economic zones. Moreover, trends toward 200-mile zones and national control over the entire continental margin limited the potential resources at the disposal of the proposed international seabed authority. Wide national jurisdiction claims therefore tended to undercut as well the significance of the obligation to share benefits from exploitation of deep seabed resources with land-locked and geographically disadvantaged states.

Coastal states tried to justify their expansive claims in terms of sovereign national prerogatives, and thereby avoid criticism by less advantaged states for the pernicious effects of such measures on the proposed internationalized deep seabed area. Accordingly, Brazil and most other major coastal states voted against a 1972 UN resolution (3029B) supported by land-locked and geographically disadvantaged states, which called for a study of the effects of the various national jurisdiction proposals submitted to the Seabed Committee on the common heritage of mankind. The resolution nevertheless passed, and the resulting study showed that wide national limits would exclude commercially significant oil resources from the common heritage.

Brazilian positions on these various international and national zone issues were primarily expressed through Subcommittees I and II of the Seabed Committee, which were converted into Committees when UNCLOS III was convened. Brazilian positions on Subcommittee III issues (marine pollution, scientific research and technological transfer) all basically derived from the territorialist position by emphasizing extensive coastal state powers and discretion. In the period under consideration, Brazil co-sponsored two proposals on scientific research, which stressed the rights and minimized the duties of the coastal state (A/AC. 138/SC.III/L.45 and A/AC. 138/SC.III/L.55).

THE CONFERENCE SESSIONS

The landlocked and geographically disadvantaged state group (LLGDS) gained cohesion at the conference sessions, thereby acquiring the potential to act as a blocking third to any global treaty adverse to their interests. Greater prominence was consequently given to the issue of equitable revenue sharing for LLGDS states in the national and international areas. At the Caracas session, the LLGDS group managed to gain considerable recognition for some sharing of living resources in economic zones with noncoastal states, but Brazil was one of the few major coastal states remaining silent about the proposal. The territorialist group did contrast sharply with the LLGDS group in stressing national rights rather than sharing, but a number of factors generally prevented a confrontation between the two groups. Few coastal states were anxious to share their economic zone resources with other states, so here the territorialists had broad support. The LLGDS group did not focus its dissatisfaction on the territorialist group or on Brazil as a prominent territorialist, since so many other coastal states were reluctant as well to share resources of their national zones. The bargaining position of the LLGDS group was also precarious, since it depended on the negotiations, not on an independent power base, for influence. LLGDS demands were later reciprocated by threats from the coastal states on whom the group depended for continuing access to the sea.

At later conference sessions, articles were incorporated into the negotiating text according a

limited right to LLGDS states to share in the fisheries of the economic zones of the coastal states of
their region. Coastal developing states did refuse
to share shelf mineral resources, save perhaps to a
limited extent beyond 200 miles to the far edge
of the continental margin. A very modest sharing
provision for these shelf resources beyond 200 miles
was incorporated into the negotiating text, and
promised to affect Brazil marginally if at all for
the foreseeable future.

In the South American context, Bolivia and
Paraguay are likewise weak, have-not states which
depend on their coastal neighbors. Both states are
contiguous to Brazil, yet they have not blamed it
for their geographical predicament or associated
problems. Instead, they are both increasingly being
drawn into Brazil's economic sphere and stand to
gain much thereby. A Brazilian official report on
the Caracas session concluded accordingly that
Brazil should study the possibility of granting
fishing preferences in its zone to both states,
which in any event "do not have sufficient fishing
potential for us to worry about."[55] In 1976,
Brazil indeed concluded a treaty with Paraguay to
provide it preferential access to living resources
in its zone in association with Brazilian enterprises. Since the agreement grants preferential
access, it contrasts with other fishing accords
Brazil has concluded on strictly commercial grounds.
The possibility of a similar treaty with Bolivia
is being studied.

As for the territorial sea issue, earlier
Brazilian willingness to compromise somewhat during
1972-1973 became more explicit at the 1974 Caracas
session of UNCLOS III. The Brazilian statement at
the Plenary Session did reaffirm sovereignty over
200 miles with a restrictive regime of innocent
passage, but also recognized the "inadequacy of old
concepts to regulate new situations." Accordingly,
"it would be possible to create a new concept which
would reflect the regime of navigation in the area
added to national sovereignty by the extension of
the territorial sea."[56] A similar pragmatic approach was evident in the statement by the Brazilian
representative at Committee II in Caracas. One of
the major obstacles to compromise, noted Ambassador
Calero Rodrigues, is that "we are trying to work out
new concepts using as our tools a traditional terminology." Hence, Brazil has encouraged compromise,
it was argued, by modifying the classic definition

of a territorial sea.

> The expression /200-mile/ 'territorial sea,'
> . . . in a way, expresses something that can
> be considered as different from the classical
> territorial sea . . . Some of the two hundred
> mile territorial sea countries expressly recog-
> nize freedom of navigation and overflight in
> that zone, or in a wider outer part of it.
> Others, as in the case of Brazil, liberalize
> in their practice the concept of what they
> still call innocent passage, so as to ensure
> that there will be no obstacles to the un-
> impeded passage of ships and aircraft that
> is indispensable to international navigation,
> transport and communications.[57]

In the 1975 third session, Brazil evinced further
flexibility in warmly supporting compromises contained in an Ecuadorian territorial sea proposal.[58]
The proposal (A/CONF.62/C.2/L.88) was ostensibly
territorialist in nature, but moved to accommodate
diverging interests by explicitly providing for "a
plurality of regimes" in which innocent passage
would apply near the coast and freedom of passage
beyond this limit. In the 1976 fourth session,
the Brazilian position at UNCLOS III moved still
further away from a hard-line 200-mile territorial
sea: "Although Brazil had extended its territorial
sea to 200 miles six years earlier, it was willing
to consider the proposal for an exclusive economic
zone."[59]
     On the domestic front, too, nationalism had
abated and positions were being reassessed. An
important segment of the press, during the early
1970s an ardent defender of a 200-mile territorial
sea, came to regard the patrimonial sea concept favorably by the Caracas session. Some former civilian
supporters of the territorialist position likewise
evolved toward patrimonial sea or economic zone
concepts by the mid-1970s.[60]
     Underlying this Brazilian evolution was a mis-
calculation in early 1970 about the political implications of declaring a 200-mile territorial sea.
Brazilian policy-makers came to recognize that it
would have been more appropriate to have couched
the area claimed beyond 12 miles in a new conciliatory concept rather than to have adopted the traditional territorial sea concept. This recognition
is implicit in the Brazilian UNCLOS III statements

cited above and has been confirmed explicitly in interviews conducted by this author.[61]

But the degree of change in subsequent Brazilian territorial sea policy is a matter of debate. When Brazil extended its territorial sea to 200 miles in early 1970, it has been argued, the patrimonial sea alternative had not yet been formulated. The apparent originator of the patrimonial sea concept, Edmundo Vargas Carreño of the Inter-American Juridical Committee, has traced the origin of the term only back to 1970.[62] The unavailability in 1970 of alternatives other than the territorial sea as an explanation of the extreme form of Brazil's claim is still questionable. Argentina in 1966 and Uruguay in 1969 had managed to limit their new 200-mile claims, and no patrimonial sea alternative was available to them either.

Some observers have similarly confused form and substance in believing that Brazil has since endorsed a patrimonialist position.[63] Instead, the content of Brazil's claim has been extensive throughout, and the new Brazilian conciliatory emphasis on the territorial sea issue seems to have involved procedure more than substance. That is, even if Brazil has made a few concessions on the territorial sea issue, it continues to claim extensive rights out to 200 miles. For example, Brazilian care in assuring unimpeded passage of ships and aircraft in the 200 miles is compatible with its strategy of conciliating the developed states and with its own interest as an emerging shipping and naval power. Yet, it continues to assert sovereignty over all other uses in the area, including residual rights of coastal states. Nationalism propelled Brazil to make an extreme 200-mile territorial sea claim in 1970, and since then the navy has emphasized the importance of security interests out to at least 200 miles and has moved to establish control over the area for that purpose.[64]

Since 1970, Brazil has therefore been consistent in claiming more extensive rights out to 200 miles than either of its regional neighbors to the south, or the patrimonialists. So if Brazilian policy-makers erred tactically in 1970 in making an extreme claim, the subsequent strategy of trying to gain as much community approval as possible at UNCLOS III for the essence of the territorialist position has been appropriate as the only one corresponding to the broad national assertion of rights

147

out to 200 miles.

Since the territorialist-patrimonalist split has proved to be an obstacle to cooperation between both of these groups in Latin America and their counterparts in other developing regions, the United States has hoped that this situation would work to its advantage. One U.S. expectation, already noted, was that the territorialists would isolate themselves because of their extreme position. Another related U.S. expectation has been that a more moderate economic zone or patrimonial sea approach would provide the basis for a compromise between most developed and developing states. The respective interpretations of offshore rights of the United States and of the patrimonial/economic zone group, it was hoped, would cluster around economic functions (resource jurisdiction) in the 188-mile zone beyond the 12-mile territorial sea and would thereby permit an overall conference compromise. The territorialists' claim to non-economic functions as well (non-resource jurisdiction, including control of navigation and overflight, security interests, etc.) out to 200 miles would accordingly isolate them. In an official U.S. statement of the results of the Caracas session, John Stevenson, Chairman of the U.S. delegation, accordingly singled out for praise the statement of the Venezuelan Chairman of the Second Committee that the 12/188 mile formula is "the keystone of the compromise solution favored by the majority of the states participating in the conference." This Venezuelan statement was circulated as an official committee document after initial opposition by the territorialists.[65]

While the United States accepted the concept of a 188-mile economic zone beyond a 12-mile territorial sea in principle at Caracas, the U.S. interpretation of coastal state rights in the zone has continued to be more limited than even the view of the patrimonialists. Like the U.S., the patrimonialist Caribbean states did support freedom of navigation in the 188-mile economic zone in the Declaration of Santo Domingo. But the declaration also provided for full coastal state control over scientific research and vessel-source pollution in the economic zone, which goes well beyond the narrowly-defined economic rights in the U.S. version of the zone. Other differences in interpretation of the zone have involved the U.S. species approach to fishing and heavy U.S. stress on a conflict resolution mechanism. U.S. acceptance in principle of an economic zone was also conditioned on a satisfactory law of the sea treaty, including provisions for un-impeded transit of international straits and a balance between coastal state rights and duties within the economic zone.

An agreed conference balance between coastal state rights and duties within the economic zone then remained elusive even for the two self-styled conciliatory partners, the patrimonialist group and the United States. Complicating the negotiating picture still more were states claiming broader coastal state rights out to 200 miles than the patri-monialists and narrower ones than the territorialists. One such group of states, the 200-mile states in South America not belonging to the territorialist group (Argentina, Chile and Uruguay), did not join the patrimonialist group either because of dis-satisfaction with its relatively limited scope for coastal state rights. For example, "The laws and other declarations on the law of the sea in Argen-tina do not permit consideration of a patrimonial sea, a concept that is not mentioned at all; furthermore, the Argentine powers in the area are broader than a mere economic content such as that suggested by the concept of patrimonial sea."[66]

This complex negotiating context encouraged the territorialists to believe that they could re-cruit new members for their group. If they could not gain full converts, they would be least try to encourage leaners and attract others sympathetic to their cause. Brazil and Peru emerged as leaders in shaping a well organized strategy for the ter-ritorialist group at UNCLOS III "to legitimize their claims for a 200-mile territorial sea or, failing that, to extend the scope of coastal state control in the economic zone to the point where it becomes the functional equivalent of a territorial sea."[67]

The first prong of the strategy, to try and legitimize claims for a 200-mile territorial sea, offered some opportunities. As long as negotiations did not advance sufficiently toward the definitive trade-offs required for a package deal, the ter-ritorialists, even if somewhat isolated, could still be hard bargainers. In view of the protracted nature of the negotiations, the Brazilian response to iso-lation consequently has not been to contract the substance of its extensive offshore claim. Several economic zone or patrimonialist states indeed have warned that if the maritime powers persist in trying to dilute coastal state powers in the zone, they may shift to a territorialist position.[68] But the increasing popularity of the economic zone approach at UNCLOS III convinced Brazilian policy-makers that any massive conversions to the territorialist cause were unlikely. So Brazil has also relied on the alternative prong of the strategy of encouraging conference consensus on expansive coastal state rights in the economic zone.

Brazilian responses to the growth in popularity of the economic zone approach therefore involved modifications in negotiating strategy more than any fundamental change in policy. Brazil has accordingly tried to pull more moderate patrimonialist/economic zone states toward a more extreme territorialist position by degrees and on questions of detail, not through formal shifts in position. The substance of the economic zone has indeed tended to expand during the course of the negotiations, and Brazil has encouraged this development. The treaty eventually emerging from negotiations, according to this line of Brazilian thinking, might list coastal state rights and duties in the 188-mile economic zone, but would leave residual rights with coastal states since the list could not be complete. An official Brazilian report on the Caracas round of UNCLOS III concluded that this would practically amount to a 200-mile territorial sea anyway: "With these characteristics and other coastal state powers of authority and control out to 200 miles, we would practically have a definition of sovereignty as a sum of jurisdictions."[69]

Resolution of the status of residual rights in the economic zone has remained a thorn in the side of conference negotiators. A residual rights clause in the successive negotiating texts merely specifies criteria to be applied in resolving cases of disagreement over attribution of rights in the economic zone. Complicating resolution of this problem of the extent of coastal state rights in the economic zone is the related problem of the legal status of the 200 miles. Its legal status might be that of high seas, a national zone, or sui generis, that is, unique in being neither high seas nor subject to unqualified national control. Here, too, Brazil found many allies in rejecting the notion of the economic zone as traditional high seas and having it categorized as national waters.

The high seas beyond 200 miles tended to get involved as well in the debate over coastal state rights in the economic zone. Were the economic zone categorized as national waters, the logic of this approach would also qualify freedom of the seas beyond 200 miles. Both territorialists and patri- monialists have supported the special interest of the coastal state in maintaining the productivity of renewable or living resources in any part of the high seas adjacent to the area subject to its juris- diction.[70]

A compromise was finally worked out in the Informal Composite Negotiating Text by defining the exclusive economic zone as sui generis, in which the coastal state would have sovereign rights over natural resources while preserving traditional high seas freedoms there. This does largely resolve the status of the economic zone, but coastal developing states will no doubt continue to push for certain rights beyond 200 miles and residual rights will re- main a source of dispute.

Pressure for still other revisions in the law derive from expansive rights of coastal developing states. Brazil was joined by 27 patrimonialists and territorialists at Caracas in co-sponsoring a hard-line technological transfer proposal for the national and international zones. It stated in part that all states "are under a duty to co-operate actively with the 'Authority'" to encourage and facilitate such transfers to developing states (A/CONF.62/C.2/L.12). Nineteen patrimonialists and territorialists, including Brazil, likewise joined hands at Caracas in a hard-line rejection of coastal state rights in the economic zone for colonial or occupying powers (A/CONF.62/C.2/L.58). In the suc- cessive sessions, Brazil continued vigorous support for broad coastal state control over scientific research and vessel source pollution in the economic zone as well.

Since Brazil has favored extensive coastal state rights, it has also opposed compulsory dispute settlement for economic zone issues. The successive negotiating texts have provided for such compulsory dispute settlement or conciliation for certain ques- tions Brazil regards as the exclusive responsibility of the coastal state.

Just as shifting circumstances, domestic and international, led to evolution in territorial sea policy, so did deep seabed policy adapt to important changes. The 1971 Latin American working paper on the deep seabed regime had achieved considerable regional unity for a strong international seabed

regime, save Brazil, which had favored a more conciliatory approach to the issue of control. But,
as noted, this really did not produce much friction
within Latin American ranks. Other factors also
tended to minimize potential conflict between
Brazil and some other developing states which might
interpret the common heritage of mankind in less
flexible fashion. In the preparatory years for
UNCLOS III, many states, especially those in the
developing world, still had not clearly defined
their ocean interests. This trend was all the more
pronounced on the deep seabed issue, which was at
once highly technical and of less immediate importance than coastal zone issues. Debates in the
Seabed Committee therefore tended to be general in
nature, and did not direct attention to details
that might divide Brazil from some other developing
states. So up to the actual convening of UNCLOS
III, the Third World consensus on the seabed issue
was limited to principles, and Brazil had been a
leader in formulating and supporting the Declaration
of Principles.

This situation began to change shortly after
UNCLOS III was convened, since the Group of 77 was
able to agree on a deep seabed text near the end of
the 1974 Caracas session (A/CONF.62/C.1/L.7). This
Group of 77 proposal contained key elements of the
1971 Latin American seabed proposal, and Latin
American diplomats have frequently argued that the
relationship between the two documents was direct
and causal. With three years of negotiations intervening between the two documents, it is difficult
to determine parentage. But one clear contrast
that emerges between them is the greater specificity
of the 1971 Latin American seabed proposal. Even
after three additional years of negotiations, it is
not surprising that the 100-odd members of the Group
of 77 were unable to reach as detailed a consensus
as the 13 Latin American states. The 1974 document
only contains a short statement of basic conditions
of exploration and exploitation for the international seabed authority. The Group of 77 proposal
nevertheless did provide for a strong Authority,
which would exercise "direct and effective control"
over all service contracts, joint ventures or other
such forms of association entered into.

Greater unity reached by the Group of 77 at
Caracas had several important implications for
Brazilian policy. Group of 77 unity did help pro-
mote the long-standing Brazilian drive to pressure

developed states to accept an international seabed
authority favorable to developing states, but the
group position still differed from the Brazilian
position on the issue of control. The Group of 77
seabed text, like the Latin American proposal before it, essentially endorsed a unitary rather than
a parallel or mixed regime by leaving discretionary
power entirely with the Authority. Control of the
Authority, in turn, would rest with the developing
states through one-state/one-vote decision making.
This left little room for the kinds of compromises
Brazil felt were required for a viable treaty.
Brazil continued to favor a mixed or parallel regime
permitting seabed mining both by the Authority and
by private or state-backed mining enterprises,
because   a unitary regime was regarded as inflexible and impractical. For example, Brazil's general
policy statement at Caracas recognized that the
Authority would have to rely on multinational corporations, so that "the intention would not be to
place any unreasonable difficulty in the way of
those who were ready to operate in the area, but to
ensure that mankind as a whole would benefit."[71]

Dissent however, had become more difficult.
Brazil had been able to avoid formally associating
itself with the detailed 1971 Latin American seabed
consensus at little cost, but strong pressures led
Brazil to endorse the less detailed but emerging
Group of 77 seabed consensus in 1974. In essence,
ideology helped promote a Group of 77 seabed consensus, which Brazil desired, but ideology also
made it difficult for Brazil to express dissent a-
bout elements of the emerging consensus with which
it did not agree.

Ideology helped unify the Group of 77 and enhanced its bargaining position in pushing for a
strong international seabed regime throughout all
the negotiating sessions. The Group of 77, after
all, grew out of UNCTAD in 1964 and shares its
determination to reshape international economic
relations. For this reason, this author has argued
that the New Law of the Sea (NLOS) supported by
developing states has become linked with the New
International Economic Order (NIEO).[72] The NLOS
has become increasingly related to the more comprehensive yet recent quest for the NIEO since the
Sixth Session of the United Nations General Assembly on the "Study of the Problems of Raw Materials and Development" in 1974. The Sixth Special
Session set the NIEO in motion and called attention

to the NLOS as one component of an emerging, more equitable global economic order. The strongest linkage between the NIEO and the NLOS emerged in the area of natural resources. The linkage involves application of the principle of permanent sovereignty over natural resources within limits of national jurisdiction, and, beyond these limits, the control and management of deep seabed nonliving natural resources through an international seabed authority. Since a resolution of the Sixth Special Session specifically entrusted all specialized UN conferences as well as other UN bodies with the implementation of the NIEO,[73] the scope and powers of the international authority became a significant test case for the NIEO. The growing linkage between the NLOS and the NIEO therefore further politicized the deep seabed debate and infused deep seabed issues with symbolic importance at times separate from the intrinsic interests involved. Compromise on the deep seabed issue between developed and developing states therefore proved particularly difficult.

For reasons of substance and timing, the strategy for implementation of the NIEO through specialized, functional conferences, as well as through other bodies, was nevertheless appropriate for the law of the sea area. With regard to substance, the question of the distribution of benefits from raw material exploitation was central to both the NIEO and the NLOS, and in the law of the sea area applied most directly to the distribution of earnings of the international seabed authority. As for the tactical advantages of timing, the first substantive UNCLOS session at Caracas followed just six weeks after the Sixth Special Session. Preparations for the related Seventh Special Session also overlapped the second UNCLOS substantive session in Geneva, and the Seventh Special Session itself preceded the third UNCLOS substantive round (held in New York City in March-May 1976) by a mere six months. So the timing of the NIEO Special Sessions permitted an opportunity for an immediate and direct impact on the UNCLOS sessions, an opportunity that indeed was seized.

A unified, numerous Group of 77 then managed to seize the negotiating initiative at UNCLOS III in pressing for an international deep seabed authority much stronger than developed states were prepared to accept. The momentum established by the Group of 77 seabed text submitted near the end of the 1974 Caracas session carried over into subsequent sessions. At the subsequent Geneva session, the Informal Single Negotiating Text of the First Committee did attempt to harmonize and synthesize the approaches of both developing and developed states, but still contained specific measures central to Group of 77 goals for an international seabed authority. These included ease of access of developing states to patented and nonpatented seabed technology (article 11.1.a), preferential treatment of developing states which either import   or export land-based counterparts of seabed minerals (article 28.xi), undetermined but "equitable" sharing of benefits and revenues for developing states (articles 26.2.x and 45), production controls (article 30.b), and price controls (annex I, part B.4.ii). Subsequent versions of the negotiating text continued to incorporate comparable articles.

These advantages of substance and timing led to Group of 77 bargaining advantages, but at a price. Such Third World insistence on a strong seabed regime, at times more on principle than with respect to concrete interests involved, contributed to the continuing impasse on the issue. The symbolic importance of a strong international ·seabed authority for many Third World states prevented flexible Group of 77 responses to concessions by developed states. Third World strategy on the deep seabed issue based on a NIEO-NLOS linkage made it difficult as well to maintain Group of 77 cohesion. Third World unity achieved through ideology and symbolism rather than through common concrete interests is precarious. The perspective and interests of developing states which opted for group cohesion on principle tended to be different from those of Brazil. While they tended to be ideologically-oriented and radical, Brazil tended to be pragmatic and conservative. They tended to put much stock on Third World cooperation in principle either because their ocean interests were not particularly important or because their influence would otherwise be limited. Brazil, in contrast, had important ocean interests, aspired to great power status, and favored Third World cooperation to the extent such concrete interests could be advanced thereby. This disparity in interests and strategy led to increasing strains in the Group of 77 coalition. When concrete interests were damaged or distorted by Third World allies, Brazil had shown its willingness to pursue policy objectives by other routes.

While the developed states rejected the 1974 Group of 77 seabed text on basic conditions in favor of some kind of licensing system, compromise still appeared possible after Caracas. For this purpose, a Working Group of Latin American states was set up at the end of the Caracas session, and was to continue even into the next Geneva session. Brazil, with its tradition of pragmatism and compromise, was appropriately one of the 9 Latin American states on the group.[74] Brazil was nevertheless faced with a dilemma by the 1975 Geneva session, when the radical, ideological faction of the Group of 77 gained the leadership initiative of the Third World coalition on the deep seabed issue. The challenge to Brazilian interests was all the more direct, since the temporary rise of the radicals to a position of leadership in the Group of 77 at Geneva aimed as well at curtailing the influence of prominent, moderate Third World states such as Brazil.

By the subsequent 1976 New York City session, Brazil undertook a major drive to shift the Group of 77 back to a more pragmatic course and strike a compromise with the developed states. As a result of a Brazilian initiative, a so-called "Brazil Group" was convened to negotiate deep seabed compromises and met simultaneously with another group convened by the Chairman of Committee I. But moderates such as Brazil were unable to sell the compromises reached to the Group of 77.[75] Radical states within the Group of 77, with a greater ideological than substantive interest in the deep seabed, resisted such compromises and prolonged the negotiating impasse. This disparity of interests and approaches continued to strain Group of 77 unity in subsequent sessions, although support among developing states did increase in the later sessions for a compromise involving some kind of parallel regime.

Brazil has favored Third World unity, but this has threatened to be at the expense of its national interests, which were concrete and substantial, not ideological and symbolic. Brazil's interests in a viable, mutually acceptable deep seabed regime are numerous. Brazil's seabed interests have become increasingly complex as it has emerged as a major power, but the basic objective of receiving multilateral approval for a relatively strong seabed regime, especially for the benefit of developing states, has been pursued throughout. The exact degree to which Brazil would benefit from a seabed regime based on the common heritage of mankind would depend on the particular scheme for distributing funds to developing states, but presumably it would receive more than most as a large, prominent developing state. Brazil is a relatively advantaged Third World state in other seabed matters as well. Unlike the major land-based producers of seabed-competing minerals, who have greatly complicated and delayed the negotiations in insisting on price and production controls, Brazil does not fear seabed mineral production as a threat to the prices of its mineral exports. The largest developing state producers of manganese ore are Brazil, Gabon, and India, but only in the case of Gabon is manganese a major source of foreign exchange earnings. So Brazil should easily be able to offset any potential earnings reductions caused by deep seabed mining, which would not be likely before 1985.[76] Brazil also appears to have a substantial reserve of nickel, but export prospects are uncertain. So, on balance, seabed mineral production would tend to benefit Brazilian industrial development by increasing supplies and holding down prices.

Brazil's emergence as a major power has also projected it into the position of a leading developing state candidate for deep seabed mining. One prominent former member of the U.S. delegation to UNCLOS III recently called attention to this distinctive position of Brazil and a few other developing states by proposing their inclusion in a seabed "mini-treaty" concluded outside the United Nations.[77] Brazil, India, Iran, Mexico, Nigeria, and Saudi Arabia were specifically mentioned as developing countries with high potential as seabed miners. Because of the continuing impasse on the seabed issue at UNCLOS III, this non-official U.S. proposal called for a more limited treaty to attract and include such potential developing state seabed miners through loan guarantees and transfer of necessary technology. The more radical or ideologically inclined developing states would be left outside the seabed mini-treaty. Of course, should a global treaty be approved, Brazil and other middle level powers still might be assisted in becoming seabed miners, with bargaining taking place inside the Authority rather than outside it.

On the official level, the United States reacted sharply to the insertion by some Group of 77 members of particularly hard-line deep seabed articles in the 1977 Informal Composite Negotiating Text by announcing that it would reappraise its

position at the law of the sea conference. The
U.S. did not carry out its implicit threat to with-
draw from the negotiations, but it did finally lend
support to interim national legislation to permit
and regulate deep seabed mining if certain conditions were met, including a revenue sharing provision for developing states. Congressional debate
on a hard minerals law paralleled negotiations at
the seventh session during mid-1978, and stepped
up pressure on the ideologically-oriented wing of
the Group of 77 to compromise. Such legislation
failed to pass Congress in the fall of 1978, but
prospects appeared good for approval in early 1979
and this would certainly influence negotiations at
the eighth session at Geneva. Other developed
states moved to pass counterpart interim legislation
to regulate national firms that would undertake deep
seabed mining.

Some critics of unilateral mining legislation
warned that extremists would be strengthened if a
North-South confrontation resulted. Moderate leadership in the developing state group, including
Brazil, has been playing an increasing role at the
conference and would be weakened by another surge
of extremist influence. A comprehensive deep seabed compromise continues to elude the negotiators,
but broad support has emerged for some kind of a
parallel regime, with certain provisions to ensure
the viability of the Authority, in the latest conference sessions.

Much bad blood has been generated by the continuing impasse on the seabed issue, and Brazil has
been severely criticized in some quarters. Vehement
criticisms have emanated from ideologically-oriented
members of the Group of 77, which regard Brazil's
search for a seabed compromise in the recent conference sessions as a grave threat to group cohesion.
In the most extreme form, Brazil has been accused
of "selling out" on the seabed issue because of an
alleged U.S. promise to help it become a seabed
miner. In addition to categorical Brazilian denials of this accusation, much evidence suggests
that Brazil has instead continued to pursue its own
distinctive national interests persistently. Most
basically, Brazil has long been inclined to compromise on the deep seabed issue and therefore did not
have to be bribed at a very late date to adopt this
policy. Moreover, the overall trend in Brazilian
foreign policy over the past decade has been toward
less subservience to the United States and greater

persistence in pursuing distinctive national interests.[78] While Brazil has not hesitated to promote its national interests, it has also been most
reluctant to alienate large numbers of Third World
states gratuitously. This it would surely do if it
signed a seabed mini-treaty outside the United Nations and received special favors from developed
states in return.

Comparison of similar Brazilian approaches to
multinational corporations domestically and on the
deep seabed issue reconfirms the distinctiveness of
Brazilian interests. Domestically, multinational
corporations have played a major role in the "economic miracle," although they have been encouraged
to transfer technology to and export from Brazil.
Brazil's ideologically relaxed attitude toward multinational corporations has been evident as well in
early and continuing support for a parallel deep
seabed regime. But here, too, part of the compromise for Brazil has included a strong Authority to
assure that a fair portion of deep seabed benefits
go to developing states through revenue sharing and
technological transfer. The 1977 Informal Composite
Negotiating Text provided both for revenue sharing
and for transfer of technology as a condition for
obtaining a contract from the international seabed
authority. In the 1978 seventh session the latter
provision was watered down somewhat by the developed
states, but Brazil insisted on the addition of a
clause with the same transfer of technology obligations to developing countries starting seabed mining
as assumed toward the Authority.

Brazil's substantial coastal zone interests constitute another reason for Brazilian preference for
an UNCLOS III treaty. Not only has an economic zone
consensus been emerging at UNCLOS III relatively
satisfactory to Brazil as a territorialist state
interested in extensive coastal state rights out to
200 miles. The negotiations have also been premised
on attainment of a consensus on both national and
international zone issues through a "package deal."
Failure to resolve the deep seabed issue at UNCLOS
III as part of a package deal would therefore
jeopardize the other part of the package deal, national jurisdiction issues, and here Brazil has very
substantial coastal zone interests. For the foreseeable future, Brazil's substantial coastal zone
interests promise to continue to overshadow any
likely Brazilian interests in the deep seabed. The extent of Brazilian coastal zone interests should be recalled. The 200-mile territorial sea encompasses over

900,000 square miles, almost one-third of Brazil's enormous land area. Brazil is consequently one of the few big Third World winners from the trend toward 200-mile zones. Of the top 10 states in terms of area of jurisdiction gained, six are developing states, with the U.S. in the lead, and four are developing states (Brazil, Chile, Indonesia and Mexico).

Recognition of expansive coastal state rights would be much less certain without an UNCLOS III treaty. In that event, coastal states would presumably define rights in their 200-mile zones unilaterally and would not recognize the validity of more extensive rights in economic zones elsewhere. For example, the U.S. 200-mile fishing zone involves much less extensive coastal state control than does the Brazilian 200-mile territorial sea. Yet, the emerging conference compromise appears much closer to the Brazilian interpretation than the U.S. one. If the global negotiations fail, this latent conflict between the United States and Brazil, settled by an interim fishing agreement pending conference consensus, might be reopened.

With the seabed issue stalemated, a package deal bringing together the emerging areas of consensus on other issues into a treaty has proved illusive. Brazil's position as an emerging power shaped its role in this outcome. Influence in the law of the sea negotiations seemed to flow indirectly from the more active, extensive presence Brazil was developing on the world scene, and Brazilian leadership was evident in numerous areas during the protracted law of the sea negotiations. Extensive, concrete marine interests also involved Brazil deeply and prominently in the national jurisdiction and deep seabed debates. Indeed, it has been shown that Brazil stands out as one of the few big potential winners in the Third World from both the seabed and non-seabed portions of the law of the sea negotiations.

But this influence has had strict limits. Not yet a great power, Brazil cannot hope to rival the influence of the existing great powers. And even within the Group of 77, Brazil was not able to exert decisive influence. On the seabed issue particularly, Brazil's relatively extensive interests vis-à-vis its Third World partners led it to adopt distinctive positions which threatened its leadership role within the Group of 77. Limits on Brazilian influence were accentuated at UNCLOS III because of the conference tendency for influence to function

somewhat separately from power.[79]   In particular,
ideologically-oriented states in the Group of 77,
frequently with limited marine potential, exercised
disproportionate influence at the expense of Brazil.
But the Group of 77 was only able to achieve a
fragile consensus on the deep seabed issue, so the
influence of ideological members of the bloc,
generally with modest ocean interests, in turn tended to be limited to that issue.   And even on the
deep seabed issue, their influence tended to decline
in later conference sessions.   In contrast, Brazil's
extensive ocean interests tended to project it
toward a prominent position on non-seabed issues as
well as seabed ones.
     Other dilemmas of an emerging Third World power
affected the internal evolution of Brazilian ocean
policy on UNCLOS-related issues.   As a developing
state, Brazil has favored revision of the traditional
order to redress the balance with the developed
states.   At the same time, as an emerging power,
Brazil has an interest in supporting a stable, open
international order.   Accordingly, Brazil's support
for a territorialist position and for a strong international seabed regime particularly benefiting
developing states has been tempered in practice.   It
remains to be seen if Brazil's potential as a constructive ocean actor will suffice to help overcome
current negotiating obstacles.

NOTES

1.   Edward Miles, "The Structure and Effects of the Decision
Process in the Seabed Committee and the Third United Nations
Conference on the Law of the Sea," International Organization
31 (Spring, 1977):   232.

2.   Wayne Selcher, Brazil's Multilateral Relations: Between
First and Third Worlds (Boulder, Colorado: Westview Press,
1978), pp. 2, 79, 15-16.

3.   Miles, "The Structure," p. 36.

4.   J. S. Nye, "Ocean Rule Making from a World Politics
Perspective," Ocean Development and International Law
Journal 3 (1975):   51.

5.   Alberto Szekely, Latin America and the Development of
the Law of the Sea: Regional Documents and National Legislation,
2 vols. (Dobbs Ferry, New York: Oceana Publications, 1976),
1:   320.

6.   Interviews not for direct attribution.

7. United Nations General Assembly resolutions 2574 (XXIV), 2749 (XXV) and 2750 (XXV), respectively.

8. Evan Luard, The Control of the Sea-bed (London: Heinemann, 1974), pp. 83-90.

9. United Nations Conference on the Law of the Sea, Official Records (A/CONF.13/42), 1958, vol. 1, p. 36.

10. See Chapter 3.

11. See, for example, a special issue on the seabed of Revista Brasileira de Política Internacional 12 (September-December, 1969).

12. Fernando Gamboa Serazzi, "Antecedentes Preparatorios de la Conferencia sobre Derecho del Mar en Santiago, (1974)," Revista de la Escuela de Diplomacia 2 (1974): 140-141. Ramiro Elysio Saraiva Guerreiro, "Aspectos Políticos, Económicos y Jurídicos do Aproveitamento do Fundo do Mar Além dos Límites da Jurisdição Nacional," Segurança e Desenvolvimento 19 (1970): 16-17, 19.

13. Barry Buzan, Seabed Politics (New York: Praeger Publishers, 1976), pp. 93, 98.

14. Saraiva Guerreiro, "Aspectos Políticos." This article was originally delivered as a speech on July 10, 1969 at the Escola Superior de Guerra. Sr. Saraiva Guerreiro has been a leading member of the Brazilian maritime community, including head of the Brazilian delegation to the Third United Nations Conference on the Law of the Sea. As Secretary-General of the Ministry of External Relations under the Geisel government, Sr. Saraiva Guerreiro was second in command, and he is Foreign Minister-designate of the new Figueiredo administration, which is to take office on March 15, 1979. See also notes 12, 48, 50, 56, and 59 for other statements by Sr. Saraiva Guerreiro.

15. Buzan, p. 144.

16. Karin Hjertonsson, The New Law of the Sea: Influence of the Latin American States on Recent Developments of the Law of the Sea (Leiden: A. W. Sijthoff), pp. 43-44. Also see Buzan, p. 96.

17. Interview with a high-ranking Brazilian diplomat in Brasília, Brazil, August 15, 1974. Also see Buzan, p. 92.

18. Buzan, p. 99.

19.   John J. Logue (ed.), The Fate of the Oceans (Villanova, Pennsylvania: Villanova University Press, 1972), p. 220. This argument by Mr. Oxman was presented in the section on "Floor Discussion."

20.   Leigh S. Ratiner, "United States Oceans Policy: An Analysis," Journal of Maritime Commerce and Law 2 (January 1971): 235-236 and footnote 24 at 235; also 260-261 and footnote 68 at 261.

21.   Hjertonsson, p. 44.

22.   See footnote 9. Also see remarks by Sergio Thompson-Flores on the United States Draft Seabed Treaty in the "Commentary" section of Logue, The Fate, pp. 195-200; further remarks by Sergio Thompson-Flores on the same subject may be found in the Proceedings of the Seventh Annual Conference of the Law of the Sea Institute, The Law of the Sea: Needs and Interests of Developing Countries (Kingston, Rhode Island: The University of Rhode Island Press, 1973), pp. 40-42.

23.   Lennox Ballah in Logue, The Fate, pp. 221. This comment was made by Ballah, Counsellor of the Trinidad and Tobago Mission to the United Nations and a member of his country's delegation to the UN Seabed Committee, during the "Floor Discussion" section. See similar comments by Mr. Ballah in the Proceedings of the Fifth Annual Conference of the Law of the Sea Institute, Law of the Sea: The United Nations and Oceans Management (Kingston, Rhode Island: University of Rhode Island, 1971), p. 33. Trinidad and Tobago and Brazil both actively led opposition to the 1969 Malta draft resolution and support for the 1970 moratorium resolution, and both were non-200 mile states at the time. Back-to-back comments of the Brazilian and Trinidadian representatives in the Logue book reflect these shared deep seabed and continental margin concerns, although by that time Brazil had moved to a 200-mile territorial sea.

24.   Margaret L. Gerstle, The Politics of UN Voting: A View from the Glass Palace (Kingston, Rhode Island: University of Rhode Island, 1970), pp. 9-10.

25.   Sylvio Heck, "O Mar de 200 Milhas," 15 Revista da Adismar (1974): 12.

26.   Written answers supplied to this author by Glycon da Paiva, Rio de Janeiro, Brazil, August 4, 1975.

27.   See Chapter 2.

28. Interviews not for direct attribution.

29. "Proyecto de Instrucciones a Uruguay sobre Proyecto Malta
L.473 en la Asemblea de las Naciones Unidas, 1969," reprinted
in Mar Territorial, Volume I (Brasília: Navy Ministry, 1972),
pp. 421-422. This interpretation by Uruguay of the Malta
proposal is implicitly supported by Brazil by way of its inclusion in the navy's compendium justifying the 200-mile decision. Brazil's concern about such 200-meter shelf proposals
and the role they played in the 200-mile territorial sea decision was confirmed in a confidential interview with a high-
level Itamaraty (Brazilian Foreign Ministry) official in
Brasília (see note 17). See, as well, Hector Gros Espiell,
"La Mer Territoriale dans L'Altantique Sud-Américain,"
Annuaire Français de Droit International, 16 (Paris: 1971),
pp. 748-749. Sr. Gros Espiell has been a leading member of
the Uruguayan maritime community.

30. Hjertonsson, footnote 138 at page 58.

31. See Chapter 2.

32. Ibid.

33. Hjertonsson, p. 60.

34. Ibid.

35. Mar Territorial, Volume II (Brasília, Brazil: Navy
Ministry), pp. 640-647.

36. Clovis Ramalhete, "Alguns Objectivos das 200 Milhas,"
Revista Militar Brasileira (April-December 1971), 78.
Italics in Original. My translation.

37. Interview with Clovis Ramalhete by this author in Rio
de Janeiro, Brazil, November 6, 1974.

38. Szekely, footnote 160 at page 284 and Document 51 in
Volume I.

39. Samuel C. Orr, "Soviet, Latin Opposition Blocks Agreement
on Seabeds Treaty," National Journal, September 12, 1970, p.
1974.

40. Buzan, p. 130 and footnote 17 at page 147.

41. R. L. Friedheim and J. B. Kadane with the assistance of
J. K. Gamble, Jr., "Quantitative Content Analysis of the
United Nations Seabed Debate: Methodology and a Continental

164

Shelf Case Study," *International Organization* 24 (Spring 1970),
see especially pages 492-493, and 501-502.

42. Ratiner, pp. 234-235.

43. Report of the Committee on the Peaceful Uses of the Sea-
Bed and the Ocean Floor Beyond the Limits of National Jurisdiction, *Official Records*: Twenty-Sixth Session. For the
Latin American list, see pages 197-200; for the Afro-Asian
proposal, see pages 202-204.

44. Report of the Committee on the Peaceful Uses of the Sea-
Bed and the Ocean Floor Beyond the Limits of National Jurisdiction, *Official Records*: Twenty-Seventh Session. For the
combined list, see pages 142-146; for the proposed amendments
to this proposal, see pages 147-154; and for the final list,
see pages 5-8.

45. Szekely, pp. 324-325.

46. Buzan, pp. 157 and 158 and footnote 13 at page 178.

47. Ambassador Carlos Calero Rodrigues, "Relações Inter-
nacionais do Brasil: Interêsses Marítimos, *Segurança e
Desenvolvimento* 22 (1973): 100. Murillo Souto Maior de
Castro, "O Direito do Mar e o Problema do Mar Territorial,"
Revista Marítima Brasileira 93 (July-September 1973): 85.

48. Statement by the Representative of Brazil, Ambassador
Ramiro Saraiva Guerreiro, in Sub-Committee II of the United
Nationa Sea-Bed Committee, Geneva, August 17, 1971. Reprinted
in *Mar Territorial*, Volume II (Brasília: Navy Ministry, 1972),
pp. 452-454. Thompson-Flores in Logue, *The Fate*, pp. 196-197
(1972).

49. John R. Stevenson and Bernard H. Oxman, "The Preparations
for the Law of the Sea Conference," *American Journal of International Law*, 68 (1974): 9.

50. Statement by the Representative of Brazil, H. E. Ambassador Ramiro Saraiva Guerreiro, March 29, 1973, before the
UN Committee on the Peaceful Uses of the Seabed and the Ocean
Floor Beyond National Jurisdiction, pp. 2, 4-5. Mimeographed
version.

51. See Chapter 2.

52. See Chapter 7.

53. "Resolution on the Law of the Sea Approved by the Inter-

American Juridical Committee on February 9, 1973, and Explanations of Votes Thereon," March 26, 1973 (OEA/Ser. P AG./doc. 345/73), pp. 3-7.

54. "Problemas do Mar: Pronunciamento do Embaixador Vincente Rao," Mar Territorial, Volume III (Brasília: Navy Ministry, 1974), pp. 1058, 1061.

55. Murillo Souto Maior de Castro, Relatório Sobre a Reunião de Caracas da III Conferência Sobre O Direito Do Mar Apresentado Pelo CMG Murillo Souto Maior de Castro (Brasília: Ministério da Marinha, Estado-Maior da Armada, September 17, 1974), pp. 22-23.

56. Statement by Ambassador Ramiro Saraiva Guerreiro, Secretary-General of the Ministry of External Relations and Head of the Brazilian Delegation, before the Plenary of the III United Nations Conference of the Law of the Sea, Caracas, June 28, 1974, p. 2 (mimeographed version). A summarized version of this statement is reproduced in A/CONF. 62/SR.21, July 3, 1974, pp. 6-8.

57. Statement by Ambassador Carlos Calero Rodrigues, before the II Committee of the III United Nations Conference on the Law of the Sea, Caracas, July 16, 1974, p. 4 (mimeographed version). A summarized version of this statement is reproduced in A/CONF. 62/C.2/Sr.5, July 18, 1974, pp. 2-4.

58. Statement by Mr. Calero Rodrigues, Third United Nations Conference on the Law of the Sea, Official Records, 4: 77.

59. Statement of Mr. Saraiva Guerreiro, Third United Nations Conference on the Law of the Sea, Official Records, 5:35.

60. See Chapter 2.

61. Both Brazilian and U.S. diplomats concur on this point. Interviews with high-level officials involved in law of the sea affairs at the State Department, Washington, D.C., May 11, 1973, and at Itamaraty, Brasília, August 15 and 16, 1974.

62. Edmundo Vargas Carreño, América latina y los problemas contemporáneos del derecho del mar (Santiago, Chile: Editorial Andrés Bello, 1973), footnote 65 at pp. 71-72.

63. A recent study asserted erroneously that Brazilian fishing zones and fishing agreements derogated from the territorial sea stricto sensu so that a type of patrimonial sea was already in de facto operation in Brazil. Ralph Zacklin, "Latin America and the Development of the Law of the Sea: An Overview," in The Changing Law of the Sea: Western Hemisphere

Perspectives, ed. Ralph Zacklin (Leiden, Holland: Sijthoff, 1974), p. 68 and footnote 20 on page 76. A more accurate description of the Brazilian claim recently concluded that it constitutes a new conception of a territorial sea considered as a unit but divided into zones for different purposes. F. V. García-Amador, "The Contribution of Latin America to the Development of the Law of the Sea," The American Journal of International Law, 68 (January, 1974). The author relied on the original Spanish mimeographed version of this article, where the description cited is located on pages 26-27.

64. See Chapters 2 and 6.

65. John R. Stevenson, Results of Caracas Session of the Third U.N. Law of the Sea Conference, statement before the Senate Foreign Relations Committee, September 5, 1974 (Washington,D.C.: Bureau of Public Affairs, Department of State, 1974), p. 5.

66. Frida M. Pfirter de Armas, "Argentina and the Law of the Sea," in Zacklin, pp. 183-184.

67. Edward Miles, "The Dynamics of Global Ocean Politics," in Marine Policy and the Coastal Community: Studies in the Social Sciences, ed. Douglas Johnston (London: Croom Helm, 1975), pp. 159-162. Sr. Murillo Souto Maior de Castro, the navy's representative on the Brazilian delegation to UNCLOS III, has explicitly articulated this territorialist strategy as well. Murillo Souto Maior de Castro, "Novos Conceitos para o Direito do Mar," Revista Marítima Brasileira 94 (October-December 1974): 28-29, 37-38.

68. Alfonso Arias Schreiber, "Las Doscientas Millas en Caracas," in Derecho del mar: Una Visión Latinoamericana, eds. Jorge A. Vargas and Edmundo Vargas Carreño (Mexico City: Editorial JUS, 1976), p. 112.

69. Murillo Souto Mairo de Castro, Relatório Sobre, pp. 10, 16, 32-33.

70. Szekely, pp. 332 and 338 and footnote 78 at page 352.

71. Statement by Mr. Thompson-Flores, Third United Nations Conference on the Law of the Sea, Official Records, 2:10.

72. Michael A. Morris, "The New International Economic Order and the New Law of the Sea," in The New International Economic Order: Confrontation or Cooperation between North and South?. eds. Karl P. Sauvant and Hajo Hasenpflug (Boulder, Colorado: Westview Press, 1977), pp. 174-188. Frederick A. Praeger,

publisher.

73. Article IX (2) and (4) of the "Programme of Action on the Establishment of a New International Economic Order." Resolution 3202 (S-VI) adopted by the General Assembly during its Sixth Special Session.

74. Szekely, p. 341 and footnote 85 at page 353.

75. Miles, "The Structure," pp. 221-222. For a recent Brazilian call for a mixed or parallel deep seabed regime, see Luiz Sérgio Silveira Costa, "A ONU e os Fundos Marinhos," Revista Marítima Brasileira 98 (April-June 1978): 77.

76. Danny M. Leipziger and James L. Mudge, Seabed Mineral Resources and the Economic Interests of Developing Countries (Cambridge, Massachusetts: Ballinger Publishing Company), pp. 135, 138.

77. Richard G. Darman, "The Law of the Sea: Rethinking U.S. Interests," Foreign Affairs 56 (1978): 394.

78. See especially Chapters 1 and 5.

79. Miles, "The Structure," p. 223.

5. Naval Trends

The growth of Brazilian naval interests and capabilities has been attracting increasing domestic and international attention. Domestically, the sea did not offer particular interest to those concerned with developing a vast country of continental dimensions. But now, increasing numbers of policy-makers and entrepreneurs are coming to recognize the importance of marine resources--and their defense--for national development. On the international front, U.S. policy-makers have become concerned that traditionally close bilateral naval contacts have been declining just as Brazil is emerging as a major power. Brazil's emergence as a major power has its naval dimension, too, and affects still other parties in different ways. Competing arms suppliers see an increasingly attractive market and possibly an opportunity to strengthen political and economic, as well as military, relations. Brazil's neighbors, most particularly Argentina, have been especially concerned about Brazil's increasing prominence, including in the naval sphere. This concern goes well beyond narrow frontier questions or contiguous resources to include speculation about possible Brazilian naval roles in the South Atlantic and beyond. Still other states, more distant, yet involved with or concerned about areas such as the South Atlantic, wonder, too, what course Brazilian naval policy will take.

THE BRAZILIAN NAVY IN TRANSITION

The 1964 military coup fundamentally altered the future of all three services, both with regard to their relationship to the political system and

their professional development. The coup brought
the armed services into politics in a deeper, more
protracted way than previously. The Brazilian Navy
is still subordinate in domestic political terms to
the Brazilian Army and is likely to remain so, with
the army being the final arbiter of the political
system in consultation with the other two services.
As for professional development, the military governments have been determined to reverse neglect of
all three services they perceived by preceding civilian governments. In fact, the navy generally did
suffer from a modest budget for naval purchases,
construction, and modernization. The security-development doctrine still has tended to keep military
spending below levels that might set back development, but very real security concerns of the new
leaders did determine that all three services would
be modernized.

Domestic politics, surveyed in detail in Chapter 2, therefore determined the basic change in all
three services toward continuing modernization and
expansion. As for the navy, it accordingly seemed
certain that when resources permitted, the service
would grow. The navy budget still remains secondary
to that of the army, but the continued growth of the
country has permitted greater sums for building up
the navy. Brazil has therefore been able to develop
a respectable naval capability in recent years and
will continue to expand the fleet, in spite of rather severe economic constraints since the 1973 oil
crisis. Closely linked to the growth of the navy
has been the expansion of naval roles, including the
expansion of the territorial sea from 12 to 200
miles in 1970.

These broad implications of military governments for the three armed services do not address
such specific questions as how fast and in what direction the navy would grow and what kind of roles
would guide that growth. About fifteen years of
military governments do provide a considerable record from which to deduce answers for such specific
questions in this chapter and the next, but ambiguities and uncertainties remain.

The continuing evolution of Brazilian naval
capabilities and roles has been paralleled by
changes on the international front. A traditional
political guideline of Brazilian foreign policy was
to cultivate close relations with the United States,
and this came to include close navy-to-navy relations. The complex network of military ties between
the United States and Brazil, including naval

170

affairs, has tended to loosen and decline in importance relative to all other Brazilian international
military contacts. Here, too, the future is not at
all clear. Change in naval policy internationally
has then been closely related to transition domestically.

The extent and implications of these broad
changes will first be examined through a comparative
analysis of the capabilities of the Brazilian Navy.
Capabilities of all three Brazilian armed services
have been growing quite rapidly, so the future of
the Brazilian Navy should be considered in relationship to the army and the air force and to national
policies that affect them all. The comparison also
focuses more specifically on navies by comparing the
naval capabilities of Brazil with those of other
states, and deriving political implications therefrom.

A subsequent section further illustrates broad
changes affecting Brazilian naval affairs. The U.S.-
Brazilian naval tradition will be explained and then
changes in the tradition will be noted. Appreciation of changes in this key bilateral relationship
will provide a basis for assessing Brazilian naval
contacts with other states and regions as well.

Finally, on the basis of naval trends analyzed
in this chapter, key Brazilian naval interests and
missions will be derived in the next chapter.

THE BRAZILIAN NAVY IN COMPARATIVE PERSPECTIVE

Around the turn of the century, Brazil was a
respectable naval power in regional terms, but subsequently national warship construction capabilities
were allowed to decline and the fleet was not reno-
vated. This situation has significantly changed
over the past decade. Larger expenditures by the
Brazilian Navy than by other Latin American navies
have led to a variety, quality, and quantity of naval vessels which stand out in the region. Brazil
has outspent other regional states in arms imports,
including naval weaponry, has surpassed them in developing a national naval construction industry, and
has even begun to export arms, although not yet naval vessels to a significant degree.

Brazil's historic competitor, Argentina, is the
only other state in Latin America with a respectable
national naval construction capability and a reason-
ably modern, diversified navy. A few other states in
the region, such as Chile, Cuba, Peru, and Venezuela

have made significant acquisitions of modern naval weaponry, but their navies lack the breadth and depth of those of Brazil and Argentina. Brazil and Argentina, too, have greater capability for and commitment to naval modernization, including their fairly advanced national naval construction industries. But none, save Brazil, promise to be a significant arms exporter as well, and even the Argentine Navy seems unable to match the across-the-board development of the Brazilian Navy. For example, over the past few years, 1973-76, Argentine arms imports averaged around $40 million annually, while those of Brazil averaged well over $100 million annually. During the same years Argentina hardly exported any domestically-produced arms, while Brazilian arms exports built up to over $80 million in 1976.[1] Estimates of Brazilian arms exports vary from $500 million to $1 billion annually by the 1980s.[2]

. Over the past decade the Brazilian military budget quadrupled to more than $2.3 billion in 1975, which was roughly equal to that of all other major South American states combined.[3] In 1976, Brazilian military expenditures were temporarily cut to $1.6 billion, yet this still amounted to about 2/3 of military spending by all other South American states.[4] Tentative estimates put Brazilian defense expenditures back up to $2.07 billion for 1977 and $2.04 billion for 1978.[5]

Relatively large Brazilian military expenditures in regional terms have not been large in relation to the national economy. Military expenditures as a proportion of Brazilian gross national product have remained modest at around 2%, which is a somewhat lower ratio than that of most other major South American states.[6] Continuing economic growth has permitted absolute increases in military spending without unduly straining national resources. For example, Brazil's growth rates during the 1970s have been nearly double those of Argentina, the most serious regional competitor, and the Brazilian gross national product has come to be about three times as large as that of Argentina.[7] Thus, Brazil can sustain at least twice as much in defense expenditures as any other South American state without exceeding or in most cases even matching their current ratio of defense spending to gross national product.

While Brazilian naval expenditures bulk large in regional terms, the navy share of the national defense budget is less prominent. In Brazil, as in most Latin American states, the army has received at least half of total defense appropriations, even though it has acquired fewer new high-cost sophisticated imports than either the air force or the navy. The Brazilian Air Force and Navy budgets have each averaged about one-quarter of total defense appropriations.[8] Each of their budgets, if respectively only about half that of the army, still has been able to support a considerable range of high-cost, sophisticated weaponry imports, in addition to growing domestic weaponry construction capabilities, and has even allowed for some exports.

Over the past decade, both domestic naval construction and imports of sophisticated naval weaponry have transformed the Brazilian Navy from a fleet of 65 largely antiquated or surplus vessels[9] to a fairly modern regional navy of well over 100 vessels.[10] Several efforts were made to modernize the navy earlier in this century, but achievements were either incomplete or of short duration. These efforts up to the initiation of a Brazilian naval construction program in the late 1960s have been characterized as "diffuse, without including a comprehensive analysis of the situation nor determination of needs, which could permit setting of priorities and implementation of a long-term program."[11]

Several years of planning led to the initial 1967 ten-year Brazilian naval construction program, which set out a blueprint for modernization and expansion of the navy. This program was quite ambitious, although the navy originally had recommended a building program for domestic construction and imports well over twice as large as that eventually approved by the army President.[12] In a first 5-year phase, 1967-72, over $300 million was eventually allocated for the program, with a comparable sum allocated for a second 5-year phase, 1973-77, although subsequent cuts in vessels projected still had to be made because of rising costs. A subsequent 10-year development program was recently approved to advance further the development of a relatively small, yet sophisticated, fleet.[13]

The Brazilian and Argentine navies do appear to have been roughly comparable until the initial 1967 ten-year Brazilian naval construction program was undertaken, although subsequent development and expansion of the Argentine Navy have been less rapid. For example, until the late 1960s Brazil's 65 largely antiquated or surplus vessels were roughly matched by an Argentine fleet of 63 ships, likewise mostly dated. In most categories of naval weaponry, the two states seemed farily evenly matched at the time.[14]

In some respects, the two navies even now are roughly comparable. Both countries have a dated aircraft carrier, each of which has recently been modernized. Both states have a number of dated and modern patrol craft, and both have a rather extensive mix of dated and modern miscellaneous craft. Both navies, too, have relied exclusively on conventional weaponry and neither has developed nor acquired nuclear vessels. Both do possess several conventional missile systems for naval defense and both appear to have the capability to develop atomic weaponry in the next few years. Neither Argentina nor Brazil, however, appears to be able or willing in the short run to develop the much more sophisticated, expensive technologies for nuclear warships or nuclear submarines armed with ballistic missiles, and such weaponry systems are currently not for sale in the international market place.

In spite of these general similarities, the Brazilian Navy still compares favorably with that of Argentina. The overall size of the Brazilian fleet. is considerably larger than that of Argentina,[15] and Brazil is ahead in most key naval warship categories in terms of numbers, with a greater lead when the additional criterion of degree of modernization is added.[16] Several of these categories of naval weaponry stand out and should be compared explicitly.

Brazil holds a considerable lead in destroyers, patrol submarines, and minesweepers, particularly with respect to the degree of modernization. Brazil has the edge in both surplus U.S. destroyers and new destroyers. In 1970, Brazil contracted with Vosper Thornycroft of Great Britain for 6 destroyers (large frigates), two of which were to be built in Rio's naval shipyard (Arsenal de Marinha do Rio de Janeiro). These large frigates, equipped with gas turbine engines, helicopters, and several kinds of missiles, are the most advanced of their kind available, and have required the bulk of funds allocated for foreign naval purchases. The missile systems are surface-to-surface, surface-to-air, and anti-submarine, from France, the United Kingdom, and Australia respectively. Three frigates have now been completed, with the other three scheduled for completion by 1980, including the two being built in Brazil. Argentina has only one similar vessel with another near completion, and while it recently placed another order in Great Britain for half a dozen additional frigates, this will not equalize

the two navies. Delivery time will take a number of
years, while Brazil's broader-based naval modernization should continue to maintain and perhaps widen
the gap. The new Argentine frigate purchase, plus a
recent order for two Type 209 submarines from West
Germany, apparently constitute the bulk of Argentine
naval modernization plans for this decade and perhaps well into the next. The Argentine frigates on
order are, moreover, smaller than the Brazilian frigates already incorporated or soon to be incorporated into the fleet.

The two projected Argentine Type 209 submarines
will be added to two already in the fleet. Brazil,
in contrast, has already incorporated three new
British Oberon class submarines into its fleet, each
of which is about twice as large as the Argentine
model. The Brazilian model is also among the most
modern conventional submarines available. For good
measure, Brazil also leads Argentina in surplus U.S.
submarines.

Other recent major additions to the Brazilian
fleet include half a dozen West German Schutze class
minesweepers. Top candidates for addition to the
fleet include a helicopter carrier, and more destroyers, frigates, submarines, coastal patrol
craft, and miscellaneous vessels, both line and supply.

Brazil's lead therefore rests on larger and
more extensive modern naval weaponry, as well as the
intention and capability to sustain a more ambitious
modernization program. Greater resources at the
disposal of Brazil have permitted a larger, more
modern and diversified navy than that of Argentina.

Complementary to Brazilian naval development is
expansion and modernization of the Brazilian Air
Force, with some $300 million invested so far in the
first phase of a modernization program. Besides
acquisition of very modern combat aircraft, such as
two squadrons of F-5E supersonic jet fighter planes
from the United States, considerable domestic production of planes has been undertaken, including the
nationally-designed Bandeirante and the Italian
Xavante produced on license. A coastal patrol aircraft has been developed from the Brazilian-designed
Bandeirante, with all other naval aircraft imported.
New, imported naval aircraft includes a variety of
helicopters and fixed-wing aircraft, with more on
order.

Since all fixed-wing aircraft belong to the air
force in Brazil, the Brazilian Air Force has considerable responsibility in the maritime sphere for

175

anti-submarine warfare, coastal fishing patrol, and shipping surveillance. This includes an anti-submarine squadron with S-2As and S2-Es, and a maritime reconnaissance squadron of P-2E Neptunes, which are being supplemented with the domestically-produced Bandeirante coastal patrol aircraft. The navy has several helicopter squadrons, with projections for a helicopter carrier and domestic production of helicopters. Argentine naval aircraft are fewer in number and somewhat less modern, and no domestic production of coastal patrol aircraft is being undertaken as in Brazil.

Also complementary to the Brazilian Navy's modernization program is the Urutu armored vehicle, which is being privately produced in Brazil in volume for export as well as domestic usage. One version of the Urutu is an armored car and the other is an amphibious troop carrier. While the Urutu has been designed basically for the army, the Brazilian Marine Corps, which in Brazil is an integral part of the navy, has relied on the amphibious version. To reinforce the potential for amphibious operations along the littoral, the navy has also acquired several landing craft for transporting the amphibious troop carriers and supplies.

Two priority areas of the new naval modernization plan are naval aviation and amphibious forces. The role of the helicopter is being particularly stressed as a versatile arm of a modern navy, and a continuing build-up of the marine corps is projected, including additional varieties of nationally-produced amphibious vehicles.

As for manpower, the Brazilian armed forces heavily outnumber any other Latin American armed forces and even surpass those of any two taken together.[17] The Brazilian lead over regional neighbors in manpower is particularly pronounced in the case of armies. Brazilian Air Force and Navy manpower, including the marine corps, together only total about half the army's manpower, as is to be expected. Since these ratios are normal and are roughly paralleled in other Latin American armed services, manpower in the Brazilian Air Force and Navy also heavily outnumbers that of regional counterparts.[18]

Although there is a Brazilian lead over regional neighbors in manpower, as in every other major quantitative indicator of military power, manpower is difficult to compare because of qualitative differences. Traditionally, larger numbers of Brazilian ground forces were counterbalanced by better

176

trained Argentine forces. Qualitatively, it is generally recognized that training of the Brazilian
armed forces has been upgraded significantly over
the last decade because of general economic development and specific efforts to modernize the military.
As the preparation of the Brazilian Army has moved
toward rough parity with that of Argentina in recent
years and quantitative growth has continued, the
traditional South American balance has been upset.

Qualitative differences between the Argentina
and Brazilian Navies were probably never as great as
in the case of ground forces, since both navies have
been elitist-oriented. Whatever differences in
quality may have existed now seem to have narrowed.
The Brazilian Navy benefited for a half century from
the technical advice of a U.S. Naval Mission and
from numerous U.S. training programs during most of
the postwar period. In fact, some U.S. naval authorities have argued on the basis of their experience in joint exercises with Latin American navies
that the Brazilian Navy is the most efficient in the
region.[19] Moreover, the Brazilian naval modernization program was intended in part to help recruiting, and, indeed, competition for entry has become
keen. A relatively large and increasingly well-
trained national manpower pool has been developed
from which the navy can choose for its elite service.
With these advantages, plus more extensive, modern
naval and air weaponry than Argentina, Brazilian
qualitative superiority in manpower may emerge as
well, if it has not already done so.

Brazil's growth, economic as well as military,
has been widely regarded as projecting it into a position of regional conventional military primacy.[20]
Superior naval strength and training comparable with
or better than that of other regional navies would
suggest that Brazil now also possesses South American naval supremacy. Some analysts have suggested
this conclusion, including Argentine military authorities.[21]

Such comparisons of military and naval power
through conventional indicators, one may argue, are
not appropriate for the contemporary Latin American
context. Traditionally, it is true, comparisons between armed forces have ultimately involved an estimate of their respective effectiveness in warfare,
while Latin American armed forces seem oriented toward national defense and protection of sovereignty
rather than toward offensive warfare. For example,
no armed forces in the region seem capable of maintaining offensive ground action against a determined

neighbor for more than a week or two.[22]   In the naval sphere, warfare between Argentina and Chile over
Beagle Channel boundary questions seems much more
likely than any kind of Argentine-Brazilian naval
confrontation.   Conventional power comparisons are
nevertheless useful.   Sea power may permit more decisive military results than ground warfare, so conventional naval comparisons still may be useful in
the Latin American context.   The very restraints of
the land milieu in Latin America, it has been argued, may increase the attractiveness of air and sea
power as a means of competing with adversaries or
potential adversaries.[23]

Moreover, in Latin America as elsewhere, naval
strength remains related to political influence.   A
recent study conceded that "peacetime force comparisons can be grossly misleading indicators of true
capabilities," but added that "these are commonly
the only variables that intrude upon the decisions
that, in turn, determine the political effectiveness
of naval forces."[24]

Brazil is a case in point of the political impact of military power, in clearly benefiting from
the prestige and influence of being generally regarded as the leading South American state and an
emerging major power.   This general image is increasingly becoming associated with regional conventional military primacy, including South American
naval supremacy.   So the Brazilian Navy is clearly
supporting key Brazilian political objectives.   Determination to defend a rapidly growing national
power base is demonstrated, and recognition that
growing national power is leading to international
great power status is achieved.

Just as regional naval supremacy has already
had a political impact within the region, so it
promises to affect events and states well beyond the
region.   We shall defer discussion of possible ex-
tra-hemispheric Brazilian naval roles and their military implications until the next chapter.   For now
we shall limit ourselves to calling attention to
some political implications for extra-regional
states of Brazil's emergence as the premier regional
naval power.   In particular, emerging regional naval
supremacy requires some rethinking about classical
kinds of comparisons between navies.   Traditionally,
blue water navies have been categorically ranked at
the top of the naval hierarchy because of their
ability to sustain continued operations in distant
waters.   This capability of blue water navies, plus
the more recent addition to their fleets of nuclear

submarines armed with intercontinental ballistic
missiles, does continue to distinguish them from
other navies, including those of emerging regional
powers such as Brazil. But in regional terms, it
may be misleading to regard navies of emerging powers such as Brazil as subordinate in all senses to
those of the established great powers.

Some difficulties with rigid hierarchical comparisons may be illustrated by a recent classifica-
tion of the world's navies into a blue water group
(the United States, the Soviet Union, Great Britain,
and France) and another group of coastal navies,
distinguished by "their common position of naval inferiority vis-à-vis the four naval powers."[25] On
the basis of this distinction, the four blue water
navies are further subdivided into first-class and
second-class navies, and the coastal navies are
further categorized as third-class, fourth-class and
fifth-class navies. Twenty-one navies are described
as third-class, including the Brazilian Navy which
is explicitly mentioned as a prototype.[26] Such an
approach leads to distortions, both in comparing the
Brazilian Navy with those of the great powers and
with those of lesser powers.

As for comparisons between the Brazilian Navy
and those of lesser powers, this approach unfortunately pairs the Brazilian Navy with dissimilar
navies. For example, ten of the 21 third-class navies are of developed states or are at least located
in developed regions, such as Europe, in close prox-
imity to one of the blue water navies (Australia,
Canada, Federal Republic of Germany, Greece, Italy,
Japan, Netherlands, Portugal, Spain, and Sweden).
Assimilation of such navies with that of Brazil, a
developing state yet a dominant power in a geographically distant region, would appear strained, since
tasks and goals are so different. China and Turkey,
two others categorized as third-class navies, would
appear to be special cases. The other nine navies
are comparable with Brazil insofar as they are from
developing regions, yet six are from Latin America
(Argentina, Brazil, Chile, Mexico, Peru, and Venezuela) and the distinctiveness of the Brazilian Navy in its region has already been noted. The three
remaining third-class navies are all from Asia (India, South Korea, and Taiwan). In contrast, this
author has argued that the Brazilian Navy is really
only comparable to the Indian Navy, since Brazil and
India are both dominant actors within their respective developing sub-regions and alone possess broad-
based economic and military capabilities, including

credible regional air forces and navies.[27] Such regional navies are clearly not yet blue water and may not evolve in that direction, but neither is their distinctive position appreciated by lumping them together with well over a hundred other coastal state navies and relegating them to third-rate status.

In any event, the same study does appear correct in placing the Brazilian Navy ahead of that of South Africa, which is classified as a fourth-class fleet.[28] Besides Argentina and Brazil, South Africa is the only other regional power in the South Atlantic which has developed a modern, fairly diversified navy. But Brazil has been outspending South Africa in defense and naval affairs, Brazil's fleet is more diversified and much larger than that of South Africa, and naval manpower is much greater. Brazil would seem able to hold the lead, with gross national product over three times that of South Africa.[29]

Regional navies of emerging powers in developing areas likewise should not be related to the blue water navies simply by "their common position of naval inferiority." The navies of the two superpowers do operate in regional waters off coastal developing states, such as the South Atlantic. However, in an increasingly pluralistic, interdependent world, including more extensive, overlapping ocean uses, rigidly hierarchical classifications of naval power may no longer be appropriate.

Contemporary legal, military, and political constraints on blue water navy operations off coastal developing states have increased, particularly in the case of regionally dominant powers such as Brazil. On the legal front, distant-water navies now operate with less freedom of action than under the traditional freedom of the seas regime. The general approval given the 12-mile territorial sea and the 200-mile exclusive economic zone at the Third United Nations Conference on the Law of the Sea has extended coastal state control into new areas. Passing naval vessels may experience no problems, but effective use of naval force or pressure is certainly becoming more restricted off coastal states because of general community political and legal.norms.[30] To be sure, the coastal state cannot forcibly constrain mobility of superpower nuclear submarines, while the superpowers might impose a solution by conventional naval force or threat of nuclear force. But the political cost, and perhaps the military cost as well, of such a strategy appear disproportionately high.

In the 1963 Lobster War, Brazil indeed did have

a naval confrontation with a much superior naval
power, France, and still managed to defend national
resource interests. France first dispatched one
destroyer to the area for a limited show of naval
force, and Brazil responded by committing a much
larger air force and naval presence to the disputed
area. Because of the political unacceptability of
escalating the conflict to match the Brazilian local
build-up and the practical difficulty of projecting
greater naval power in a distant theatre, France
eventually negotiated a settlement.[31]

In 1963, Brazil was not an emerging power nor
had naval modernization even begun, yet it still was
able to mount a credible local defense and deter es-
calation by a superior power. Now that Brazil is an
emerging power in a developing area with a reasona-
bly strong regional navy and air force, the constraints on the maritime powers tend to be reinforced. A respectable regional navy and air force,
particularly when associated with broad-based national emergence as a major power, appear both to
elicit restraint from the superpowers and command
greater respect from them. Over the last decade,
superpower naval air power has declined relative to
air forces of some regional powers in their respective local theatres, and in local coastal waters
"the sea-based missile has emerged as the great
equalizer" of a superpower fleet presence.[32] Defense of national maritime territory through Brazilian air and naval power accordingly seems more
credible and deterrence appears enhanced.

Such changes counsel revision of traditional
classifications of navies, most particularly that
regional navies are third-rate simply because they
are smaller and less sophisticated than those of the
established maritime powers. Regional navies generally have more influence than other putative
third-class navies and may even influence actions of
the superpowers. U.S.-Brazilian naval relations, to
which we now turn, indicate how one emerging regional power indeed has gradually been able to redefine
its relations with one of the superpowers, with implications for the other superpower as well, from
dependence to relative autonomy.

U.S.-BRAZILIAN NAVAL RELATIONS

A tradition of convergent U.S.-Brazilian military interests, including those in the naval sphere,
was gradually built up during much of this century

and received expression through a number of institutions. This complex network of military ties between the United States and Brazil has gradually
loosened and declined in importance relative to all
other Brazilian international military contacts over
the last decade. In the naval sphere, this relative
decline has been evident, but has varied from sector
to sector. Accordingly, the future of different
components of U.S.-Brazilian naval relations likewise varies.

A Tradition of Convergent Naval Interests

The United States began to wean Brazil away
from British naval traditions in the early part of
this century. A Brazilian naval visit to the United
States in 1907 and another visit by a U.S. fleet to
Rio de Janeiro in 1908 played an important part in
promoting a rapprochement between the two states'
foreign policies.[33] Then in 1914, by invitation,
the United States assigned a naval officer to help
establish the Brazilian Naval War College, and by
1917 the Brazilian government requested that six
U.S. Navy officers be detailed to Brazil as instruc-
tors at the Naval War College and elsewhere.
Admiral William B. Caperton played a major role
in cultivating closer U.S.-Brazilian relations during the war years, 1917-1919, when he commanded a
South Atlantic patrol force based in Brazil.
Through astute use of goodwill tours by the squadron,
personal diplomacy, and encouragement of a U.S. Naval Mission rather than one from Great Britain,
Caperton helped promote U.S. influence. While
Caperton hoped to contain British influence as well
as extend U.S. influence, Brazil hoped to strengthen
its hand against Argentina through the presence of a
United States naval force in its waters.[34]
In 1922 a U.S.Naval Mission was indeed established in Brazil to assist in modernizing and training the navy. The Brazilian decision to choose a
U.S. rather than a British Naval Mission has been
attributed to greater familiarity with U.S. officers.[35] The naval mission contined in operation for
about half a century, with a gap only between 1930-
36 when Brazil allowed the contract to lapse because
of adverse national financial conditions. Even then,
some U.S. naval officers remained in Brazil on an
individual basis.
The official purpose of the naval mission was
to increase "the efficiency of the Brazilian Navy,"

but the close bilateral naval relationship was also intended to limit other foreign influence. For example, one provision of the agreement establishing the naval mission explicitly stated the exclusiveness of the position granted the United States: "So long as this agreement, or any extension thereof, is in effect, the Government of Brazil shall not engage the services of any personnel of any other foreign government for duties of any nature connected with the Brazilian Navy except by mutual agreement between the Government of the United States and the Government of Brazil."

A related aim of the naval mission through the years was to encourage reliance on U.S. naval weaponry and limit the position of the European powers in the Brazilian arms market.[36] The naval mission did help develop a strong navy-to-navy relationship, symbolized by the incorporation of the mission into the Brazilian Navy's organizational chart. But the United States did not emerge as the predominant arms supplier to Brazil and the rest of Latin America until World War II, partly because of restrictions on the export of weapons and munitions. A recent tabulation showed that prior to World War II European yards accounted for the major share of Latin American naval tonnage, and in the case of Brazil, from 1890 through 1939, 75% of warships were British-built, 15% were products of continental Europe, and 10% came from Brazilian yards.[37]

In 1934, a counterpart U.S. Army mission to Brazil was established, which succeeded a French Military Mission for the same area, and in 1940 a U.S. air mission was added. The only other Brazilian instance of such bilateral cooperation with another country for a military training mission is the Brazilian-Paraguayan Military Mission, which has functioned since 1942, and in that case it is Brazil which helps train the Paraguayan Army.

The U.S.-Brazilian tradition of military cooperation was not without problems involving Argentina. An unfortunate effect of the U.S. Naval Mission was to flame Argentina's suspicions about potential Brazilian naval expansion. In 1924, for example, two years after the arrival of the U.S. Naval Mission, the Argentine government made strong protests to Washington about a projected Brazilian naval expansion program, and the United States denied that the mission had any part in this. As matters turned out, the Brazilian government was not able to finance the naval program.[38] Then in 1937 Argentina managed to block the planned transfer of three old

U.S. destroyers to the Brazilian Navy, in spite of
the recent return of the U.S. Naval Misison to Brazil. As a result, Brazil felt compelled to turn to
Europe for military and naval equipment, since it
had become dependent on foreign shipyards, not having constructed a new warship itself in nearly fifty
years. Brazilian determination to reequip and modernize its armed forces from whatever external
source possible was reinforced in 1938, when Argentina began buying large quantities of arms in
Europe.[39] As matters turned out, this was only a
temporary interlude. In World War II, Brazil managed to cement its military ties with the United
States, while Argentina became isolated because of
pro-Axis sympathies. In 1956, a similar episode
occurred when the United States refused to sell Brazil an aircraft carrier because of Argentine objections. The negative effects of the episode for bilateral relations were contained in that case, too.
Brazil went ahead and purchased an attack carrier
from Great Britain while the United States still remained its predominant military supplier, and Argentina eventually matched the Brazilian purchase without an arms race ensuing.

Another significant aspect of U.S.-Brazilian
military ties has involved international operations.
Brazil was the United States' only South American
ally during World War I, when Brazilian officers saw
duty on American warships in the South Atlantic. A
Brazilian naval force was also on its way to the
Mediterranean when the war ended, although it was to
be placed under British, not U.S., command. Brazil
was likewise the only South American state to provide substantial forces to the allied cause in World
War II, when the navy performed anti-submarine and
convoy escort duties in the South Atlantic in cooperation with the United States. Subsequent instances of Brazilian defense alignment with the
United States include contributions to international
peacekeeping operations, such as the U.N. peacekeeping missions in the Suez and the Congo, and the
Dominican Republic in the mid-1960s, when Brazil was
one of only two South American countries to provide
substantial forces after the U.S. intervention. But
these postwar instances of military cooperation did
not include a significant naval component.

Close collaboration between the Brazilian and
U.S. militaries during World War II had a decisive
impact on subsequent military relations. Close personal relationships and a common outlook on security
matters grew out of the wartime partnership. But

184

close military cooperation was also regarded as
serving distinctive Brazilian interests. It will be
recalled that distinctive national interests had
already led Brazilian policy-makers temporarily to
question the wisdom of exclusive military ties with
the United States during 1937-38. In general, Brazilian policy-makers expected that their support for
the United States would be reciprocated by U.S. support for Brazilian preeminence in South America.
More particularly, a complex mixture of domestic and
international motives prompted the Vargas administration to extend traditional bilateral cooperation
more decisively in the military sphere during World
War II. Among Vargas' considerations in deciding to
intervene with force outside the hemisphere on the
side of the United States was a desire to secure a
stronger international position and to keep the
armed forces out of politics. Brazilian policy-
makers also hoped that another result of participation in the war would be the development of national
maritime power.[40]

The pursuit of distinctive national interests,
albeit in the context of dependency on the United
States, is evident in another example of wartime naval cooperation. Vice-Admiral Jonas H. Ingram, who
commanded the South Atlantic Force, later designated
the United States Fourth Fleet, is credited with a
decisive role in encouraging Brazil to enter the war.
In fact, "Vargas agreed to give Ingram full authority over the Brazilian navy and air force, and complete responsibility for defense of the entire Brazilian coast."[41] This extraordinary measure was
seen by some on the U.S. side as fostering an ex-
cessive measure of dependency for a self-respecting
country. Instead, Vargas, "as one imbued with the
'patron' outlook, ... believed that the weak should
stand in the shadow of the strong, and, conversely,
that the strong should protect the weak." Thus, to
Brazilian policy-makers, U.S. predominance in the
military partnership did not connote dependency at
the expense of national interests, and was instead
regarded as necessary for maintaining national independence.[42] As Brazil became stronger, more self-
reliant, and less in need of a "patron," this attitude began to change.

Among the most enduring products of the World
War II military partnership were a Joint Brazil-
United States Defense Commission in Washington and a
Joint Brazilian-United States Military Commission in
Brazil (JBUSMC), which were established in 1942 to
coordinate common military interests and activities.

For over thirty years, JBUSMC was the principal agency in Brazil for facilitating military cooperation with the United States. On its creation in World War II, it incorporated all three preexisting U.S. military missions, which have since been of approximately equal size.

JBUSMC was distinctive and important for several reasons. It was a semi-autonomous institution, separate from the armed services ministries and with high-level representatives on both the Brazilian and U.S. sides. For example, a four-star general headed the Brazilian delegation to JBUSMC, which he also chaired. The existence of such a forum played a vital part in the development of cordial U.S. relations with the Brazilian military, at the middle as well as the top levels. The importance placed on JBUSMC by both sides contrasted with lower level representatives and less institutionalized, less intimate contacts with other Latin American militaries through military assistance advisory groups (MAAGs).[43] On the other side, the Joint Brazil-United States Defense Commission was incorporated into the organizational chart of the Joint Chiefs of Staff, which was a distinction accorded to only two other bilateral military bodies, ones with Canada and Mexico. JBUSMC then provided the opportunity for continuous dialogue about security issues affecting the two states.

Brazil did have the counterpart of a MAAG since 1952, when a Military Assistance Agreement was signed with the United States to provide for transfers of military equipment, materials, and services. The distinctive aspect of this military assistance agreement was that it was established at Brazilian request within the more intimate context of JBUSMC. A previous MAAG offer by the United States had been rejected by Brazilian authorities, who preferred that these functions be carried out by the U.S. delegation to JBUSMC.[44]

The U.S. Naval Mission, also the navy section of JBUSMC since World War II, likewise promoted close relations between the middle and upper levels of the U.S. and Brazilian Navies. For example, the U.S. Army, Navy, and Air Force sections of JBUSMC were located directly in the respective service divisions of the Brazilian Ministry of War (Army, Navy, and Air Force). They were assigned offices alongside Brazilians, wore civilian clothes, and mixed freely with their Brazilian counterparts. A half century of close cooperation between the United States and Brazilian Navies helped promote common

186

interests, even though naval contacts have diminished in the last few years.

A. U.S. advisory mission also helped establish the National War College (Escola Superior de Guerra) in 1948, remained until 1960, and made an important impact on the formation of the armed services' National Security Doctrine. The U.S. Naval Mission likewise assisted in starting the Naval Research Institute (Instituto de Pesquisa da Marinha), just as U.S. naval officers had earlier played an important role in the creation of the Brazilian Naval War College.

Several other cooperative naval arrangements have also reinforced U.S.-Brazilian naval relations. The Navy Communications Technical Group Rio (NAVCOMMTECHGRU RIO) is a collaborative U.S.-Brazilian communications facility for training Brazilian naval personnel and providing essential communications for navy ships transiting the South Atlantic around Cape Horn and the Cape of Good Hope. This was the only existing facility of its kind at the time. The more recent 1972 IANCA (Inter-American Naval Cooperation Agency) agreement is another example of naval cooperation between the United States and a number of Latin American states, including Brazil, for control of maritime traffic.

Several different kinds of regular naval exercises also involve the United States and Brazil. Operation UNITAS is an annual series of exercises between the U.S. Navy and several South American navies, including that of Brazil. Over more than a decade the annual UNITAS naval exercises have helped promote good U.S.-Brazilian naval relations. A U.S. task force steams down one coast of South America and returns up the other, and carries out a series of bilateral or occasional trilateral exercises en route. Over the last decade, Operation SPRINGBOARD has been carried out as well in the Caribbean by allied navies, including those of Brazil and the United States, and related bilateral amphibious operations in Puerto Rico have been undertaken as part of the VERITAS series. The only other annual military exercises Brazil carries out with another state are the Ninfa series with Paraguay, the seventh of which was held in July 1978. In this series, fluvial anti-guerrilla exercises are carried out by the Brazilian Navy and Marine Corps in collaboration with the Paraguayan Navy.

Certain aspects of U.S.-Brazilian military relationships also involved substantial expenditures and numerous personnel. U.S. military assistance in loans and grants to Brazil amounted to about $300 million by the late 1960s, which was about a third of the total for all of Latin America for those years.[45] The bulk of these funds was for arms transfers, with smaller sums used to train several thousand members of the Brazilian armed forces by 1970.[46] Foreign arms transfers to Brazil were mostly from the United States during the postwar period up to the late 1960s. With the onset of World War II, European arms sources to the region dried up, and after the war, the United States dominated the market, largely through the sale of surplus·weapons, up to the late 1960s.

This survey of the historical relationship indicates that there is an approximate relationship between the degree of intensity of U.S. naval ties and cooperation with Brazil and the extent of U.S. influence with the Brazilian Navy. The relatively large U.S. training program for Brazilian naval officers, for example, was "very influential in persuading the Brazilians that the U.S. strategic capabilities enable them to keep their military equipment procurement primarily limited to their needs for internal security and defense of contiguous maritime communications."[47] More broadly, interviews conducted by this author with both Brazilian and U.S. Army, Air Force and Navy officers were in consensus that navy-to-navy relations have been closer than those involving the two armies and air forces. Several interviewees added that relations between the U.S. and Brazilian Marine Corps tended to be even closer than navy-to-navy relations.[48] While the marine corps is an integral part of the Brazilian Navy, its relatively small size has permitted particularly close cooperation. For example, the Brazilian Marine Corps numbers about 13,000, of which about 4,500 are combat ready, so the 600 marines who participate on a rotating basis each year in Operation VERITAS with the United States Marine Corps is a relatively large number. Similarly, most of the five admirals of the Brazilian Marine Corps have received at least a year of military training in the United States.

Just as the United States was pursuing certain national interests, such as influence, through bilateral military cooperation, including the maritime sphere, so was Brazil. Consistent Brazilian pursuit of distinctive national interests indicates that bilateral military cooperation was never an end in itself, but was regarded as a means toward achievement of other concrete objectives. For over half a

century, policy considerations did continue to counsel bilateral naval cooperation, and this cooperation did develop its own tradition and momentum.
But the domestic and international contexts shaping
Brazilian policy objectives continued to evolve and
in time gradually loosened military and naval ties.
In response to the changing policy context, Brazilian policy-makers came to believe that diversification of international military and naval ties would
be more advisable.

Readjustments in U.S.-Brazilian Naval Relations

While the historical record demonstrates that
close navy-to-navy ties led to considerable U.S. influence, the converse is not necessarily true. That
is, loosening of naval ties will not necessarily
lead to a steady decline of U.S. influence. Influence depends on many factors and not just on the intensity of naval ties. It is well to recall that
the sources of U.S. influence in Brazilian naval affairs traditionally have been multiple, including
power, prestige, personal relationships, mutual
self-interest, and general compatability of naval
interests. It follows that the gradual loosening of
bilateral naval ties would have equally complex effects on U.S. influence. One such effect, it will
be argued, is that the very meaning of influence is
evolving.
The extent of change varies with the particular
component of bilateral relations, so each major component will be analyzed in turn. Central to the
changes is the arms trade, since the United States
no longer occupies the predominant position in the
Brazilian arms market, including naval weaponry, it
did up to about a decade ago. Part of this change
is due to internal developments in Brazil, part is
due to U.S. policy, and part is due to international
arms competitors.
As for internal developments, three objectives
of the Brazilian armed forces--modernization, self-
sufficiency, and diversification--have tended to alter the context of bilateral military relations.
Growing national aspirations to great power status
seemed to require a modern military establishment
that would be as self-sufficient as possible and no
longer dependent on one major foreign arms supplier,
the United States. For example, the commander of
the Brazilian Marine Corps remarked several years
ago that "A nation is independent when it

manufactures its own arms." These changes in domestic policy and capabilities would have tended to have reduced the dominant U.S. presence in the Brazilian arms picture regardless of international developments.

Two periods with different characteristics have conditioned the Brazilian armed forces' efforts to modernize, become as self-sufficient as possible, and diversify sources of arms imports.

The Brazilian armed forces, including the navy, began a concerted drive toward modernization in a first period from the late 1960s to the early 1970s, which was a time of dramatic upswing in the national economy. Modernization was broadly paralleled throughout much of Latin America, if on a more modest scale, with a burst of spending and arms purchases from about 1967-1973. A modern core of weaponry was purchased from abroad, especially by air forces and navies, and expectations were raised for carrying through rapid modernization during the rest of the 1970s. Six Latin American states dominated foreign arms purchases during this first period (97% or $1.6 billion), including Brazil, whose share was alone about one-third.[49] During this first spending cycle, 75% of the region's imported military equipment, most of which was relatively sophisticated, was of Western European origin. The United States share in the Latin American arms import market declined to 13%, which was composed of less sophisticated weaponry.[50]

Particularly since the oil crisis of 1973, the modernization programs of Latin American militaries have had to be reconciled with tighter finances. Modernization continued in this second period, but at a more modest rate since economies were relatively less affluent and some basic modernization needs had already been met. Brazil will still likely be able to sustain a considerably higher level of spending for arms imports and domestic weaponry production than any other South American state, as demonstrated previously. For its part, the United States tried to regain its position as the major arms supplier to the region in the second period, after having declined precipitously as an arms supplier in the first period. Shifting domestic trends then influenced and interacted with a shifting foreign arms picture.

Self-sufficiency illustrates both problems and opportunities, domestic and international, in modernizing the navy. The Brazilian drive to establish a viable domestic arms industry and eventually to

190

become as self-sufficiant as possible necessarily
involves reshaping relationships with traditional
foreign arms suppliers, but obstacles are many.
Self-sufficiency is particularly difficult with respect to naval armament, which involves considerable
technological sophistication and heavy capital outlays. Consequently, about three-fourths of the
budget for the naval construction program has had to
remain allocated for foreign purchases, which have
been the only source of high-technology naval weaponry. National naval warship construction has also
received less priority than expansion of the merchant marine, which likewise requires heavy capital
investments and advanced technology for both domestic construction and imports. On this basis, the
Brazilian Navy Minister concluded that the navy
would still have to continue to rely on foreign imports for an uncertain period in spite of the policy
of relying on national production as much as possible.[51]

Heavy reliance on both importation of foreign
warships and on expansion of the national merchant
marine nevertheless can assist national naval warship construction capabilities in the long run.
Particularly in Brazil, national merchant marine
construction and national naval warship construction
tend to be complementary. Because of the general
similarities between the two industries and the
existence of a military government, most key executive positions in merchant marine construction are
occupied by ex-navy men. The navy is likewise responsible for training merchant marine personnel.[52]
Both industries, moreover, benefit from Brazil's
relatively sophisticated industrial infra-structure,
so that local production of components can frequently be feasible and efficient, and, with modifications, can be used by each.[53] Numerous ships in the
navy's fleet have already been built on contract in
national civilian shipyards, and the navy's shipyard
(Arsenal de Marinha do Rio de Janeiro) in turn has
built ships for the civilian secotr. It is also
expected that by the 1980s civilian shipbuilding capacity will have expanded sufficiently to be able to
place greater emphasis on exports or naval warship
construction, as needs then dictate.

National naval warship construction likewise
benefits from a foreign presence in several ways.
Heavy foreign investment in national merchant marine
construction, especially Dutch and Japanese, helps
encourage shipbuilding which is efficient and responsive to technological innovations. Dutch and

Japanese entrenchment in the Brazilian civilian
shipbuilding industry occurred well before either
of the naval modernization periods under discussion
here, but did involve an important U.S. lost opportunity. Recent naval arms purchases from West
European states have also tended to encourage efficiency and technological innovation in national warship construction because of co-production agreements, if likewise to the exclusion of the United
States.

All recent major Brazilian arms purchases--
frigates, minesweepers, and submarines--either provide for or envisage co-production. Recent co-production agreements with Great Britain provide for
upgrading of Brazilian naval construction technology, with two of the original six British missile
frigates being built in part in Brazil. Argentina
also has an agreement with Great Britain for local
assembly of one of its missile frigates. A similar
co-production arrangement had been included in the
Brazilian minesweeper deal with West Germany, but
was later canceled because of shortcomings of the
Brazilian firm. The Brazilian Navy's procurement
chief recently declared in like fashion that "the
next submarine to be incorporated into our fleet
will be of Brazilian manufacture."[54] Brazilian naval planners have contended that their experience in
building the British frigates and repairing and re-
fitting the British submarines has now prepared Brazil to build its own conventional submarines, possibly in continuing association with Great Britain.[55]

Such co-production arrangements can therefore
be an important step toward a self-sufficient naval
warship manufacturing capability. While such arrangements may be initially limited largely to assembly, Brazil has shown its ability to progressively acquire and adapt foreign technologies through
license production, from automobiles to combat aircraft. While European arms suppliers have been responsive to the Brazilian desire for co-production
and are actively negotiating new weaponry co-production agreements, U.S. practice has generally not
favored such arrangements.

Some advances have been made with little or no
foreign input. On their own, Brazil and Argentina
have gone much further toward developing viable arms
industries than any other states in the region. Naturally, both states have moved first to satisfy
domestic requirements for basic, less sophisticated
military hardware. The strategy is to move gradually toward production of more sophisticated military

items, and to phase out foreign arms purchases accordingly. With only about one-quarter of the budget of the naval construction program, national naval construction potential has still been developing fairly rapidly. Home production already is responsible for much light and intermediate naval equipment. Several examples may be cited to supplement the earlier discussion of Brazilian naval capabilities. Coastal craft and vessels for riparian operations have already been constructed domestically, and naval shipbuilding capabilities can handle a variety of support craft as well. National civilian shipbuilders are being considered for contracts for additional coastal patrol boats, and may be able to contribute toward self-sufficiency here, too. Chile recently purchased some Piratini coastal patrol craft from Brazil, although home production of naval weaponry has generally been hard pressed to meet domestic needs and no other significant export sales have been made. Cost is still much less than that of more sophisticated naval imports, so the new naval construction plan projects construction of 43 warships locally over the next 10 years.

Home production of naval weaponry has therefore made some notable strides, but still lags behind the other armed services. Aircraft production has a history dating back several decades, and now supplies domestic designs, as well as foreign models through licensing and co-production agreements, for both national consumption and export markets. Two examples have been cited. The Bandeirante C-95 is domestically designed and developed, and is being used nationally and exported to other countries as well. Of particular relevance for the naval sector, nine units of a maritime military reconnaissance version of this plane were recently sold to Chile for $9 million, 3 have been delivered to the Brazilian Air Force, and 18 more are initially projected. The Urutu armored vehicle is another example of a weapon basically designed for the army yet also used by the marine corps. Considerable strides toward self-sufficiency by the army and air force therefore complement the navy's strategy, and are gradually reshaping relationships with foreign suppliers.

The third and final Brazilian policy objective is diversification of the source of arms imports, also carried out with increasing resolve over the last decade. International events likewise tended to have this effect, including U.S. reluctance to conclude naval weaponry co-production arrangements or invest in civilian shipbuilding, U.S. opposition to sophisticated arms exports, and increasing European competitiveness. Naval aims were consequently achieved more fully in diversification than in self-sufficiency.

On the international side, part of the decline of the position of the United States in the Brazilian arms market in the first period, the late 1960s to early 1970s, was consequently of its own making. A number of statutory limitations on types of U.S. military equipment export sales and on the amount of government credit available for arms transfers made it particularly difficult for the United States to respond to the desire of Latin American militaries to modernize their military establishments in the 1960s. In 1967, Congress limited government involvement in foreign military sales and credits to Latin America to $75 million annually. Legislation likewise prohibited the export of sophisticated weapons to Latin America, at a time when such advanced weaponry was often regarded as necessary by militaries in the region to carry out their modernization programs. Such legislative restrictions contributed to a shift from the United States to Western Europe as the primary source of arms exports to the region, although congressional action did later lift certain restrictions placed on availability of equipment.

In the case of Brazil, the navy and air force were precluded from purchasing modern ships and aircraft from the United States for their expansion programs, primarily due to legislative restrictions imposed by Congress on sales of sophisticated weapons and on credit sales. Brazilian policymakers eventually felt obliged to turn to Great Britain, France, West Germany, and other nations for these military items. From the late 1960s to the early 1970s, U.S. arms sales to Brazil stagnated at modest annual levels, while Brazilian arms imports increased rapidly. For example, in fiscal year 1968 U.S. foreign military sales agreements with Brazil reached a low of $2.265 million, and in fiscal year 1969 they remained modest at $11.348 million.[56]

Military grants for matériel support and training were reduced rapidly from the late 1960s as well. While Brazil's share of U.S. grant military assistance was about one-third of the total dispensed to Latin American nations during the 1950s and 1960s, in more recent years its share of U.S. military assistance to Latin America declined. Congress also moved to reduce and eventually eliminate military assistance grants, and correspondingly smaller quantities were available to Latin America. Grants for matériel support to Brazil, as well as several of the larger Latin American states, were discontinued altogether by 1969 because the U.S. deemed that the growth of the national economy increased the Brazilian ability to purchase needed goods. Accordingly, by the 1970s Brazil was receiving less than $1 million annually in military grants, all exclusively for training assistance.

These cuts were alone not responsible for the marked decline in U.S. arms sales to Latin America, but they did have a negative effect being accompanied by restrictions on credits and sophisticated weaponry. A recent authoritative study called instead for ending promotional aspects of U.S. arms transfer policy, such as grant military assistance, as well as eliminating restrictionist aspects, "in the interest of seeking a less politicized and more competitive market system."[57]

As U.S. military credits, grants, and sales declined, U.S. military personnel in Brazil were also cut. As part of "Operation Topsy," from 1966-1972, JBUSMC was cut from 150 to 54 officers and men, with other cuts also made in personnel in the Military Attaché's office. In making these cuts, U.S. Ambassador to Brazil Tuthill challenged the conventional wisdom that more numerous U.S. military personnel led to closer contacts and therefore more influence with the Brazilian armed forces. Tuthill argued that a smaller U.S. presence would lead to greater efficiency, and would be more responsive to Brazilian nationalism. Technical aspects of military relations could largely be handled by reciprocal visits, he argued, with more responsibility being given the Brazilians.[58] Indeed, positive results from Tuthill's action in Brazil motivated successive rounds of personnel cuts elsewhere in the world. Unfortunately, such positive readjustments in U.S.-Brazilian military relations were offset by failure to respond to Brazilian aspirations in other areas.

As for international arms competitors, several Western European states moved to fill the Latin American demand for sophisticated weaponry in the late 1960s. To stimulate their arms sales, European suppliers stepped up sales efforts, offered attractive financial arrangements, and negotiated some co-production arrangements. From 1968-1972, Brazil purchased $499 million in arms from "third country" states, mostly in Western Europe, and only $76

million from the United States.[59] The Soviet Union
is the major arms supplier to Cuba, but so far has
only made an occasional arms sale to other Latin
American states and no major arms sale to Brazil.
Other arms suppliers, such as Canada and Israel,
have largely been limited to supplying certain
specialty items to the region.

The trend toward diversification of arms supplies to Latin America was particularly pronounced
in naval weaponry, in which Western European states
are highly competitive, particularly Great Britain.
In the first period or spending cycle, naval vessels
worth $658 million were purchased for Latin American
navies from Western Europe, or 95% of the total.
Only $4 million of naval weaponry purchases were
made from the United States, although this figure is
undervalued because costs to buyers for rehabilita-
tion of surplus vessels acquired were not included.[60]

Counterpart trends affected the Brazilian Navy.
The three most expensive foreign acquisitions--frig-
ates, submarines, and minesweepers--were all provided by Western European states and the first two
were particularly sophisticated. The political significance of these purchases may be even greater
than the large initial outlays suggest. For example,
the millile frigates are expected to remain operational through the 1980s, such large advanced weaponry sales often require training from the country
of origin, and new supply and maintenance patterns
are established. Still other types of contacts may
be stimulated, such as related military and nonmili-
tary exports. A case in point is the Brazilian purchase of British Lynx helicopters for the missile
frigates. Successive frigates supplied Brazil also
have introduced technological advances as they became available, and a similar moderniazation option
is available for continued buying in series. Brazilian naval development therefore may remain deeply
involved with Great Britain throughout the 1980s and
perhaps beyond. With the assistance of ample military credits and careful attention to weapons requirements for Brazil's naval modernization program,
Western European suppliers should be able to retain
a substantial portion of the Brazilian naval arms
market even though the United States has now re-
entered the competition.

Fears have been expressed in the United States
that large and perhaps increasing West European
weapons sales to Brazil will tend to increase West
European influence with the Brazilian armed services,

including the Brazilian Navy. This concern would be justified were past trends and political-economic relationships extrapolated into the future. In Latin America, the United States indeed has tended to regard arms transfers as an extension of political relationships which promote the supplier's influence. In contrast, Western European states have tended to regard arms transfers as a commercial transaction in the sphere of international trade.[61] European states can be expected to continue to limit their role in promotion of arms transfers to the region to commercial interests, since it is clear that no Western European state aspires to fashion any kind of a dominant political role such as that traditionally played by the United States. Moreover, on the Latin American side there is general determination to lessen traditional dependency and not to substitute one paramount for another. This includes Latin American determination to diversify arms purchases and thereby prevent becoming dependent again on a single foreign arms source which can use resultant leverage to influence the direction of national security policy.

Accordingly, an increasingly multipolar world environment will tend to create new opportunities for commercially oriented arms sales without political obligations or vulnerabilities on the part of the purchaser. This is particularly true for a purchaser such as Brazil, which has become a power in its own right. Determination to keep pursuing a policy of self-sufficiency and diversification will encourage multiple suppliers as all foreign weaponry purchases gradually tend to decline.

Arms transfers nevertheless may help promote general European political relations, as well as commercial interests, with Brazil. But such improvements in the general political-economic climate probably will not be able to generate traditional kinds of influence for significant changes in national security policy. For example, increasing numbers of Western Europeans have been stationed in Brazil to service or give advice regarding weaponry acquired abroad, but most are civilians on short-term assignments.[62] Likewise, the Brazilian Navy has held exercises with both the British and French Navies, but only on an irregular basis, in contrast to the annual series of U.S.-Brazilian naval exercises. The Brazilian Naval Commission in Europe is similarly limited to technical and commercial matters relating to arms sales, and does not become directly involved in national political and security matters like the U.S. Naval Mission did.

The specific circumstances of the recent Brazilian arms purchases from Western Europe also illustrate the complexity of changing political-economic relationships. For example, diversification of arms sources was a consideration in the Brazilian decision to purchase frigates from Great Britain, but the decisive factors were availability of advanced technology, promise of continued technological innovation, and favorable financial conditions.[63] U.S. legislative restrictions on arms transfer policy at the time did block the sale by the United States on each score. Still, Brazil had first tried to buy frigates from the United States in spite of its diversification strategy, because unit cost was less and supply and part replacement was easier than in the case of Europe.

Because of such considerations U.S. weaponry is still frequently preferred, particulary for the air force and army, but in a number of areas of naval weaponry European countries have a competitive advantage.[64] British sales of sophisticated conventional submarines and West German sales of modern minesweepers to Brazil are examples of areas where the United States has not been sufficiently competitive. A problem of lack of U.S. competitiveness even arose later in the frigate case, making U.S. reentry into the market more difficult. At first, there was concern in Brazil about problems with the British method of gas turbine propulsion for the frigates, but this method has since proved satisfactory.[65] The United States is not competitive in gas turbine propelled frigates, although costs escalated and delivery times were considerably extended for the frigates, so enthusiasm for European naval weaponry remains qualified.

Even as the navy began to rely more heavily on European sources, it continued to benefit from surplus U.S. weaponry. Surplus U.S. destroyers, submarines, and auxiliary ships have all been transferred to the Brazilian Navy since the late 1960s. The U.S. vessels are useful for training, and provide a stopgap until the Brazilian Navy's modernization program is further advanced since they are available within several months after purchase. For example, Brazil still only has ten submarines, including the three new British submarines. Yet, World War II vintage craft from the United States have had increasingly short life spans when purchased and have involved serious repair problems, so new units with full life spans are now preferred.[66]

Several of the surplus U.S. submarines are already being retired. Surplus S2-E planes were also bought from the United States over the past few years for patrol and submarine surveillance off the aircraft carrier Minas Gerais, with similar problems and advantages.

A number of factors besides U.S. policy then contributed to the United States' decline as the dominant Latin American arms supplier. Latin American demand for sophisticated weaponry was greater than before, and European suppliers were active and competitive in meeting this demand, particularly in naval weaponry. The Brazilian naval case nevertheless indicates that the national goals of modernization, diversification, and self-sufficiency were compatible with a continuing major U.S. role as an arms supplier, and would have led to a much more gradual decline in the United States' position had U.S. responses been more positive. There clearly was not a deliberate naval policy of turning away precipitately from U.S. suppliers. The potential has therefore remained for the United States to reestablish a significant, if not a dominant, position in the Brazilian arms market in the late 1970s and 1980s.

Even trends during the first period, 1967-1973, suggested that European and U.S. suppliers would eventually divide the Latin American arms market more evenly. European arms sales to Latin America built up from an annual low of $59 million in 1967 to a peak of $589 million in 1970 as Latin American modernization programs gained momentum, and then declined to $177 million in 1971 and $138 million in 1972.[67] European arms sales to Latin America are likely to remain substantial, but are not likely to reach the earlier peak again because subsequent orders will tend to be limited largely to supplementing earlier modernization efforts, particularly since economic constraints have markedly increased. Similar trends characterize the Brazilian naval arms market. The volume of naval arms imports, while remaining considerable for the foreseeable future, is not likely to surpass the peak reached in the late 1960s and early 1970s. The first naval construction plan built up the nucleus of a modern, technologically sophisticated regional navy. The emphasis on self-sufficiency, plus subsequent economic constraints, promise to limit future naval imports largely to sophisticated warships that will flesh in earlier modernization efforts.

By 1972, U.S. policy also began to adapt to

accommodate the Latin American armed forces' modernization programs by raising the credit limit for
arms sales to the region from $75 million to $100
million, with an additional $50 million permitted at
the President's discretion. In December 1974 the
regional ceiling on arms credits for Latin America
was terminated altogether. On June 5, 1973, former
President Nixon announced another significant policy
change by authorizing the sale and financing through
military credits of F-5E supersonic jet fighter
planes to Brazil and four other South American countries (Argentina, Chile, Colombia and Venezuela).
At the time, Congress still barred the sale of relatively sophisticated jet aircraft to Latin American
countries, so the President used his authority to
waive the restrictions when important for national
security. The United States, it was argued, should
no longer attempt to determine for Latin American
governments what their reasonable military needs
should be, since the attempt to discourage them from
buying advanced military equipment had failed and
the United States was losing markets to other suppliers.

Policy readjustments on the U.S. side contributed to its reemergence as a major arms supplier to
Latin America. U.S. arms sales to the region jumped
from a low of $30 million in 1967 to $80 million in
1972.[68] Over the next few years, the United States
benefited from a continuing Latin American preference for U.S. weaponry and again managed to become
the largest single arms supplier to the region. But
the United States did not come to occupy a dominant
position as before, and the U.S. reemergence was
much less pronounced in the naval sector, where West
European states are particularly competitive, than
in aircraft sales.

In spite of the U.S. reemergence as a major
regional arms supplier, it is unlikely that Brazil
will again become extremely dependent on the United
States as an arms source. Particularly in the case
of naval weapons, in which European states are especially competitive and Brazilian imports will be
selective, the United States will not likely come to
dominate the market. The United States itself seems
to have become more aware of the pitfalls of a dependent diplomatic relationship in which close military, economic, and political ties with Brazil heavily influenced the policies of the client state.
But the readjustments in bilateral relations required for greater equality or mutual respect have
not been easy in practice.

Recent U.S. attempts to pressure Brazil in various areas related to naval affairs smack of expectations nurtured in an earlier patron-client relationship. Now inappropriate in an altered context, they have been counterproductive. The U.S. effort in the late 1960s to limit Latin American arms purchases and to discourage purchases of advanced weaponry failed and U.S. policy has subsequently been modified, but sales of major combatant vessels to Latin America are still barred, such as cruisers and aircraft carriers. In the areas of nuclear proliferation and human rights, the Carter administration has again tried to pressure Brazil, with a negative impact on general diplomatic relations and on naval relations as well. The Carter administration's drive to block the purchase by Brazil of nuclear reprocessing facilities from West Germany strained bilateral relations. Further aggravation occurred because of a March 1977 State Department report criticizing Brazilian human rights practices, which was required in connection with Congressional consideration of the security assistance appropriation.

In response to the 1977 State Department report, Brazil canceled the 1952 military assistance agreement with the United States, which although small at the time, did symbolize Brazilian displeasure. This terminated any further U.S. military aid, but did not affect accumulated credit or cash sales of arms. In a follow-up measure, several related arrangements were later canceled in September 1977, including the U.S. Naval Mission and JBUSMC. Actual termination of these accords occurred one year after the official requests for cancellation, in accord with the terms of reference of the accords.

Brazil's refusal to accept further military aid and the severing of special military ties does tend to weaken naval relations. The U.S. Naval Mission and JBUSMC historically helped promote close navy-to-navy relations, while common interests now must be pursued outside these traditional institutional channels. It is also feared by U.S. officials that resultant Brazilian ineligibility for foreign military sales purchases from the Department of Defense will lead to increased reliance on other sources for new equipment as problems of maintaining existing U.S. equipment worsen.[69] In fact, Western European arms manufacturers have stepped up their drive to negotiate weaponry co-production deals with Brazil since the military agreements with the United States were cancelled, and to some Brazilian officials the cancellation "was our declaration of military

sovereignty, and with these new /Western European7
deals we will have even more independence."[70] The
Brazilian government at the time did affirm its
willingness to continue cooperating with the U.S.
government both on the bilateral and multilateral
levels, but "also expressed its desire to keep the
relations between the two countries on the traditional basis of mutual respect and noninterference
in each other's internal affairs."[71]

Shared U.S.-Brazilian military and naval interests are still considerable. There is a broad consensus about the nature of the Cold War and the
communist threat. The conservative Brazilian military regime endorses the Western tradition and cap-
italism, and regards communism as posing a fundamental threat to these commonly held values. Military alliance with a superpower is consequently regarded as a necessary protection for Brazilian security in a hostile world, and the Rio Pact (Inter-
American Treaty of Reciprocal Assistance) continues
to commit Brazil and the United States to hemispheric defense. The U.S. Navy has similarly been regarded as an essential element in the defense of the
West by Brazilian naval planners.[72]

Brazil's 200-mile territorial sea is likewise
regarded by Brazilian planners as complementary to
U.S. strategic interests, since Soviet and other
ships with a potential for spying are placed therein
under increased vigilance and restrictions.[73] In
contrast, the U.S. Navy has been concerned that the
200-mile territorial sea would set a dangerous precedent in limiting world-wide naval mobility, so U.S.
global interests have outweighed any advantages
gained by restrictions on the activities of Soviet
warships in Brazilian territorial waters. Basic
shared security interests have nevertheless helped
minimize immediate practical difficulties. U.S.
officials have acknowledged that in spite of problems involving the 1970 200-mile territorial sea extension, Brazil continues to be interested in contributing to hemispheric defense and U.S. warships
are always welcome in Brazilian waters.[74] For example, Brazil and the United States cooperate in
tracking Soviet submarines, and U.S. subs are not
required to surface and show their flag when in the
Brazilian territorial sea, which strict enforcement
of Brazil's territorial sea claim would require.[75]

In addition to basic shared values, the joint
annual naval exercises organized by the United
States still include Brazilian participation. The
latest UNITAS operation, the nineteenth in the

series, was carried out in August 1978, and in February 1978 the latest operation in the Caribbean, READEX-I, was also carried out as part of a continuing series, both with Brazilian participation.

Close personal relations also continue between the two navies, albeit not now through special military and naval institutions. In fact, the extraordinary influence exerted by individuals such as Admirals Caperton during World War I and Ingram during World War II would not be compatible with the trend toward greater Brazilian independence. Naval contacts continue through the regular joint naval operations and the naval attachés. Frequent reciprocal visits of high-ranking U.S. and Brazilian naval officers, Inter-American Naval Conferences, and meetings with chiefs of staff and naval ministers of Latin American states also help promote close relations. For example, close navy-to-navy relations have been credited with a major role in working out a 1972 U.S.-Brazilian Shrimp Agreement, which accommodated differences over the territorial sea issue.[76]

The State Department, over opposition by the U.S. Navy, did complicate resolution of differences over the territorial sea issue at the time by threatening to recall U.S. naval vessels on loan if Brazil seized U.S. shrimp boats.[77] Such heavy-handed U.S. tactics linking weapons supplies with ocean resource issues, on at least this one occasion with Brazil and on numerous occasions with west coast South American states, have been poorly received in Brasília. This difference, plus other problems cited above, have strained bilateral military relations, but a mutually beneficial basis for military cooperation remains.

Continuing U.S.-Brazilian military links should benefit from a new institutional framework for mutual consultations more compatible with Brazil's status as an emerging power. A February 1976 memorandum of understanding between former Secretary of State Kissinger and Brazilian Foreign Affairs Minister Silveira provided for twice-yearly ministeral level discussions on outstanding issues, and was explicitly designed to recognize Brazil's new, larger role in world affairs. In the event military differences arise, this framework provides for discussions on a basis of equality rather than on a donor-recipient basis, which unavoidably had come to characterize the traditional institutional military links. This new institutional framework survived the dismantling of military institutional ties in 1977, and indeed could provide for a more viable, if looser, long-term military relationship.

Changing trends in U.S.-Brazilian naval relations then reflect some fundamental changes in regional and international politics, which require rethinking about traditional relationships between influence and international military contacts. Changing diplomatic relationships have made it difficult,
for example, to correlate the volume of supplier
arms sales with the degree of supplier influence.
In particular, the expected political impact of the
changing pattern of foreign arms suppliers on the
Brazilian Navy--declining U.S. influence and rising
West European influence--has been delayed for a number of reasons. The United States, it is true, was
not able to influence the course of Brazilian naval
modernization, navy-to-navy ties loosened on multiple fronts, and the navy, like all Brazilian armed
services, has wished to avoid a return to excessive
dependency. But U.S. influence still can prosper
through a more mature, equal partnership.

The Brazilian Navy clearly sees continuing cooperation with the United States as desirable and
as broadly complementary to political relationships,
if on a basis of mutual respect and equality. Ample
opportunities still exist for bilateral naval cooperation, which on more than one occasion has had a
beneficial effect on general diplomatic relations.
A basic core of political-military interests is
shared by Brazil and the United States, it is still
believed, which is not shared as completely by Brazil and Western Europe. U.S.-Brazilian naval relationships, it appears, are already being recast in a
more flexible, cooperative political mold. This
will not involve a regionally dominant, yet pliable,
proxy, as has apparently been envisaged in the Nixon
Doctrine. Evidence in this and the following chapter still indicates that a bilateral partnership can
continue to rest on important shared interests if
accommodations are made to Brazil's rising status.

NOTES

1. U.S., Arms Control and Disarmament Agency, World Military
Expenditures and Arms Transfers, 1967-1976 (Washington, D.C.:
Government Printing Office, 1978), pp. 121, 123.

2. "Brazil: A Major Contender in the Arms Business," Business
Week, July 31, 1978, p. 45. This estimate puts Brazilian arms
exports at $500 million annually by the 1980s. A Brazilian of-
ficial was recently reported as claiming that arms exports

would reach $1 billion by 1980. Larry Rohter, "W. Europeans Seek to Join Brazil in Production of Arms," Washington Post, May 8, 1978, p. 17.

3. World Military Expenditures..., p. 36 and passim. Brazil's 1975 military budget is cited as $2.38 billion in both current and constant dollars.

4. Ibid. The $1.6 billion is in current dollars, which in constant dollars is $1.5 billion.

5. The Military Balance: 1977-1978 (London: The International Institute for Strategic Studies, 1977), p. 68. The Military Balance: 1978-1979 (London: The International Institute for Strategic Studies, 1978), p. 72.

6. World Military Expenditures..., p. 36. Brazil's ratio is listed at 2.2% for 1975 and 1.3% for 1976. Because of the growth of the Brazilian economy, The Military Balance lists the same ratio for Brazil for 1977 as only 1.1%. The Military Balance: 1978-1979, p. 89. Military expenditures as a proportion of gross national product of other major South American states for 1975 and 1976 were respectively for Argentina, 2.3% and 2.4%, Chile, 4.3% and 1.9%, Colombia, 1.2% and 0.9%, Peru, 4.5% and 5.2%, and Venezuela, 2.1% and 1.8%. World Military Expenditures..., passim.

7. Latest World Bank estimates for growth rates for gross national product per capita from 1970-1975 are 6.2% for Brazil and 2.9% for Argentina. Gross national product for Brazil for 1975 is listed as $110.13 billion and that of Argentina as $39.33 billion, and preliminary estimates for 1976 are respectively $125.57 billion and $39.93 billion. World Bank Atlas (Washington, D.C.: World Bank, 1977), pp. 22, 30.

8. Boletim Federal, February 1973, p. 134ff. Diário Oficial, December 16, 1974.

9. Raymond V. B. Blackman, ed., Jane's Fighting Ships, 1968-69 (London: Sampson Low, Marston and Co., Ltd., 1968), p. 22. Practically all 65 Brazilian naval vessels were over a decade old in 1965 and many were at least two decades old, according to a table prepared by Paulo Lafayette Pinto, "A Marinha e a Construção de Navios de Guerra no Brasil," Revista Marítima Brasileira 94 (April-June 1974): 39.

10. Bases of calculating the size of the fleet vary, but estimates concur that there are around 100 ships in the Brazilian Navy. Jane's Fighting Ships lists 110 ships in the Brazilian pennant list. John E. Moore, ed., Jane's Fighting Ships, 1977-78 (New York: Franklin Watts, Inc., 1977), p. 40. The

Military Balance lists 100 ships for Brazil for 1977 and 95 for 1978. The Military Balance, 1977-1978, p. 68. The Military Balance, 1978-1979, p. 72.

11. Euclides Quandt de Oliveira, "Renovação dos Meios Flutuantes," Revista Marítima Brasileira 89 (January-March 1969): 48.

12. Adalberto de Barros Nunes, A Nova Marinha (Brasília: Serviço Gráfico do Senado Federal, 1970), pp. 9-11.

13. Jornal do Brasil, July 21, 1977, p. 15. The then navy minister estimated that the short-run size of the navy would be between 121-124 vessels and the long-term size would be more than 135. Adalberto de Barros Nunes, "Administração Naval," Revista Marítima Brasileira 93 (July-September 1973): 37.

14. Jane's Fighting Ships, 1968-69, pp. 2, 22, 520-521.

15. Jane's Fighting Ships lists 73 ships in the Argentine pennant list. Jane's Fighting Ships, 1977-78, p. 9. The Military Balance lists 74 ships for Argentina for 1977 and 75 for 1978. The Military Balance, 1977-1978, p. 67. The Military Balance, 1978-1979, p. 71. See also comment in footnote 10.

16. Jane's Fighting Ships, 1977-78, pp. 8-19, 40-50, and 796-797.

17. Brazil's armed forces total 273,800, while the next largest Latin American armed forces are those of Argentina, Cuba, Mexico, and Peru with 132,900, 159,000, 97,000 and 70,000 respectively. The Military Balance, 1978-1979. pp. 71-77, 91.

18. Ibid. The Brazilian Navy and Air Force respectively number 49,000 and 42,800, while the same armed services of Argentina respectively number 32,900 and 20,000. The Brazilian Marine Corps numbers about 13,500, which is included in the 49,000 figure for the navy.

19. Interviews.

20. Norman A. Bailey and Ronald M. Schneider, "Brazil's Foreign Policy: A Case in Upward Mobility," Inter-American Economic Affairs 27 (Spring 1974): 22-25. William Perry, "The Brazilian Armed Forces: Military Power and Conventional Capabilities of an Emerging Power," Military Review 58 (September 1978): 10-24.

21. Ibid. See also the following sources for references to regional Brazilian naval superiority. Kenneth E. Robert, U.S. Defense and the South Atlantic (Carlisle Barracks,

206

Pennsylvania: U.S. Army War College, 1976), p. 21. "Brazil: Naval Power," Latin America, November 3, 1972, p. 351. Eduardo Machicote, La Expansión brasileña: Notas para un estudio geohistórico (Buenos Aires, Argentina: Editorial Ciencia Nueva, 1973), pp. 44-46.

22. Luigi Einaudi, Hans Heymann, Jr., David Ronfeldt, and Cesar Sereseres, Arms Transfers to Latin America: Toward a Policy of Mutual Respect (Santa Monica, California: The Rand Corporation, 1973), pp. 25-26.

23. Geoffrey Kemp, "The Prospects for Arms Control in Latin America: The Strategic Dimensions," in Military Rule in Latin America: Function, Consequences and Perspectives, ed. Philippe C. Schmitter (Beverly Hills, California: Sage Publications, 1973), p. 217.

24. Edward N. Luttwak, The Political Uses of Sea Power (Baltimore: The Johns Hopkins University Press, 1974), p. 40. Italics in original.

25. Mark W. Janis, Sea Power and the Law of the Sea (Lexington, Massachusetts: D.C. Heath and Company, 1976), pp. 63-64.

26. Ibid., p. 63.

27. Michael A. Morris, "Brazil and India as Emerging Third World Powers," paper delivered at the annual meeting of the Latin American Studies Association, Pittsburgh, Pennsylvania, April 5-7, 1979.

28. Janis, p. 64.

29. The Military Balance, 1978-1979, pp. 72, 49, 89. World Military Expenditures...., p. 61.

30. Janis, pp. 84-92.

31. Several accounts have explicitly analyzed military aspects of the lobster war. T. Paul Messick, Jr., Maritime Resource Conflicts--Perspectives for Resolution (Chapel Hill, North Carolina: University of North Carolina Sea Grant Program, Sea Grant Publication UNC-SG-74-06, May 1974), pp. 5-18. D.P. O'Connell, The Influence of Law on Sea Power (Annapolis, Maryland: Naval Institute Press, 1975), pp. 7, 12, 115.

32. Luttwak, pp. 49-52.

33. E. Bradford Burns, The Unwritten Alliance: Rio-Branco and Brazilian-American Relations (New York: Columbia University Press, 1966), pp. 115, 132-135, 142, 176, 200.

207

34. David Healy, "Admiral William B. Caperton and United States Naval Diplomacy in South America, 1917-1919," Journal of Latin American Studies 8 (November 1976): 297-323.

35. Malcolm Lynn Pearce, "A Marinha Brasileira de 1900 à 1930," Navigator: Subsídios para História Marítima do Brasil 12 (December 1975): 70. 50.⁰ Aniversário da Missão Naval Americana no Brasil (Brasília: Marinha do Brasil, Relações Públicas, 1972), p. 4. Robert G. Nachman, "Dollars, Diplomacy and Dependency: The Failures and Success of the First United States Naval Mission to Brazil (1922-1930)," pp. 3, 8. (Unpublished manuscript)

36. Nachman, pp. 10ff. Frank D. McCann, Jr., The Brazilian-American Alliance: 1937-1945 (Princeton: Princeton University Press, 1973), pp. 328, 457.

37. Robert L. Scheina, "South American Navies: Who Needs Them?," U.S. Naval Institute Proceedings (February 1978): 63.

38. Lawrence F. Hill, "The United States," in Brazil, ed. Lawrence F. Hill (Berkeley: University of California Press, 1947), pp. 364-365.

39. McCann, pp. 43, 113.

40. Ibid., pp. 302-307 and passim.

41. Ibid., p. 294.

42. Ibid., pp. 295-296, 302.

43. The agreement setting up the Commissions "institutionalized a program of high-level exchange on security issues that is not found in other bilateral treaties in Latin America." Alfred Stepan, The Military in Politics: Changing Patterns in Brazil (Princeton: Princeton University Press, 1971), p. 129.

44. U.S., Congress, Senate, Hearings before the Subcommittee on Western Hemisphere Affairs of the Committee on Foreign Relations, United States Policies and Programs in Brazil (Washington, D.C.: U.S. Government Printing Office, 1971), p. 52. Testimony of Major General George S. Beatty, Chairman, U.S. Delegation, Joint Brazil-United States Military Commission.

45. Foreign Military Sales and Military Assistance Facts: December 1977 (Washington, D.C.: Data Management Division, Comptroller, DSAA, 1977), pp. 2, 5, 10, 18, 22, 27.

46. United States Policies..., pp. 84-85. Beatty testimony.

47. Ibid., p. 55.

48. Interviews not for direct attribution.

49. U.S. Department of State, <u>Arms Sales in Latin America</u>, Office of Media Services (July 1973), p. 2. <u>World Military Expenditures...</u>, p. 117ff.

50. <u>Arms Sales in Latin America</u>, p. 7.

51. "Marinha acha impossível interromper importações de equipamento militar," <u>Jornal do Brasil</u>, July 11, 1975, p. 13. The U.S. Admiral who was the last head of JBUSMC estimated that Brazil could not attain complete self-sufficiency in weaponry for at least ten years. U.S., Congress, House of Representatives, Hearing before a Subcommittee of the Committee on Government Operations, <u>United States Embassy Operations - Rio de Janeiro</u> (Washington, D.C.: U.S. Government Printing Office, 1978), p. 34. Testimony of Rear Admiral William Callaghan.

52. A recent article also noted that private shipbuilders frequently have benefited from personnel trained at the navy's shipbuilding school (Escola Técnica do Arsenal de Marinha). Yvon de A. Luz, "E Tempo de Construir," <u>Mar: Boletim do Clube Naval</u> 86 (September-October 1974): 10.

53. The navy minister, for example, called attention to coordination between naval and civilian shipbuilding in the electronics area and cooperation between private industry and the naval shipbuilding yard (Arsenal de Marinha do Rio de Janeiro). "Henning diz que plano de renovação da Marinha terá caráter nacionalizante," <u>Jornal do Brasil</u>, April 27, 1975, p. 2. A recent article likewise described measures taken by the navy to encourage the national electronics industry to develop a wide range of products for civilian and military use. José Lauria Sobral Morães, "A Indústria Eletrónica Brasileira e a Marinha de Guerra," <u>Revista Marítima Brasileira</u> 89 (April-June 1969): 85-93.

54. Larry Rohter, "U.S. Military Aid Rejected: Brazil Stepping Up Arms Output," <u>The Washington Post</u>, December 18, 1977, p. 1. Admiral Maximiano Eduardo da Silva Fonseca, besides being deeply involved with national naval warship construction as the navy's procurement chief (Diretor-Geral de Material da Marinha) under the Geisel administration, is also to be the new navy minister with the Figueiredo administration, which will take office on March 15, 1979.

55. Carlos Eduardo Rodrigues da Costa, "Submarinos: Reparo-Construção, O Gerente do Projeto, Sinopses," <u>Revista Marítima</u>

Brasileira 98 (April–June 1978), pp. 9–26. Larry Rohter's article cited above, "W. Europeans Seek to Join Brazil in Production of Arms," reviews the major weapons co-production agreements either concluded or being discussed with Western European states, including warships and submarines.

56. Foreign Military Sales..., pp. 2, 5.

57. Einaudi et al., p. 53.

58. John W. Tuthill, "Operation Topsy," Foreign Policy (Fall 1972): 62–85. A recent Rand Corporation study made a similar recommendation of reorienting the present advisory mission system to provide a small interservice group acting as liaison on professional problems of management, organization, and training. Einaudi et al., p. 68.

59. Einaudi et al., p. 13.

60. Arms Sales in Latin America, pp. 8–9.

61. Ibid., p. 44.

62. United States Policies..., p. 152. Beatty testimony.

63. A Nova Marinha, p. 17.

64. For explicit official U.S. acknowledgement of European competitive advantage in a number of areas of naval weaponry with respect to Latin America in general and Brazil in particular, see United States Foreign Policy, 1971: A Report of the Secretary of State (Washington, D.C.: U.S. Government Printing Office, 1972), pp. 134–135.

65. Euclides Quandt de Oliveira, pp. 49–50.

66. Ibid., pp. 54–55, 57.

67. Arms Sales in Latin America, p. 10.

68. Ibid.

69. United States Embassy Operations..., pp. 33–34. Callaghan testimony.

70. Larry Rohter, "W. Europeans Seek to Join Brazil in Production of Arms."

71. Several recent authoritative U.S. studies have concurred in recommending such an approach to arms transfers to Latin America as a "policy of mutual respect." Einaudi et al.,

especially Chapter VI. Report by the Commission on United States-Latin American Relations, The Americas in a Changing World (New York City: Center for Inter-American Relations, 1974), pp. 23-26. A Second Report by the Commission on United States-Latin American Relations, The United States and Latin America: Next Steps (New York City: Center for Inter-American Relations, 1976), pp. 12-13.

72. Hilton Berutti Augusto Moreira, "Mar: Caminho do Progresso do Brasil," Segurança e Desenvolvimento 20 (1971): 141. Fernando Paulo Nunes Baptista, "O Mar Territorial Brasileiro," Revista Marítima Brasileira 91 (January-March 1971): 51. Footnote 50 in Chapter 6 refers more specifically to Brazilian expectations about the need for continuing U.S. involvement in the South Atlantic.

73. Mucio Piragibe Ribeiro de Bakker, "Soberania Marítima," in Mar Territorial, 2 (Brasília: Marinha do Brasil, 1972), pp. 541-542. A Questão do Mar Territorial Brasileiro (Brasília: Gabinete do Ministro da Marinha, n.d.), p. 12.

74. United States Policies..., pp. 282-283. Testimony by U.S. Ambassador to Brazil William M. Rountree. Admiral Hill, the former chief of the U.S. Naval Mission to Brazil, likewise confirmed that the Brazilian President had stated that the U.S. Navy was welcome at any time in Brazilian waters. But he also cited a December 1970 example in which Brazil, supported by the U.S. political officer, requested that an upcoming U.S. naval exercise to be held in the 200-mile territorial sea be held outside the area instead. The navy went on ahead and quickly held the exercise, including flight operations for training, within the 200 miles without further immediate repercussion. Clarence A. Hill, "U.S. Law of the Sea Position and Its Effect on the Operating Navy: A Naval Officer's View," Ocean Development and International Law Journal 3 (1976): 342. But no other U.S. unilateral naval exercises have been held since in Brazil's 200 miles. In fact, Hjertonsson reports that "The United States Air Force is said to avoid flying over the area" (the Brazilian 200-mile territorial sea), because "Asking for permission would imply recognition, while flying without permission could lead to politically undesirable clashes." Karin Hjertonsson, The New Law of the Sea: Influence of the Latin American States on Recent Developments of the Law of the Sea (Leiden, Holland: A.W. Sijthoff, 1973), p. 60. Each side therefore has remained concerned with legal precedent, although this has not led to actual bilateral military clashes.

75. Elio Monnerat Solon de Pontes, Professor of International Law at the Universidade Federal Fluminense, was consulted by the Brazilian Navy on this matter of policy toward U.S. submarines in late 1972. He reported that lack of strict

adherence to the law with respect to U.S. submarines would not compromise Brazilian control over the 200 miles and would instead complement bilateral military cooperation with the U.S. and global deterrence. This permission view toward mobility of U.S. submarines was endorsed de facto by the navy. Professor Monnerat's view was all the more significant, since he was a central figure in the 1969-1970 campaign to extend the territorial sea to 200 miles, as indicated in Chapter 2. Interview with Elio Monnerat Solon de Pontes, Niterói, Brazil, November 26, 1974.

76. Robert O. Keohane and Joseph S. Nye, Power and Interdependence: World Politics in Transition (Boston: Little, Brown and Company, 1977), pp. 116, 252. Keohane and Nye state that they reached this conclusion on the basis of interviews. Interviews by this author corroborate their conclusion.

77. Clarence Hill, p. 345.

6. Naval Interests and Missions

Naval trends surveyed in the last chapter reflect a larger process of change in the hierarchy of Brazilian naval interests. First, the impact of change on the hierarchy of Brazilian naval interests will be analyzed, which in turn will allow us to distinguish between core naval interests and secondary naval interests. Naval missions will be deduced therefrom.

A CHANGING HIERARCHY OF NAVAL INTERESTS

Naval interests can be categorized as core and secondary, but such a hierarchy of naval interests can only be relative during a period of change. Changing U.S.-Brazilian naval relations, analyzed in the last chapter, illustrate both the problems and possibility of categorizing and ordering naval interests.

Close relations with the United States, including close navy-to-navy relations, were always regarded as a means toward larger ends. Policy ends have subsequently evolved, but a shared community of interests still remains. The prognosis for U.S.-Brazilian naval relations was accordingly somewhat uncertain because of the complex blend of change and continuity in Brazilian naval interests, as well as the complexity and ambiguity of events extraneous to those interests but still affecting them. Certain basic conclusions were nevertheless possible. Domestic factors were the decisive considerations in gradually reassessing naval relations with the United States, most particularly the objectives of modernization, diversification, and self-sufficiency, which motivated and sustained the related

foreign policy goal of greater independence.
Brazil's growth facilitated achievement of these
objectives, and itself reinforced the determination
of policy-makers to lessen dependency on the United
States. International events helped determine the
exact shape and rate of implementation of these domestic objectives.

Similar conclusions characterize the larger
hierarchy of Brazilian naval interests. Core interests are basically domestic in nature or orientation, and secondary interests involve broader international roles. Similar ambiguities qualify this
conclusion. The dividing line between domestic and
international interests is by no means clear. Offensive and defensive naval missions and equipment
functions likewise overlap. For example, anti-submarine warfare weaponry generally can help perform
other functions as well, such as coastal patrolling
and maintenance of internal security. The six frigates are a case in point, since they can be targeted
toward either coastal or deep water roles, with four
frigates designated as anti-submarine in nature and
the rest general purpose. Finally, naval policy
sometimes has been guided by purpose, yet at other
times it has been propelled by events extraneous to
the navy. Each of these kinds of ambiguities will
be illustrated, in order to suggest the relativity
between core and secondary interests.

Defense and development of the 200-mile territorial sea is the central core interest, but here,
too, ambiguity is present. The extent to which this
core interest is domestic or international in nature
is a matter of debate. To Brazilian naval planners,
this is an area of exclusive domestic responsibility
under national sovereignty, with foreign ships only
enjoying a right of innocent passage. Establishment
of such exclusive control over the 200 miles necessarily involves national security functions, although from the Brazilian perspective, as noted previously, this is compatible with U.S. security interests. Brazil has been edging away from this
extreme territorialist position, and would likely
accept some compromise emerging from the law of the
sea negotiations, such as free transit. But navy
interest in maintaining responsibility for the 200
miles still infuses the Brazilian position with a
claim to manage security in the area. The U.S.
perspective, in contrast, recognizes no legitimate
national security functions beyond a twelve-mile
territorial sea which are exclusive in nature or can

214

exclude others. The law of the sea negotiations have brought U.S. acceptance of national resource responsibilities beyond twelve miles, but the U.S. still insists that for security purposes waters beyond that limit are high seas. Accordingly, the United States has regarded the Brazilian drive to assert sovereignty and perform exclusive security functions out to 200 miles as either illegitimate or as an expansion of international roles by the Brazilian Navy.

Just as the dividing line between domestic and international interests in the 200 miles has been fuzzy, so have purposes there been unclear. The drive for a 200-mile territorial sea was not primarily motivated by navel interests, as noted in Chapter 2, and the navy eventually only threw its support behind the measure when it became evident that institutional roles would grow and prosper therefrom. This ambiguity of purpose of the 200 miles resulted in some ambiguity of roles. Increasing attention and effort have been directed toward patrolling of the broad swath of territorial sea claimed, in order to establish a Brazilian presence and to prevent unauthorized foreign fishing, research, or military activities. But the frigates are more appropriate for repelling foreign military threats out to considerable distances from shore than for such routine patrol activities.

A final element of ambiguity affecting the entire hierarchy of Brazilian naval interests is related to Brazil's growth. Growth provides a dynamic, changing environment for both domestic and international interests, and tends to encourage expansive, relative definitions of each.

Progress toward great power status, at the present initial stage, is seen as resulting primarily through rapid internal integration and development, since domestic growth can be an engine for promoting international status. For example, a recurring theme in Brazilian foreign policy statements is that as a nation grows, so do its foreign interests and involvement in international relations. Expansion of foreign policy interests is accordingly regarded as largely a function of the domestic economy, which has been growing quite rapidly, and time is regarded as working in Brazil's favor. In this view, international interests will tend to expand as opportunities arise, and interests which are now secondary may gradually acquire greater importance.

From a somewhat different perspective, the
security-development doctrine links national growth
to expansion of security responsibilities as well.
Adequate security measures are required to provide
a congenial environment for development, so as development proceeds, security responsibilities will
need to grow accordingly. Such a broad, expansive
definition of national security also encourages
involvement of the armed services, including the
navy, in economic development tasks, especially
those vital for integration or progress but not
easily performed by the private sector or civilian
ministries. In 1970, when the territorial sea was
extended, the ocean focus of the security-development doctrine was implicitly expanded as well from
12 to 200 miles.

This general domestic and foreign policy orientation toward Brazil's emergence as a major power
finds explicit expression as well in naval affairs.
In particular, considerable navy thinking has been
devoted to elaboration of the concepts of Brazilian
maritime power (poder maritimo brasileiro) and its
relationship to naval power or sea power (poder
naval).[1] Maritime power refers to the support all
economic and military factors related to rivers and
the sea provide toward achievement of security and
development goals. Maritime policy is what actually
mobilizes, coordinates, and directs the elements of
maritime power toward these goals, and the navy has
the key role in coordinating maritime policy. The
navy accordingly provides security for all economic
activities in the maritime sphere through naval
power, which is the military component of maritime
power, and itself carries out important economic
development and national integration functions. Because maritime affairs are of increasing importance
for Brazil, naval power is particularly important
for continued national emergence as a great power
and naval expansion is a necessary concomitant to
national growth. Just as other great powers have
relied and still rely heavily on maritime and naval
power, Brazil requires a navy worthy of its status
as an emerging major power. In fact, the navy's
responsibilities are so important that it has "to
grow more rapidly than Brazil grows," according to
the then navy minister.[2]

Brazilian attitudes toward great power status, the security-
development doctrine, and the maritime-naval power doctrine then
all tend to encourage expansion of naval interests. Sometimes
pressure for expansion is directly related to navy responsibili-

216

ties, while at other times, expansion of naval interests tends to be spurred by factors extraneous to the navy, such as the rate of national growth and the rapidity of expansion of general foreign policy interests. Either way, secondary interests involving broader international roles than are currently feasible may gain favor as Brazil grows. In fact, Brazilian naval interests have been expanding concomitantly with Brazil's emergence as a major power.

Growing naval capabilities, too, make ambitious roles more feasible, and very well may tend to stoke Brazilian ambitions and expand naval interests. The first 10-year naval expansion program built the foundation of a credible regional navy, on which the second 10-year expansion program is now elaborating. Future expansion has been facilitated, and, should circumstances or policy eventually so require, expansion could be more easily accelerated.

In spite of pressures for expansion of naval interests, naval security responsibilities will probably tend to grow only gradually as long as Brazil continues to enjoy a relatively benign security environment. No immediate security threat has been posed for Brazilian frontiers or coastal waters, or in the South Atlantic, in recent years. Concern has mounted recently about a Soviet threat in the South Atlantic, but this has not yet altered the basic naval policy priority of domestic over international interests. Should a more immediate security threat be posed or perceived, it could shift policy emphasis toward international security responsibilities. It has also been argued that South American militaries are placing renewed emphasis on external defense missions, because of increasing regional autonomy resulting from the tendency toward multipolarity, as well as the external defense emphasis of geopolitical thought.[3] However, hallmarks of Brazilian foreign policy under the successive military governments have been caution and moderation, and the navy still remains targeted primarily toward domestic development and security concerns.

In sum, ambiguity of Brazilian naval interests stems more from the complexity of circumstances and the continuing growth of national power than from confusion or disagreement within the navy. The bitter debate between the air force and the navy over respective jurisdictional rights over naval aviation, settled in 1965, was inter-service rather

than intra-service in nature. The 1969-1970 200-
mile territorial sea debate seems to have been the
only instance of a great debate splitting the navy
since 1964, when the military came to power. Even
this only involved determination of the proper legal
and political framework for defending naval interests and carrying out naval roles, rather than
disagreement over what those interests and roles
ought to be. Accordingly, there has been considerable consensus within the navy about threat perception and appropriate roles, including which interests are core or vital in nature and which are
secondary. However, ambiguities mentioned could
lead to subsequent disagreement about roles and
interests.

CORE INTERESTS

The general internal focus both of the security-development doctrine and of successive military
governments since 1964 has determined that domestic
concerns would likewise guide the evolution of naval
interests and missions. The predominant policy
thrust has been protection and promotion of national
security and development, although within these
general guidelines, as noted, there has been much
ambiguity.

National Security and Development

In brief, the navy is responsible for providing
security for all internal waterways and for the territorial sea, in order to provide a stable environment favorable for development. This basic security
mission of the navy is broadened at times to include direct responsibility for and involvement in
development tasks.

There is vivid awareness in the navy that the
core security-development mission must be firmly
assured before the navy can contemplate seriously
other more ambitious roles. The focus of the navy
on domestic security and development is not only
determined by broad policy guidelines, but is also
reinforced by the immensity of the tasks assigned.

As a result of the one policy measure extending
the territorial sea from 12 to 200 miles in 1970,
the area of naval responsibility was multiplied about
16 times to 920,000 square miles. This enormous
maritime zone, which extends out 200 miles from the

4,500 mile maritime frontier all along the littoral and around the islands, is the equivalent of almost one-third of Brazil's huge 3.3 million square mile land surface. The broad continental shelf averages 100 miles all along the littoral, but does not extend beyond 200 miles at any point. In comparative terms, Brazil's land surface is fifth largest in the world, the littoral is nineth longest, and the area of the continental shelf out to a depth of 200 meters is eighth. In spite of the recent modernization and expansion of the navy and the air force, capabilities are still spread thin in trying to defend the 200-mile territorial sea.

The nation's extensive 31,000 mile river network, of which more than a third is navigable, involves the navy in numerous security and development tasks as well. The 1.6 million square miles of the Brazilian portion of the Amazon basin alone cover practically half of the national territory, and, with the other river networks, lend a riverine environment to many of Brazil's frontier regions with ten other states.

The strictly military portion of the key security-development mission reflects certain common Latin American perceptions about maritime threats. All countries in the region are developing and none are a great power, although there is increasing regional determination to lessen both the economic and strategic vulnerability which have traditionally flowed from subordinate status. This broadly shared determination, both to promote national development and to deter or discourage great power strategic interference or intervention in internal affairs, includes ocean areas over which national jurisdiction or sovereignty is claimed. Latin American ocean policies, including that of Brazil, have accordingly stressed national control of resources in broad offshore zones to promote both economic development and territorial defense.

Great maritime powers, so the Latin American argument goes, oppose extensive offshore claims of developing states and support freedom of the seas in order to "assure hegemony over the seas, as an instrument of political and military domination, or of commercial and economic exploitation."[4] Naval threats to Latin American ocean interests may occur indirectly through unilateral great power encroachments on the common heritage of mankind, represented through the prospective international seabed authority, or directly through encroachment on national ocean zones. In particular, the Latin American concern has been that the increasing turn of the superpower arms race toward the oceans threatens to lead to the military colonization of the deep seabed and superjacent waters.[5] Superpower interests are defined so expansively, Latin American spokesmen also fear, that their high seas military activities will extend as well into the national ocean space of other states. Conflicts which could arise involving the coastal state include superpower attempts to dominate areas claimed as national waters, to assure maximum mobility for nuclear submarines, and to place military installations on the continental shelves of other states.[6]

From a different perspective, U.S. policymakers have also foreseen conflicts between resource and military uses of the deep seabed, the high seas, and national zones. The U.S. concern has been that strong economic powers of an international seabed authority could extend into areas affecting superpower military interests, while creeping jurisdiction in national zones might eventually restrict traditional high seas freedoms enjoyed by naval powers.

It is consequently misleading to argue, as many have, that Latin American ocean policies have been solely resource-oriented.[7] Rather, there is general regional concern with both strategic and economic vulnerability of ocean, as well as continental, space. In order to prevent further alleged abuses by the great maritime powers sanctioned through traditional ocean rules, Latin American and other developing states have increasingly united to support a New Law of the Sea, in turn part of a larger drive for a New International Economic Order. This trend has been expressed in the law of the sea negotiations, analyzed in Chapter 4, but the focus of the conference on economic resource issues has led to the misleading conclusion that Latin American concerns are exclusively economic in nature. Measures calling for restraint in naval activities have not figured explicitly on the UNCLOS III agenda, but are inherent in the main theme of the conference, the peaceful use of ocean space, so that security considerations have played "an important role in the shaping of individual states' positions on practically all the issues involved."[8]

Developing states, including those of Latin America, then tend to regard great-power military, economic, and political interests as a multifaceted challenge to their own policies, and have reacted in opposition on each front to build a new order for the oceans and for the world economy. With military governments in most important South American states, sensitivity to security interests is understandable.

Brazil shares the general Latin American concern with maintaining the integrity of national ocean space, but national circumstances and tradition distinguish its pursuit of this key objective. Brazil's growing navy and increasingly sophisticated foreign policy establishment contrast with more limited naval and diplomatic capabilities of other states in the region. Brazil has therefore been able to take a particularly active, multifaceted approach toward control of national ocean space. Active Brazilian concern with maintenance of security out to 200 miles dates from the March 25, 1970 decree-law, whose introductory exposition of motives explicitly mentions the needs of national security and defense.

> . . . each state has competence to fix its territorial sea within reasonable limits, taking into account geographical and biological factors, as well as the needs of the population and its national security and defense.[9]

Article 3 of the main body of the March 1970 Brazilian decree explicitly stated as well that the claim asserts control over military activities out to 200 miles: "The Brazilian Government shall issue regulations that, for reasons of security, it deems necessary to be observed by warships and other ships belonging to a foreign state."[10] This has been called the "first explicit reference in Latin American 200-mile legislation" to security interests.[11]

Ambiguities have subsequently emerged in the Brazilian claim, as noted, including special privileges for the U.S. Navy, although Brazil continues to oppose U.S. unilateral naval exercises within its 200-mile territorial sea.[12] Access to the 200 miles provided to the U.S. Navy is still regarded as subject to national regulation, and Brazil has consistently expressed its intention to exclude Soviet warships from the 200-mile territorial sea.

Since all Latin American states are concerned with maintaining the integrity of national ocean space, Brazilian concern with maintaining security out to 200 miles does not really set it apart from other states in the region. Instead, it would be more accurate to conclude that greater ambiguity of ocean claims and lesser naval capabilities distinguish other Latin American states from Brazil. Ocean security interests elsewhere in the region are less directly expressed and less capable of enforcement. For example, it has been debated for years whether the ocean claim of Peru, perhaps the most prominent Latin American state in revising the traditional law of the sea, is to a territorial sea or to some kind of resource zone. The extent of Peru's resource and security aims has consequently remained rather unclear, although by design. Peruvian planners and negotiators, from a position of relative naval weakness, have intentionally relied on this ambiguity to promote and protect their claim.[13]

The claim of Argentina, Brazil's traditional rival and most credible regional naval competitor, is likewise ambiguous. Argentina's claim is generally regarded as less extensive than a territorial sea, but evidence nevertheless suggests that it does seek to regulate foreign military activities in the 200-mile area, including the operation of nuclear submarines.[14] Argentina still has been hesitant to support a 200-mile territorial sea, in part because of concern that such a precedent might allow Brazil to prohibit northbound navigation and overflying in the event of eventual hostile relations. Chile shares a similar navigational and overflight concern vis-à-vis its northern neighbor, Peru.[15]

While Brazil's ocean security interests out to at least 200 miles are not unique in Latin America, Brazilian doctrine and capabilities have gone further in fleshing out and sustaining such interests. A central ocean security interest is defense, not just patrolling, of the 200 miles. All the modern naval weaponry recently acquired by Brazil--submarines, frigates, and minesweepers--is more appropriate for maintenance of security within and perhaps even beyond the 200 miles than for routine patrolling, for which less sophisticated equipment can suffice. Brazilian sea and air power are becoming sufficiently developed, according to military planners, to deter great power intervention or unfriendly acts in Brazilian waters and to make Brazilian cooperation desirable in defending the major maritime trade routes of the South Atlantic.[16]

The defense of sea lanes has become increasingly important to Brazil as the merchant marine has

grown. Exports carried by the merchant marine have
played a key role in Brazil's continuing economic
expansion,[17] and have contributed to greater interest in the defense of sea lanes than other Latin
American states. While defense of sea lanes in the
South Atlantic will necessarily involve cooperation
between allies for the foreseeable future, Brazil
has moved unilaterally to secure shipping in its own
waters. The Brazilian Navy stands out in Latin
America in having a growing, respectable anti-submarine warfare capability, while other Latin American navies are largely limited to anti-surface warfare capability. Only Brazil has been developing
a significant capability for anti-submarine warfare,
as well as anti-surface and anti-air warfare,
through a sizable mix of submarines, frigates,
destroyers, minesweepers, planes and helicopters,
and associated weapons systems.[18]

Several other 200-mile security interests
involve deterrence of sea-based threats to Brazilian
waters. For example, increased surveillance out to
200 miles can discourage or prevent foreign spying,
particularly by spy vessels in the guise of fishing
craft. This would deny the enemy knowledge of
coastal defenses, prevent unauthorized mapping or
research about the continental shelf and superjacent
waters for possible military uses, and tend to enhance Brazilian maritime defenses accordingly.[19] It
is debatable whether there ever was any significant
foreign spying off the Brazilian coast, but this was
a frequent claim during the 1969-1970 territorial
sea debate. Accordingly, foreign fishing vessels
have been monitored for their compliance with
security, as well as fishing, regulations.

Still another security interest reinforces
Brazil's continuing determination to meet and repel
challenges in the 200-mile territorial sea. A
Brazilian naval presence out to 200 miles, instead
of six or twelve miles as previously, substantially
"broadens the first line of maritime security" protecting the Brazilian littoral. This has been
regarded by navy planners as significantly enhancing
deterrence of overseas support for subversion
through clandestine arms shipments or infiltration
of terrorists.[20] The then air force minister has
likewise stressed seaborne revolutionary warfare
threats to Brazil, as well as more conventional
maritime threats posed by foreign warships and
planes, including a possible repetition of the
Lobster War, all of which require particularly close

inter-service cooperation.[21]

A related 200-mile security interest is to prevent and deter foreign powers from locating military weaponry on the continental shelf, while permitting Brazil to do so, if necessary, at some future date.[22] Several measures have been taken to protect this security interest in the broad Brazilian shelf.

First, on the naval front, Brazil has moved to assert military control over waters superjacent to the continental shelf, which would also facilitate military control of the shelf itself. The growing surface combatant capability has been complemented in this respect by an increasingly sophisticated submarine force and anti-submarine warfare capability, which in normal circumstances might exercise a deterrent effect. But it still would be very difficult for Brazil to try to prevent a determined adversary with nuclear submarines from making military use of the shelf. Accordingly, Brazil has relied on legal, as well as naval, means to deter any foreign military presence on the shelf.

Second, on the negotiating front, from 1968-1971, Brazil emerged as a particularly influential advocate of extensive coastal states' rights at the twenty-five state Geneva seabed arms control negotiations.[23] Brazil favored complete demilitarization of the seabed in principle, but objected to the Soviet proposal for immediate and complete seabed disarmament. Instead, it supported the United States' proposal for a ban on nuclear weapons only beyond a twelve-mile seabed zone as a first step toward comprehensive seabed disarmament. Brazil did compromise in accepting a twelve-mile seabed area for the purpose of the treaty, but bargained hard throughout the negotiations to assure that the ban would be compatible with extensive coastal states' rights out to 200 miles. For example, Brazil supported an unsuccessful Canadian drive for recognition in the treaty of a coastal state right to rely on defensive weaponry in the 200-mile zone. More successful was Brazilian insistence that coastal states be entitled to participate in any verification activities and that such activities not restrict the rights of coastal states with respect to exploration and exploitation of their continental shelves. Both Brazilian demands were included in clauses in the 1971 treaty, primarily because Brazil went further than any other state in the negotiations in bluntly refusing to sign the treaty if its core interests were not protected in this way.[24]

224

The seabed arms control negotiations, 1968-1971, overlapped the 1970 Brazilian 200-mile territorial sea decision, although strong coastal state rights over the continental shelf was an interest supported by Brazil throughout the negotiations. The seabed disarmament negotiations therefore illustrate a theme developed previously in this study from an historical perspective--continuity of policy and interests in spite of changes flowing from the 1970 territorial sea decision.[25]

Related negotiations leading to the 1967 Latin American nuclear weapons-free zone agreement (Treaty of Tlateloco) evoked similar Brazilian security concerns, but this time with less direct reference to ocean affairs. The treaty prohibited nuclear weapons in both continental territory and coastal zones subject to national sovereignty of Latin American states. Both Argentine and Brazil have had serious misgivings about the treaty, because they have regarded it as restricting their desire to develop peaceful nuclear explosives. Argentine and Brazilian opposition to the treaty has focused so much on the nuclear option issue that the applicability of the ban to ocean space, as well as to continental territory, has not been a key factor in the debate. Dominance of national security interests over regional and global interests nevertheless links Brazilian attitudes toward the 1968 Tlateloco treaty and the 1971 seabed arms control treaty. Brazil ratified and signed the treaty, but is still not bound by its provisions until all other Latin American states likewise sign and ratify it, and until protocols are also signed and ratified by all nuclear weapons states and all foreign states with territories in the region. Since these conditions will not easily be met, Brazil does not feel constrained by the treaty provisions.

A final naval mission in the 200-mile territorial sea is defense of economic resources, especially fishing and offshore petroleum. The need for greater protection of fishing resources from alleged foreign depredations was one of the reasons cited for declaring a 200-mile territorial sea. In the first year of extended patrolling out to 200 miles, 1971, when foreign challenges to Brazilian fishing regulations were at their peak, the navy undertook 106 patrol missions, with 61 in the north, 31 in the northeast, and 14 in the southeast.[26] Besides the gradual build-up of patrol capabilities of the air force and navy, naval deployment toward the major

fishing zones in the southeast, northeast, and north
has been facilitated by diversification away from
Rio de Janeiro. Greater naval decentralization is
being achieved through expansion of naval facilities
in Belem, the gateway to the Amazon, and at Natal
and Bahia (Aratu) in the northeast, and through
development of a new base at Santa Maria in Rio
Grande do Sul.

Offshore oil was also a consideration, if not
the key one, in declaring a 200-mile territorial
sea, since the 1958 Geneva provision for sovereignty
over the continental shelf for resource purposes
only was regarded as insufficient protection. Offshore oil wells might need to be located beyond the
traditional narrow limits of the territorial sea,
it was believed. There, associated surface installations would not benefit from national control. A
200-mile territorial sea would guarantee national
sovereignty over both the shelf and superjacent
waters, and therefore would provide a firmer basis
for protecting offshore oil.[27] Indeed, recent
Brazilian oil finds on the continental shelf have
been well beyond even the maximum traditional territorial sea limit of twelve miles. As offshore
oil production has grown, plans for the defense of
offshore oil wells have recently been prepared as
well.[28]

Control of resources on the continental shelf
and in superjacent waters may have to be sustained
at times by threat of use of military force, but
defense of resources is not primarily responsible
for the growth of naval capabilities. It was noted
that all the modern weaponry recently acquired by
Brazil is more appropriate for maintenance of security within and perhaps even beyond the 200 miles
than for routine patrolling, for which less sophisticated equipment can suffice. In fact, relatively
modest patrol forces spread out somewhat thinly have
sufficed to prevent unauthorized foreign fishing
activities. For example, only ten ocean patrol vessels were eventually approved in the naval modernization program to cover the 200-mile territorial sea
all along the extensive littoral, although the navy
had originally requested fifty such vessels to patrol a territorial sea at the time only six miles in
breadth.[29] Since 1970 there has still been increasing international respect for Brazilian regulation over fishing out to 200 miles, due to general
recognition of such coastal state fishing rights at
the third law of the sea conference as well as to

226

relatively modest Brazilian air and naval patrolling activities. With national fishing rights already being consolidated with existing capabilities and defense of offshore oil facilities only a recent concern, more versatile, extensive naval forces have consequently been built up through the successive naval modernization programs to support the other, more ambitious security roles in the 200-mile territorial sea.

Both security and development missions have also involved the navy in numerous activities along the littoral and throughout the nation's extensive riparian network. Security in riverine environments, both near the frontier and in the sparsely settled interior, is being reinforced by more vessels and more frequent naval patrols, assisted by the marines. Anti-guerrilla fluvial exercises with Paraguay, mentioned earlier, are also held annually. A wide variety of civic action and developmental activities are carried out by the navy as well along the littoral and throughout the riparian network. The navy is responsible for security and training for the merchant marine, management of ports, contentional coast guard duties, riverine and maritime mapping and navigational aids, and a variety of services for civilians, particularly medical and dental services for isolated communities. All three armed services have been heavily involved in such developmental activities, for which almost one third of their budgets have been allocated.[30]

Naval activities in the Amazon illustrate both security and developmental missions. The Amazon has been a security concern because of imputed foreign designs on a neglected, but allegedly wealthy, area and because of occasional guerilla activities. The Amazon has been a developmental concern as well because of the failure to integrate this vast, sparsely populated area into the national economy and life. More positively, maintenance of security and rapid development of the Amazon through collaboration among the three armed services is viewed as a key factor in projecting Brazil as a great power.[31] The impact of Amazonian roadbuilding has not been as great as originally expected, but fluvial transportation still provides a relatively cheap alternative at a time of high energy costs for access to the world's largest hydrographic net.

The Amazon Fleet has accordingly been expanded to five river patrol ships, all of which were locally produced and equipped for civic action missions

as well as for more conventional riverine patrol
duties. In 1977, in nineteen missions the Amazon
Fleet performed patrol duties covering 24,327 miles,
and made further progress in mapping and researching
the Amazonian network. Civic action activities included 14,512 medical treatments, 7,872 dental treatments 68 laboratory tests, and 36,896 vaccina-
tions[32] While not large in absolute numbers, these
statistics are nevertheless impressive because of
the sparse Amazonian population, much of which had
previously been inaccessible to modern medical attention. Similar civil action missions are performed by the smaller Mato Grosso Fleet, as well as
along the ocean littoral.

     The River Plate basin has been prominent on the
diplomatic front, primarily because of the inability
of Argentina and Brazil to agree on sharing of hy-
dro-electric resources. But in this case, unlike
the Amazon, the navy has not become heavily involved
on either the security or development fronts, and
hence there are no significant linkages here between
non-maritime international water resources and maritime policy. More generally, it will be recalled
that Brazilian geopolitical thinking has not integrated ocean issues with its major focus on land
masses.[33] On the Argentine side, such linkages have
existed, apparently as a defensive reaction to
numerous Brazilian continental and maritime initiatives. In particular, much Argentine geopolitical
thought has linked expansion of Brazilian influence
in the River Plate basin with Brazilian continental
and maritime expansion elsewhere as part of a master
plan for achieving South American hegemony. Brazilian expansion in the River Plate basin is accordingly regarded as part of a larger Brazilian strategy to expand influence in the Amazon toward the west
coast of South America and the Caribbean, in Mato
Grosso toward the west coast of South America and
southwards, in the South Atlantic, and toward
Antarctica.[34] In the next section, these various
alleged elements of Brazilian strategy will be discussed insofar as they indeed do relate to ocean
affairs.

SECONDARY INTERESTS

     Brazil's emergence as a major power and its
associated rise as Latin America's premier naval
power promises to alter the regional diplomatic con-

stellation, and hence has been the object of much speculation. Unfortunately, speculation about likely Brazilian major power and naval roles has often been based more on emotion and imagination than on evidence, and perhaps because of this has received disproportionate attention. Such uninformed interpretations share an exaggerated notion of Brazilian naval capabilities and intentions.

A changing hierarchy of Brazilian naval interests does make it difficult to distinguish unambiguously between core and secondary interests. But it does seem quite certain that the most likely candidate for eventual transformation from a secondary interest to a core one is the Brazilian naval presence in the South Atlantic. Some speculation has indicated that such a transformation is imminent, while other lines of speculation have posited Brazilian naval roles even beyond the South Atlantic. First, roles speculated for the Brazilian Navy beyond the South Atlantic will be listed and dispatched. Then, projected Brazilian roles in the South Atlantic will be examined.

Speculative Naval Roles

Some observers have regarded the transamazonian highway network as part of a larger Brazilian movement westward toward the Pacific. Direct Brazilian land communication with the west coast of South America would allegedly provide the opportunity for establishing a naval base and developing a Brazilian Pacific fleet. Through such a presence, Brazil allegedly would be able to dominate both the Atlantic and Pacific coasts of South America.

Only extrapolation from some rather unrelated events supports such allegations. No Brazilian policy statements have advocated a Pacific coast naval role, nor have existing or projected weapons acquisitions or deployments lent plausibility to such a course of action. A two-ocean navy is but a distant possibility until a firmer presence is established in the ocean of greatest immediate importance for Brazil, the South Atlantic.

West coast South American states, especially Peru, have still been suspicious at times about Brazilian designs toward the Pacific, allegedly expressed through development of the Amazon, and consequently have not themselves proposed any naval cooperation with Brazil. Cooperation for economic development is much more likely. Peru and seven

other states bordering the Amazon signed the Brazil-
ian-inspired Amazon Cooperation Treaty in July 1978,
which may help defuse suspicions through mutually
complementary development approaches to jungle regions.

Insofar as Brazil may have tried to shape a
sphere of influence for projecting naval power or
for whatever reason, it has only occurred with respect to the small neighboring states, Bolivia,
Paraguay, and Uruguay, not with respect to west
coast states. Bolivia has been regarded by some as
a potential land bridge for Brazil to the Pacific
via Chile, Brazil's historic west coast ally. But
Chile has its own maritime tradition, which would
not easily be subordinated to that of non-contiguous
Brazil. For its part, Bolivia would not be likely to
allow its long nationalistic battle with Chile for
access to the sea to become a mere stalking-horse
for Brazil.

Brazil does place some importance on the Caribbean and the southern portion of the North Atlantic.
In terms of geography, Brazil's north coast is contiguous with the Guyanas, which have conventionally
been considered as part of the Caribbean. The major
north coast port of Belem is almost on the Equator,
only 1250 miles from Trinidad and 1850 miles from
Puerto Rico, and the remainder of the north coast
and territorial sea up to the Guyanas is above the
Equator. Belem has been emerging as a major new
center of naval activity, benefiting from its position at the mouth of the Amazon and near the juncture of the North and South Atlantic. In recent
years, Brazilian trade and diplomatic contacts with
the Caribbean have also increased, and at least in
the case of the Guyanas, it is often speculated
that Brazil would act unilaterally if political
events there were to evolve in a radical or menacing
direction.

Any Brazilian strategic involvement in the
Caribbean is likely only in association with the
United States, since the U.S. has long regarded
strategic interests in the area as its particular
concern. Brazil has cooperated with the United
States in the Caribbean during the annual series of
naval exercises, through participation in the
Organization of American States' peacekeeping force
in the Dominican Republic, 1965-1966, and through
vigorous condemnation of Cuban subversion. But any
unilateral naval action resulting from expanding
trade and diplomatic contact with the Caribbean is

highly unlikely. The only possible exception might
be the Guyanas, but threats and responses involving
contiguous Brazil in that case have been regarded
as land-based.

As for the North Atlantic, much of Brazil's
large and growing trade must pass through the area
to ports in the United States and Europe, so that
defense of both parts of the Atlantic has been regarded as interrelated. Some proposed Brazilian
strategies have accordingly extended a unilateral
or multilateral South Atlantic defense zone up to
the southernmost limit of NATO's sphere of responsibility at the Tropic of Cancer in the southern North
Atlantic. But North Atlantic defense remains largely a responsibility of NATO, and any projected
Brazilian role in the southern North Atlantic appears premature before any significant naval presence has been established closer to home in the
South Atlantic.

Speculation about ambitious naval interests and
roles has also related to Brazilian dependence on
global sea routes. Because of a global merchant
marine, rapidly growing exports, and large oil imports, Brazil allegedly has a vital interest in the
defense of global sea lanes. In particular,
Brazilian dependence on South Atlantic sea lanes
has been adduced as a compelling reason for
Brazilian participation in defense of these maritime
routes. While the argument is plausible, so is the
related, more ambitious view that Brazilian dependence on Persian Gulf oil and growing commerce
with Africa and Asia create important Brazilian
interests in the defense of sea lanes and security
of the Indian Ocean. On this basis, an occasional
Brazilian naval presence in the Indian Ocean has
been proposed.[35] By extension of the same logic,
Brazil should have global naval interests and a
global navy, since it has a heavy stake in security
of sea routes as well in areas such as the North
Atlantic and Mediterranean.

Brazilian foreign policy and naval interests
are gradually expanding, to be sure, but at a considerably slower rate than commercial interests,
and Brazilian military leaders over the last decade
have consistently resisted any attempt to alter
these basic priorities. Ambitious proposals for
defense of sea lanes are not only implausible in
terms of this domestic policy context, but are also
not feasible in the international arena. Even the
two superpowers are not able to provide comprehen-

sive naval protection for their global merchant
marines and fishing fleets, and have to rely heavily
on maritime law and order for their protection.
Brazilian Naval War College war games do concentrate
on deep-water missions, such as defense of sea lanes
in the Mediterranean, the South Atlantic, and the
Indian Ocean, but this appears to be more the result
of influence of U.S. advisors and methods than a
reflection of actual naval priorities and missions.[36]

Yet another speculative role involves Brazilian
designs on the Antarctic, which are allegedly part
of a larger naval drive to expand influence southwards in the South Atlantic. Some unofficial writings have indeed urged that Brazil make an Antarctic
claim based on a modified sectoral theory, which
would encompass over a million square miles of land
and adjacent sea and overlap Argentina's Antarctic
claim. Antarctica could pose an eventual military
threat to Brazil, either through enemy bases or control of adjacent waters, it has also been argued in
unofficial channels.[37] Recent mineral discoveries
in Antarctica have been presented as well as an
important interest for energy-scarce Brazil in the
region, in addition to some rich fishing grounds.

But here, too, Brazilian policy-makers have
been most cautious in avoiding any unnecessary prov-
ocation to South American neighbors, who are already uneasy about Brazil's rise. So far, only a
Brazilian scientific expedition to Antarctica has
been projected, and no official claim to the region
has been made. Actual overlapping Argentine,
British, and Chilean claims have led to more friction than any potential overlapping Argentine-
Brazilian claims, Argentine planners have recognized. In any event, only a conflict of interests rather than armed conflict would be involved.[38]
Brazilian law of the sea negotiators have also recognized that national policy toward the Antarctic
has remained largely undefined,[39] so allegations of
a conspiracy to expand Brazilian influence seem misplaced.

Brazilian interest in the Antarctic is still
growing. The Brazilian government finally did adhere to the 1959 Antarctic treaty in 1975, and in
the official document of adhesion it declared that
Brazil, as the state with the most extensive littoral in the South Atlantic, had substantial interests in the Antarctic, and that it was already
involved in defense of the region through the Rio
Pact (Inter-American Treaty of Reciprocal Assis-

232

tance). The Antarctic treaty does prevent Brazil
from making a claim in the immediate future, but it
also holds others' claims in abeyance. The treaty
provides both that claims made up to 1959 be frozen
for thirty years from the date of entry into force
of the treaty (1961), and that new claims not be
made during that period either. Brazilian signing
of the treaty does facilitate presentation of a
claim in 1991 when the freeze on current claims ex-
pires, should this course of action then appear
desirable, by allowing participation in scientific
investigations and discussions about the region in
the meantime.

Political uses of naval power have also been a
source of some speculation. Some political benefits
have already resulted from regional conventional
military primacy, including South American naval
supremacy, such as demonstration of determination
to defend a rapidly growing national power base and
recognition that growing national power is leading
to international great power status.[40] Such political benefits from naval power have directly supported the key security-development mission in a
relatively unprovocative way. More ambitious use
of naval power has been proposed to support overseas
political interests. This would involve support of
diplomacy and expansion of influence, particularly
in the case of small African and Latin American
states, or the use of naval presence in selected
cases of political instability around the South
Atlantic.[41]

Proposals for gunboat diplomacy, whether direct
or indirect, appear most unlikely to gain official
favor. It is well to recall that Brazilian foreign
policy behavior has generally been cautious, and
that Brazilian naval capabilities are still relatively modest. The small border states, Bolivia,
Paraguay, and Uruguay might be the only exceptions,
where Brazil has apparently been interested in
building a "security perimeter" and has been sus-
pected of influencing internal security matters.[42]
Threatened political uses of naval power near home
might be credible because of growing amphibious,
naval, and air power, but in these border state
cases, as with the Guyanas, threats and responses
involving contiguous Brazil have been regarded as
land-based.

Speculation about naval roles and interests
focuses in part on projected capabilities, as well
as alleged Brazilian motives. Steady expansion of

Brazilian naval capabilities and projected future
expansion have led to considerable concern in neighboring states that naval roles and interests must be
expanding concomitantly, perhaps at their expense.
Since direct evidence documenting alleged ambitious
naval missions has been flimsy, one line of argument has stressed instead that growing weapons capability is itself proof of such ambitious naval
roles. Continuing Brazilian naval modernization and
expansion do support the contention that naval interests are expanding, but conventional naval capabilities have not yet sufficiently outdistanced
those of Argentina to support allegations of inordinate naval ambitions. The specter of a
Brazilian nuclear navy has been more alarming to
critics, who see such a development supporting extensive naval activities throughout the South
Atlantic, including Antarctica.[43] While such concerns emanate mainly from Argentina, it is ironical
that some concern has been expressed in Brazil that
Argentina will acquire nuclear submarines.[44]

Brazil, like Argentina, has never foregone the
nuclear option in any international agreement, including the Tlatelolco treaty and the nuclear non-
proliferation treaty, so that it may eventually
develop or purchase nuclear warships. Brazilian
naval planners have openly discussed the possibility
of purchasing a nuclear submarine for years. The
last two navy ministers have commented favorably on
a gradual transition from conventional to nuclear
submarines,[45] and others have gone so far as to argue that the navy and merchant marine of the future
will need to be nuclear.[46] Such discussion favoring
nuclear submarines clearly envisages their supporting a more active Brazilian role in the South
Atlantic, but Brazil has yet to acquire any nuclear-
powered vessel, and tentative weapons acquisitions
projections for the next few years have only included the purchase of one nuclear submarine
abroad.[47]

In addition to the formidable difficulty of
finding a willing seller of nuclear naval weaponry,
the naval budget has had to impose a tight rein on
foreign warship acquisitions, so ability to acquire
particularly expensive nuclear warships would be
limited in any event. Good progress has been made
in developing an indigenous armaments industry,
especially weaponry for the army and air force, but
development of a national naval warship construction
capability has been slower and Brazil has yet to

build even conventional submarines.[48] National
construction of nuclear warships appears possible
only in the more distant future. Even supporters
of national construction of nuclear surface com-
batants and submarines have acknowledged that "this
matter appears remote for immediate interests of the
navy."[49]

The South Atlantic

Brazilian naval involvement in the South Atlantic has been real and protracted rather than
speculative, if not sufficiently extensive to
qualify as a core interest. Important interests
nevertheless support Brazilian naval involvement in
the South Atlantic. Brazil fronts on the South
Atlantic, and the islands extend the 200-mile territorial sea even further seawards. Much of
Brazil's growth is generated by seaborne trade,
which is coming to include east-west routes between Africa and Brazil across the South Atlantic,
as well as the more traditional north-south routes.
Brazilian concern about the vulnerability of South
Atlantic shipping lanes is heightened by heavy
dependency on imported oil, most of which has to
come around the Cape route in supertankers. There
are therefore important Brazilian interests in the
area, but, as indicated, national security and development missions of the navy are very extensive
and must be further consolidated before still more
ambitious missions can be undertaken seriously.
The nature of past and present Brazilian naval
involvement in the South Atlantic may be briefly review-
ed. World Wars I and II involved the Brazilian Navy in South
Atlantic operations, the Rio Pact (Inter-American Treaty of
Reciprocal Assistance) includes hemispheric maritime defense,
and the anti-submarine warfare UNITAS exercises are targeted
toward protection of Western merchant marine traffic in the
event of hostilities. These and several other related arrangements for naval cooperation have included the U.S. and were
discussed in the last chapter. Some other aspects
of Brazil's South Atlantic involvement have been
through multilateral defense cooperation with
regional neighbors.
Within the purview of the Rio Pact is the
Inter-American Defense Board of the Organization of
American States, which plans hemispheric defense,
including protection of maritime traffic. In 1959,
this board approved a Plan for the Defense of Inter-
American Maritime Traffic, from which the South

Atlantic Maritime Area Command (CAMUS) was later created. CAMUS is composed of representatives from Argentina, Brazil, Paraguay, and Uruguay, whose leadership alternates between a leading Argentine and Brazilian naval officer every other year. This is a combined control of shipping organization, to be converted into an integrated command in wartime to which national air and naval forces would be subordinated. Protection of maritime traffic in the South Atlantic was primarily intended, most particularly to counter any Soviet threat, although coordination between merchant marines and navies of member states has been promoted as well. CAMUS-related activities have accordingly included Atlantis operations to simulate wartime convoy conditions, frequent communications exercises, and regular tracking of ships in the South Atlantic.

These kinds of bilateral and multilateral involvement in the South Atlantic have been oriented particularly toward the possibility of total war or sizable limited warfare. In such situations of sizable conflict or confrontation, Brazilian naval planners have clearly recognized that they must rely on the United States, perhaps in the context of the Rio Pact, and cannot protect their own or Western interests in the South Atlantic alone. But it is still expected that Brazil's growth will allow it to play an increasingly autonomous role in most naval contingencies.[50]

In addition to these traditional kinds of involvement in the South Atlantic, Brazilian interest in the region is increasing. Much speculation, if misplaced in part, does correctly recognize that Brazil's growth is expanding Brazilian political and commercial interests into the South Atlantic and beyond, and will tend to be complemented by more extensive naval roles. External pressures for more extensive Brazilian naval involvement in the South Atlantic are mounting as well. A Soviet naval and diplomatic presence in Africa and the South Atlantic has been increasing at just the time when Brazil has been aspiring to fashion a role for itself in those areas. An increasing Soviet threat to the South Atlantic, it is often argued, is paralleled by increasing strategic importance of the area for the West and calls for vigorous response.

In response to strategic changes in the South Atlantic, Brazil's traditional kind of involvement and way of thinking about defense of the region will likely change, it is frequently argued. For ex-

ample, naval cooperation between indigenous South
Atlantic naval powers, especially Argentina, Brazil,
and South Africa, has often been predicted. But
such a maritime alliance would be neither militarily
nor politically viable. Were these regional powers
to act alone, without association with the United
States, they would not be able to counter a determined Soviet threat, which has been one of the key
objectives. None of these regional naval powers
have a nuclear navy nor are likely to develop one
in the near future, and none have a substantial
deep-water capability. Accordingly, such a regional
maritime alliance, it is predicted, might be associated with the United States and/or NATO through a
South Atlantic Treaty Organization (SATO). While
this would make such a pact militarily viable, it
would not make it politically viable.

South African membership in a South Atlantic
maritime alliance would be a distinct military
advantage because of its strategic location, but
the excesses of apartheid would constitute a heavy
political liability. Any kind of South Atlantic
maritime alliance in which South Africa played a
part would inevitably associate treaty partners
with the South African regime. For its part, South
Africa has regarded such an alliance as a way to
gain political allies and respectability, which is
an objective apparently shared at times by Argentina.
Both Brazil and the United States have been reluctant to pay the high political cost of engaging in
any military alliance or commitment with South
Africa. During 1968-1969 Brazil nearly participated in naval exercises with Portugal and South
Africa in the South Atlantic, and subsequently
Argentina did participate in exercises with the
South African Navy. Since then, Brazil has avoided
any military cooperation with South Africa and has
strengthened political and economic ties with black
Africa.

Brazilian policy-makers have also been hesitant to unnecessarily militarize the South Atlantic
with a new naval alliance as long as the Soviet
threat remains relatively low-key. Speculation
about a South Atlantic maritime alliance has generally been linked to exaggerated portraits of the
Soviet threat to the area. Spreading Soviet influence in Africa threatens Western security, it is
argued, and Soviet sea power threatens shipping in
the South Atlantic. The military necessity of a
South Atlantic alliance, in this view, should con-

sequently override political disadvantages.

At least with respect to the South Atlantic, Soviet behavior has been more restrained and Soviet capabilities have been more modest than suggested. The Soviet Union is interested in stability at sea and is reluctant to interfere with the free passage of ships. In the unlikely event of limited war engagements in the South Atlantic, U.S. capabilities compare well with those of the Soviet Union. On the basis of present Soviet naval shipbuilding rates through the 1980s, it has been estimated that a Soviet task force formed for operations in the South Atlantic would probably have to be at the expense of some element of existing deployments.[51] Soviet responses have likewise been restrained in response to enforcement of South American fishing policies. Both before and after the Soviet Union eventually acquiesced to South American ocean resource claims, it did not respond with force to seizure of fishing vessels. In the case of recent Argentine forceful seizure of Soviet fishing vessels, the response was limited to denials of operating within the 200-mile limit.

Brazilian policy-makers have still not been pleased with the growing Soviet presence in Africa, but have not regarded this as an immediate national security threat. Soviet support of the Popular Movement for the Liberation of Angola (MPLA), including troop involvement through a Cuban proxy in a civil war, had the most direct impact on Brazil and on the kind of role it might play in the South Atlantic. The conflict posed several dilemmas for Brazil. It had aspired to play a role in Portuguese Africa while perhaps also expanding commercial relations with South Africa, yet had often regarded the potential advent of radical states along the African littoral of the South Atlantic as a threat. MPLA control in Angola would lead to the creation of just such a radical state from Portuguese Africa. Another alleged Brazilian consideration in choosing sides was the desire to gain access to Angolan oil.

With apparent military predominance of the MPLA, Brazil reconciled its traditional dislike for radical states with other interests, and moved quickly in late 1975 to become one of the first states to recognize the MPLA government, apparently in order to identify itself with black African nationalism. Domestic criticism followed the Brazilian recognition, including within the armed forces, and related rumors of an imminent South Atlantic naval alliance attracted interest as an alternative policy course. But subsequent Brazilian actions remained relatively consistent. Accommodation was sought with black African nationalism, security threats to the South Atlantic were downplayed, and relations with South Africa were reassessed. Efforts were made to promote commercial relations with Angola and other black African states, and Brazil began to respond to African pressure to loosen relations with South Africa. Commercial relations with South Africa continued, but criticism of apartheid stepped up somewhat and on several occasions, most recently in late 1978, Brazilian Foreign Minister Azeredo da Silveira declared that Brazil would not co-operate with South Africa for the defense of the South Atlantic.

Apparently a new equilibrium has been estab-lished in support of these various Brazilian policy initiatives toward Africa and the South Atlantic. Domestic criticism of the Brazilian recognition of Angola of late 1975 and related rumors of an imminent South Atlantic naval alliance peaked in 1976. Since then, there has been considerable do-mestic and international acceptance of Brazil's moderate response to Soviet activities in Africa and the South Atlantic. Internationally, there has been general unwillingness in the West to make a vigor-ous response. On the domestic front, all sectors of the Brazilian Navy regard the Soviet presence in Africa and the South Atlantic as potentially dan-gerous, so that the debate within the military over recognition of Angola and related issues was limit-ed to whether a harder-line toward Soviet involve-ment should be pursued. This rather limited area of disagreement promises to remain latent if the Soviet role in the South Atlantic remains re-strained.

Argentina has tended to react differently to Angola and related events affecting the South Atlantic. The Argentine Navy in particular has been more willing to cooperate with South Africa for South Atlantic defense, but overall policy has held back from formal institutional arrangements. Both Argentina and South Africa have regarded Soviet involvement in Angola as linked to significant Soviet penetration into the South Atlantic. Argen-tina's small neighbor, Uruguay, has leaned toward the Argentine approach on this issue as well. Argentine suspicion of Brazil has been so pronounced

in some quarters that Brazil's approach to Angola
has been regarded as placing it in a position to
"make the South Atlantic a Brazilian sea with the
explicit backing of the State Department."[52]

But tactics, rather than strategy, seem to
separate Argentine and Brazilian responses to
Soviet activities in the South Atlantic. Tactical
differences include how and with whom to cooperate.
Brazil is clearly opposed to South African membership in any South Atlantic defense arrangements, and
fears that a SATO-type organization might needlessly
promote superpower confrontation. In this view, the
Rio Pact already provides for hemispheric continental and maritime defense in a less provocative way.
Argentina is more favorably disposed toward South
African membership and new formal organizational
arrangements. Important strategic interests, however, are shared.

Both Argentine and Brazil have right-wing military governments which have taken a stern line
toward any domestic communist activities and inter-
nationally-sponsored subversion, and cooperate in
controlling both. Argentina and Brazil also tend
to regard Soviet foreign and naval policies as fundamentally antagonistic to national interests, even
though both states are interested in expanding commercial relations with the Soviet Union. In both
countries, the military governments have assigned
the navy key tasks, including defense of the South
Atlantic, and have been relatively generous in allocating available resources to them, with the
Argentine Navy currently being more active and influential in domestic politics and foreign policy
and more inclined toward interservice rivalry than
the Brazilian Navy.

Similar Argentine and Brazilian attitudes and
responsibilities have led to considerable naval
cooperation. There have been rather frequent and
cordial naval visits and contacts, both bilateral
and multilateral, in spite of areas of national
rivalry. In addition to visits and contacts, it
will be recalled that these South American navies
also carry out joint exercises with the United
States and themselves cooperate jointly in South
Atlantic defense, which distinguishes them from the
less cosmopolitan orientation of the other two
services.

Bilateral and multilateral cooperation in a
South Atlantic crisis would therefore be probable
even though a formal South Atlantic defense pact has

been regarded as undesirable by Brazil. Over a decade ago, when there was no appreciable Soviet threat in the South Atlantic, a prominent U.S. diplomat reported, on the basis of interviews, unanimous agreement among Latin American officers studying at the U.S. Naval War College "that there is no real impediment to very active co-operation and coordination of activity as between the Latin American navies, particularly in ASW operations."[53] Argentine anti-submarine warfare capabilities do not match those of Brazil, but existing capabilities do form the basis of a carrier strike force[54] so that joint cooperation might be increasingly effective in helping defend the South Atlantic.

While Brazil is already involved in South Atlantic defense, especially through multilateral channels, development of a unilateral Brazilian naval role in the South Atlantic is more speculative. The nature of such a projected unilateral role varies considerably according to the particular author, but some general conclusions are possible by surveying some representative proposals. In particular, fears in some Argentine quarters that Brazil intends to establish continental hegemony and monopolize the South Atlantic appear much more intemperate than Brazilian ambitions.

For example, a Brazilian naval officer, in an unofficial capacity, recently recommended a reformulated naval strategy to reflect the increasing importance of the South Atlantic for Brazil. The strategy would include expansion of Brazilian naval activities throughout the South Atlantic, including the African and Antarctic coasts, Brazilian bases around the periphery of the region and on strategic islands, and an accelerated build-up of naval, naval aviation, and amphibious forces. This allegedly would allow Brazil to dominate the focal points of the South Atlantic, particularly the Recife Gap (Natal-Dakar or Atlantic corridor) separating West Africa and Brazil. Such naval expansion would not be a case of commerce following the flag, but rather would respond to and help protect already extensive Brazilian overseas economic interests, which are dependent on access to major sea lanes.[55]

An equally ambitious "South Atlantic strategy" proposed by a prominent Brazilian general, Meira Mattos, called for greater Brazilian air and naval capability to support Brazilian interests throughout the region. Brazil should gradually assume greater responsibility for South Atlantic defense, but for

the present, defense of key South Atlantic maritime
routes would need to rely on the United States.
Naval cooperation with a "Southern Cone Community"
of South American states would be encouraged, and
later would include African states.[56]
    Even these ambitious proposals for a unilateral
Brazilian naval role in the South Atlantic are tempered by moderation. While such proposals envisage
a distinctive Brazilian role in the South Atlantic,
they also recognize the desirability of and need for
continuing bilateral cooperation with the United
States, at least in strategic affairs, and more extensive multilateral cooperation in the conventional
sphere. Meira Mattos' geopolitical vision of
Brazil's role in the South Atlantic emphasizes multilateral cooperation to the fullest extent possible,
and has been regarded as updating General Golbery
do Couto e Silva's similar influential vision a
decade previously.[57] Even proposals for Brazilian
bases would require multilateral cooperation, and
strategy primarily oriented toward defense of sea
lanes would be defensive, not offensive, in nature.
    Calls for a more extensive Brazilian presence
in the South Atlantic are also tempered by recognition of limitations of current resources. The navy
should grow as Brazil grows, it is argued, but this
will apparently entail only gradual expansion of a
naval presence in the South Atlantic, not rapid
expansion. Even those who emphasize the need for a
larger Brazilian role in the South Atlantic recognize the primacy of consolidation of control of the
200-mile territorial sea.[58]
    The expansion and modernization of the
Brazilian Navy has still been creating a limited
deep-water capability. For example, the Oberon
submarines are capable of navigating for six weeks
without surfacing and the missile frigates can cover
the 3,800 mile route between Rio and Capetown, South
Africa without refuelling. The Brazilian Navy accordingly has been described accurately as being
simultaneously oceangoing, coastal, and fluvial.[59]
Modern warships of the oceangoing force can perform
some deep-water missions, and can also back up, when
necessary with air support, the smaller vessels of
the coastal fleet, either within the 200 miles or
beyond that limit. Moreover, it has been indicated
here that 200-mile missions of the navy cannot be
separated unambiguously from deep-water missions.
This is particularly the case with respect to protection of sea lanes for merchant marine traffic,

which is the interest of most immediate importance for Brazil in the South Atlantic.

Were attack on sea lanes to occur relatively close to the Brazilian littoral, even if beyond 200 miles, it is probable that Brazil might feel compelled to respond with air and/or naval power. At least for such limited purposes and with land-based air cover, Brazilian naval power would seem capable of deep-water operations. Nuclear submarine activities against maritime shipping in the South Atlantic are regarded as unlikely, so that more modest conventional weaponry, including land- and sea-based air power, could provide sufficient protection for shipping against limited threats.[60] Convoy support, however, would stretch Brazilian capabilities seriously if carried out alone throughout the South Atlantic.

Defense from attack from the South Atlantic has been another concern. Brazilian strategists have argued that missile frigates, plus other relatively small missle-equipped craft and hopefully missile submarines, in combination with shore-based air power, could hold a larger, more powerful adversary up to hundreds of miles off the western South Atlantic littoral. But the additional argument that Brazil might be able to respond along the eastern South Atlantic littoral similarly by relying on bases[61] is much more problematical, since cooperation with South Africa is unlikely on Brazil's part, and black African states, for their part, are unlikely to concede base rights to Brazil. In fact, a Brazilian fear has been that Soviet planes based in west Africa could hit major Brazilian population centers.[62]

Operations in mid-ocean would face additional difficulties. At great distances from the coast, sea control would be much more difficult. For example, operations carried out from strategically located areas along the littoral, even in the relatively narrow eastern portion of the Recife Gap (Natal-Dakar or Atlantic corridor) separating West Africa and Brazil, would not suffice to control traffic through the entire 1,600 mile breadth. Naval and air engagements distant from the coast would also be difficult. Air cover would pose a problem, since the aircraft carrier. Minas Gerais, only carries anti-submarine aircraft, not attack planes. The effectiveness of a small Brazilian task force would be limited by even more mundane considerations. Particularly since the oil crisis, naval maneuvers have been largely limited to training to conserve petroleum, and refuelling capability remains limited.

The development or acquisition of relatively sophisticated conventional weapons systems by certain developing coastal states, such as Brazil, still enhances defense against major powers. But this new advantage is particularly applicable to coastal zones and narrow international waterways contiguous to the national littoral. In the case of the South Atlantic, passage through narrow waters or straits is not required and control over the wide expanses of ocean involved is beyond current Brazilian capabilities. In any event, such ambitious roles are reserved only for war-time emergencies, and would likely involve the United States.

In sum, there is much the Brazilian Navy does and can do, but naval capabilities and missions still lag well behind the increasingly far-flung scope of commercial and diplomatic activities. It is to Brazil's credit that in its emergence as a major power, naval interests and missions continue to be defined with moderation, and that development is not distorted by security demands. This has not led toward democracy, but the modernizing, if authoritarian, military governments have held to their promise to promote development.

NOTES

1. The following sources explicitly relate national growth to Brazilian maritime power and naval power. Mario Cesar Flores, ed., Panorama do Poder Marítimo Brasileiro (Rio de Janeiro: Serviço de Documentação Geral da Marinha, 1972). A Marinha Crece com o Brasil (Brasília: Ministério da Marinha, Relações Publicas, n.d.). Gustavo Francisco Feijó Bittencourt, "Conotações do Poder Marítimo Necessárias ao Processo de Engrandecimento no Brasil," Revista Marítima Brasileira 91 (October-December 1971): 107-121. See also the discussion of Brazilian naval doctrine and domestic politics in Chapter 2.

2. Adalberto de Barros Nunes, "Administração Naval," Revista Marítima Brasileira 93 (July-September 1973): 26.

3. David F. Ronfeldt, Future U.S. Security Relations in the Latin American Contexts (Santa Monica, California: The Rand Corporation, 1975), pp. 11-13.

4. Alfonso Arias Schreiber, "Las 200 Millas en Caracas," in
Derecho del Mar : Una Visión Latinoamericana, eds. Jorge A.
Vargas and Edmundo Vargas Carreño (Mexico City: Editorial
JUS, 1976), p. 79. My translation. The Brazilian foreign
minister, Azeredo da Silveira, has expressed exactly the same
view that great powers support freedom of the seas in order
to have "carte blanche for the exercise, de facto, of antiquated aspirations of hegemony or domination." Azeredo da
Silveira, "Políticos e diplomatas: o diálogo indispensável,"
Resenha de Politica Exterior do Brasil 1 (March-June 1974):
44.

5. Luis Valencia Rodríguez, "Los Usos Militares de los Fondos
Marinos y Oceánicos," in Vargas and Vargas, pp. 267-268.

6. Ibid., pp. 255-256; 261, 268-269.

7. Mark Janis, _Sea Power and the Law of the Sea_ (Lexington,
Massachusetts: D.C. Heath and Company, 1976), pp. 68-69.
Clarence A. Hill, Jr., "U.S. Law of the Sea Position and Its
Effect on the Operating Navy: A Naval Officer's View,"
Ocean Development and International Law Journal 3 (1976):
341-359. For a refutation of Admiral Hill's article by this
author, see Michael A. Morris, "Have U.S. Security Interests
Really Been Sacrificed?: A Reply to Admiral Hill," _Ocean
Development and International Law Journal_ 4 (1977): 381-397.
Robert L. Friedheim has similarly called attention to the
symbolic, territorial aspect of Latin American ocean claims,
which makes any compromise retrenching national ocean claims
very difficult. Robert L. Friedheim, "A Law of the Sea
Conference--Who Needs It?," in _International Relations and
the Future of Ocean Space_, ed. Robert G. Wirsing (Columbia,
South Carolina: University of South Carolina Press, 1974),
pp. 57-58.

8. Jozef Goldblat, "Law of the Sea and the Security of
Coastal States," in _Law of the Sea: Caracas and Beyond_, eds.
Francis T. Christy et al. (Cambridge, Massachusetts: Bal-
linger Publishing Company, 1975), p. 301.

9. Section A-2 of the 1956 Principles of Mexico on the
Juridical Regime of the Sea does contain a provision with almost exactly the same wording as the section cited here from
the 1970 Brazilian decree-law, but the historical context was
very different. The 1956 measure was directed against recognition of a 3-mile territorial sea rather than for maintenance
of security over a 200-mile territorial sea. Brazil did vote
for the 1956 resolution, but made an explicit reservation,
including a dissent from Section A-2. A translation of the
document is presented as Document 3 and the Brazilian state-

ment as Document 5 in Alberto Székely, Latin America and the Development of the Law of the Sea: Regional Documents and National Legislation, 2 vols. (Dobbs Ferry, New York: Oceana Publications, Inc., 1976), 1: Part IIA. Chapter 3 of this study provides the historical background to this subject. The Declaration of Montevideo on the Law of the Sea of May 8, 1970 and the Declaration of the Latin American States on the Law of the Sea (Lima) of August 8, 1970 also have very similar provisions, but without any reference to national security and defense. See Chapter 4 of this study for analysis of these documents. Translations of these documents are presented as Documents 29 and 36 in Volume I of Székely.

10. "Decreto-Lei No. 1.098, de 25 de Marco de 1970," in Mar Territorial (Brasília: Marinha do Brasil, 1971), 1: 19-20. My translation.

11. Edmundo Vargas Carreño, América latina y los problemas contemporáneos del derecho del mar (Santiago, Chile: Editorial Andrés Bello, 1973), p. 36. My translation. Chapter 4 of this study also noted Brazilian reaffirmation of the importance of security interests in the 200 miles in dissenting from part of a 1973 law of the sea resolution of the Inter-American Juridical Committee.

12. See footnote 73 in Chapter 5. For a general Brazilian policy statement opposing any military activities by third states within the 200 miles, see "Delegation of Brazil, Statement by Professor Vicente Marotta Rangel before the II Committee of the III U.N. Conference on the Law of the Sea," Caracas, August 5, 1974, pp. 203. (mimeograph)

13. David C. Loring, "The Fisheries Dispute," in U.S. Foreign Policy and Peru, ed. Daniel A. Sharp (Austin: University of Texas Press, 1972), pp. 91, 93, 96.

14. Frida M. Pfirter de Armas, "Argentina and the Law of the Sea," in The Changing Law of the Sea: Western Hemisphere Perspectives, ed. Ralph Zecklin (Leiden, Holland: Sijthoff, 1974), pp. 179-180.

15. Ibid., p. 180. Also see Karin Hjertonsson, The New Law of the Sea: Influence of the Latin American States on Recent Developments of the Law of the Sea (Leiden, Holland: Sijthoff, 1973), p. 60.

16. Mario Cesar Flores, "Na década dos setenta," in Panorama do Poder Marítimo Brasileiro, pp. 153-154, 127-128.

17. See Chapter 8.

18. Robert L. Scheina, "Latin American Naval Purpose," U.S. Naval Institute Proceedings (September 1977): 116-117, 119.

19. Alex Hennig Bastos, "Mar Territorial Brasileiro," Revista Marítima Brasileira 90 (October-December 1970): 54, 60.

20. H. M. Caminha, "O Mar Territorial Brasileiro de Duzentas Milhas," Revista Marítima Brasileira 92 (July-September 1972): 41.

21. Marcio de Souza d Mello, "A Aeronáutica no Esforço De-senvolvimentista," Segurança e Desenvolvimento 20 (1971): 85.

22. Alex Hennig Bastos, "Mar Territorial Brasileiro," pp. 54, 60. Fernando Paulo Nunes Baptista, "O Mar Territorial Brasileiro," Revista Marítima Brasileira 91 (January-March 1971): 53, 55.

23. Bennett Ramberg, The Seabed Arms Control Negotiations: A Study of Multilateral Arms Control Conference Diplomacy (Denver: Department of Graphics of the University of Denver, 1978), parts 4 and 5 passim. Evan Luard, The Control of the Sea-Bed: A New International Issue (London: Heinemann, 1974), pp. 100-109. Ramiro Elysio Savaiva Guerreiro, "Aspectos Políticos, Econômicos e Jurídicos do Aproveitamento do Fundo do Mar Além dos Limites da Jurisdição Nacional," Segurança e Desenvolvimento 19 (1970): 19-21.

24. Bennett Ramberg, pp. 69, 88, 91.

25. See Chapter 3.

26. Relatório Sucinto, 1971 (Brasília: Ministerio da Marinha, 1972), p. 4.

27. Alex Hennig Bastos, "Mar Territorial Brasileiro," p. 52.

28. O Globo, September 5, 1977, p. 5.

29. Adalberto de Barros Nunes, A Nova Marinha (Brasília: Serviço Gráfico do Senado Federal, 1970), pp. 10-11.

30. Antonio Carlos da Silva Muricy, "O Exército como Instru-mento da Ação Política Nacional," Segurança e Desenvolvimento 20 (1970): 72-75. Marcio de Souza e Mello, pp. 89-90. Participação e Desenvolvimento da Marinha (Brasília: Serviço de Relações Públicas da Marinha, n.d.), p. 1.

31. General Rodrigo Octavio Jordão Ramos, "As Forças Armadas e a Integração da Amazônia," Revista Brasileira de Política

Internacional 14 (March-June 1971): 81-89.

32. "Noticiário Marítimo," *Revista Marítima Brasileria* 98 (January-March 1978): 156-157.

33. See Chapter 2.

34. Florentino Dias Loza, "Geopolítica del Brasil," *Estrategia* 29 (May-June 1974): 30-40. Juan E. Guigialmelli, "Argentina. Política nacional y política de Fronteras. Crisis nacional y problemas fronterizos." *Estrategia* 37-38 (November 1975-February 1976): 7-21.

35. Aguinaldo Aldighieri Soares, "O Oceano Indico e Os Interesses Brasileiros," *Revista Marítima Brasileira* 92 (April-June 1972): 20-52.

36. Interviews not for direct attribution.

37. Faust Cardona, "Geopolítica da Antártida," *Adismar* 4 (August-September 1974); 20-26. Therezinha de Castro, "Chama-se Antártica e faz parte do nosso destino," *Journal do Brasil*, July 13, 1975, p. 1, Section 3.

38. Jorge A. Fraga, "El Futuro incierto político-económico de la Antártida," *Estrategia* 43-44 (November-December 1976-January-February 1977): 41-42.

39. *Relatório Sobre a Reunião de Caracas da III Conferência Sobre O Direito do Mar Apresentado Pelo CMG Murillo Souto Maior de Castro* (Brasília: Ministério da Marinha, 1974), pp. 31-31.

40. See Chapter 5.

41. Domingos Pacífico Castello Branco Ferreira, "Algumas Formulações Estratégicas," *Revista da Escola de Guerra Naval* 3 (December 1973): 52-53. Mario Cesar Flores, "Mísseis Táticos na Guerra Naval," *Revista Marítima Brasileira* 90 (October-December 1970): 30.

42. William Perry, *Contemporary Brazilian Foreign Policy: The International Strategy of an Emerging Power* (Beverly Hills, California: Sage Publications, 1976), pp. 45-47.

43. José Enrique Greño Velasco, "La Adhesión de Brasil al Tratado Antártico," *Revista de Política Internacional* 146 (July-August 1976): 75.

44. "Argentina construirá submarinos atômicos," *Jornal do*

Brasil, September 11, 1974, p. 2.

45. Adalberto de Barros Nunes, "A Marinha no Governo Medici," Revista da Escola de Guerra Naval 3 (December 1973): 12. "Henning revela que Armada terá helicópteros pesados," Jornal do Brasil, November 11, 1974, p. 4.

46. Domingos Pacífico Castello Branco Ferreira, "A Exploração do Atomo pelo Brasil e Suas Implicações Internacionais," Revista Marítima Brasileira 92 (April-June 1972): 88, 90-91.

47. Adalberto de Barros Nunes, "A Marinha no Governo Medici," pp. 10-11.

48. See Chapter 5.

49. Adhemar Garcia de Paiva Filho, "A controversia sôbre reatores nucleares e sua implicação na Marinha," Mar: Boletim do Clube Naval 86 (March-April 1974): 35.

50. Mario Cesar Flores, "Na década dos setenta," pp. 154, 160. Mario Cesar Flores, "A Marinha de Guerra no Brasil atual," in Panorama do Poder Marítimo Brasileiro, pp. 170-171. Fernando Paulo Nunes Baptisa, "Análise da Estratégia Naval Soviética," Revista Marítima Brasileira 92 (January-March 1972): 108-109, 112. Newton Ferreira Campos Junior, "Importância da Marinha de Guerra em Face da Conjuntura Atual," Revista Marítima Brasileira 90 (October-December 1970): 84-85. Footnote 72 in Chapter 5 referred more generally to Brazilian expectations about the role of the U.S. Navy as an essential element in the defense of the West.

51. Michael MccGwire, "Soviet Interests and Capabilities in the South Atlantic Region: 1977-1990," pp. 50, 61-63. (unpublished manuscript, March 2, 1977).

52. Carlos P. Mastrorilli, "Una actualización da la doctrina Golbery: Brasil geopolítica y destino del General Carlos Meira Mattos," Estrategia 39 (March-April 1976): 38. Juan Guglialmelli, "Golbery do Couto e Silva, el 'destino manifesto' brasileño y el atlántico sur," Estrategia 39 (March-April 1976): 5-22.

53. Robert McClintock, "Latin America and Naval Power," U.S. Naval Institute Proceedings (October 1965): 36.

54. Robert L. Scheina, "South American Navies: Who Needs Them?," U.S. Naval Institute Proceedings (February 1978): 65.

55. Domingos Pacífico Castello Branco Ferreira, "Algumas Formulações Estratégicas," pp. 52-53, 49-50.

56. Carlos de Meira Mattos, A Geopolítica e as Projeções do Poder (Rio de Janeiro: Livraria José Olympio Editora, 1977), pp. 119-124.

57. Mastrorilli, pp. 37-47. Golbery did apparently favor a unilateral Brazilian role in the entire South Atlantic, but with U.S. consent and support. Golbery do Couto e Silva, Geopolitica do Brasil (Rio de Janeiro: Editora José Olympio, 1967), p. 200.
    Both Meira Mattos and Golbery are discussed briefly in Chapter 2 insofar as their geopolitical thought relates to the navy and domestic politics.

58. Paulo Lafayette Pinto, "Os Pequenos Navios de Guerra," Revista Marítima Brasileira 92 (January-March 1972); 23, 25. Hilton Berutti Augusto Moreira, "O Brasil e suas responsabilidades no Atlântico Sul," Revista Marítima Brasileira 92 (October-December 1972): 30-31, 34.

59. Mario Cesar Flores, "A Marinha de Guerra no Brasil atual," pp. 168-176.

60. Mario Cesar Flores, "Mísseis Táticos na Guerra Naval," p. 32. Alex Hennig Bastos, "A Guerra A/S de uma Perspectiva Ampla," Revista Marítima Brasileira 92 (July-September 1972): 21-24.

61. Mario Cesar Flores, "Mísseis Táticos na Guerra Naval," pp. 30-31, 8-12.

62. Ibid., pp. 25-26, Aguinaldo Aldighieri Soares, "O Continente Africano ou as Muitas Africas," Revista Marítima Brasileira 98 (July-September 1978): 48, 50.

7. Ocean Resources

Ocean resource issues of interest to Brazil fall into three groups, living and non-living resources in areas of national jurisdiction and deep seabed resources in the international zone. A fourth group of ocean resources, living resources of the high seas, is of marginal interest to Brazil, since no significant deep-water fishing capability is planned. All these issues have long been of central concern to law of the sea negotiations and to national ocean policies because of political differences over how to allocate ocean resources. After years of interaction between national ocean policies, both within the outside negotiating forums, certain basic trends have emerged in each area of ocean resources.

There was early postwar recognition, both in international forums and in Brazilian legislation, of the right of national jurisdiction over non-living resources on the continental shelf. By the 1970s, a consensus also emerged favoring extension of national jurisdiction out to 200 miles over living resources, and coincided with a similar trend in Brazilian ocean policy. This chapter is limited to fleshing in some of the details about how national and international trends in these two ocean resource areas, offshore oil and fishing, have tended to parallel and complement one another. The third ocean resource area, deep seabed resources in the international zone, has been dealt with almost exclusively within the context of the Third United Nations Conference on the Law of the Sea. For an analysis of how deep seabed trends relate to Brazilian ocean policy, the reader is referred back to Chapter 4. Trends in the fourth ocean resource area, high seas fisheries, have pointed toward some-

what greater international regulation, but, as
noted, this area is of marginal concern for Brazil
and will not be discussed in this chapter. Again,
the reader is referred back to Chapters 3 and 4,
where Brazilian preferences were noted for some
coastal state fisheries powers beyond 200 miles
and greater community control over high seas fisheries in general.

OFFSHORE OIL

     National control of mineral resources of the
continental shelf has been a continuing concern of
Brazilian ocean policy. It has been shown that
Brazil followed the lead of others at a relatively
early date in asserting jurisdiction over the shelf.
National shelf control likewise continued after the
1970 extension of the territorial sea to 200 miles,
and was indeed reinforced through an altered legal
regime. The principle of national shelf control
has been reaffirmed as well at every major postwar
international maritime conference, and only rarely
has been challenged. Since by general agreement
continental shelf mineral resources fall within
the scope of national politics, global politics,
the perspective of this book, has generally been
involved only indirectly. Accordingly, in this
section discussion will be limited to certain important recent developments affecting Brazilian offshore oil.
     The 1973-1974 oil crisis had a particularly ad-
verse impact on Brazil, because the country must import about four-fifths of its petroleum. With successive oil price hikes, oil imports have mounted in
value to over a quarter of total imports, thereby
aggravating an already precarious balance of payments situation and contributing to a serious rise
in inflation. Because of the growing energy demands
of Brazil's relatively large, expanding economy,
the country has been importing more oil in recent
years than any other developing state. In response,
Brazil has moved vigorously at home to explore alternative sources of energy, enforce conservation, and
accelerate exploration and production of offshore
oil. On the international front, Brazil has moved
to develop assured sources of supply of foreign oil
through joint ventures.
     Only in the past several years has offshore
oil held out a promise of lessening dependency on
imported oil. This promise has not yet been real-

ized, but offshore oil exploration and production
have been accelerated over the past few years. Because expectations about offshore oil potential are
of quite recent origin, offshore oil was not a key
consideration in extending the territorial sea to
200 miles in 1970. Oil exploration on the continental shelf only began in the late 1960s and no important offshore oil finds were made until the early
1970s.[1]

Acceleration of offshore oil exploration and
production was hampered by concern about foreign
involvement in the national oil industry. National
policy favored limiting foreign involvement in both
on-shore and offshore oil exploration as much as
possible, because Petrobrás, the state oil company,
was established in 1953 as a national monopoly on
the crest of a nationalist campaign declaring that
"the oil is ours" ("o petróleo é nosso"). The national oil monopoly accordingly has been dedicated
to national control of a vital sector of the economy in order to spur independent economic development and contribute to eventual great power status.[2]

The symbolic importance of a national oil monopoly made it politically very difficult to associate foreign firms with offshore oil development
when the need arose in the early 1970s, just as it
had precluded any significant foreign involvement in
developing land-based oil since 1953 when Petrobrás
was created. As late as 1973, the request of several foreign oil companies, including Texaco, to
explore Brazil's continental shelf for oil was categorically rejected.[3] The United States was still
involved indirectly in various ways in development
of Brazilian offshore oil resources. For example,
a U.S. firm helped survey the continental shelf and
carried out related geological experiments during
1971. Similarly, in 1973, an $11 million contract
was concluded between Petrobras and a joint venture
company, equally owned by U.S. and Brazilian concerns, to furnish and operate an offshore drilling
platform, and a $6.6 million sale of U. S. support
boats for Brazilian offshore drilling operations
was made. The U.S. Export-Import Bank provided or
guaranteed most of the financing for these 1973
transactions.[4] But such kinds of foreign involvement were essentially limited to service contracts
for carrying out specifically assigned technical
tasks. Only later would foreign oil firms be invited to actively explore for oil through risk contracts.

During 1974-1975 a debate was carried on in
the public media over whether the government should
invite foreign oil firms to explore for oil through
risk contracts. On October 9, 1975, President
Ernesto Geisel finally approved risk contracts for
foreign oil companies to explore on-shore and offshore, and several risk contract negotiating rounds
have been held since the 1975 policy change. Risk
contracts provide for limited foreign participation
in the national oil industry by contracting an
international oil firm to explore for petroleum in
specified blocks or areas. In the event of a com-
merically exploitable oil discovery, the firm would
be remunerated for exploration expenses and would be
given a share of production profits. In the event
no significant oil find were made, the firm would
pay for all its expenditures.

Geisel, in his position as head of Petrobrás
up to being named president of the country, had become acutely aware that pragmatic economic imperatives might need to override political expediency
and ideology in energy affairs. As for politics,
nationalists within and outside the military bit-
terly opposed reopening the Brazilian oil industry
to more active involvement by foreign companies.
But economic imperatives were compelling. Land-based
reserves and production ("on-shore oil") were de-
cling at just the time increasing resources were
required to finance oil imports. Offshore oil potential appeared more promising by the 1970s, but
rapid development of offshore oil would require
particularly heavy investments because of the difficult maritime environment. Risk contracts promised to speed development of offshore oil while
shifting a significant portion of the heavy financial burden to foreign investors. Most risk contracts have indeed been let for offshore oil production, and about eighty per cent (80%) of current
Brazilian oil exploratory efforts are offshore.[5]
Offshore oil production has been increasing as well,
although no big offshore oil finds have yet been
made by the international oil companies and the
demand for and consumption of oil continue to grow.

Risk contracts do leave the state oil monopoly
intact, since on-shore and offshore oil development
remains under national control. Foreign oil companies are now permitted to explore oil in Brazil,
but only according to conditions and in designated
areas specified by the government. Risk contracts
by themselves therefore do not bring international

254

politics directly to bear on continental shelf mineral exploitation, which is still a national prerogative.

But international oil politics has affected offshore oil development in indirect ways. Successive oil price hikes, with their particularly heavy impact on oil-scarce Brazil, did spur accelerated development of offshore oil and required consideration and eventual approval of risk contracts. In essence, international economic realities required readjustments in domestic politics. Petrobrás' own international joint venture exploration activities through its subsidiary Braspetro (Petróbras Internacional S.A.) did help make risk contracts for national oil exploration more acceptable to domestic opinion as well as to international investors. Still, in foreign policy, heavy dependence on foreign oil, especially from the Middle East, led Brazil to alter its relatively even-handed approach to the region by tilting toward the Arab states.

In the longer run, Brazil hopes both to diversify sources of foreign oil supply and to lessen dependence altogether on foreign oil, technology, and capital. While relying on risk contracts with foreign oil firms for part of oil exploration efforts nationally, Petrobrás has itself been developing expertise in offshore oil operations and now operates numerous drilling rigs offshore. In turn, Braspetro probably will move gradually into offshore oil exploration to complement present on-shore exploration in foreign states. Yet another Petrobrás venture with international maritime implications, the national tanker fleet (Fronape), will be discussed in the next chapter.

FISHING

Largely negative findings have been reached so far in this study about Brazilian policy toward fisheries resources--fisheries have bulked much larger in west coast South American ocean policies than in those of east coast countries, including Brazil; Brazilian fisheries politics, especially alleged foreign depredation of national fisheries, has been a function of nationalism and the exigencies of national politics rather than of important economic interests; and fisheries have accordingly appeared much more important for Brazilian ocean policy than has been the case.[6]

A few statistics document the rather limited
economic importance of fisheries for Brazil. Revenue from fishing as a percentage of gross national
product was only .31% in 1976 and 2.5% of total agricultural value that same year.[7] Brazilian fish exports have been relatively modest as well, averaging
some $40 million annually in recent years out of
total exports reaching over $10 billion annually.
Of Latin American states, Peru has exported considerably more fisheries products by value and volume than Brazil. Brazilian fisheries imports have
also been somewhat larger than fisheries exports.
    However, these comparisons can be misleading.
The relatively large size of the Brazilian economy
and the relatively small size of Brazilian fisheries
suggest that the latter is uniformly insignificant,
which is not the case. For example, fisheries exports are highly concentrated by product. The two
species of fish resources which have involved serious international problems, lobsters and shrimp,
together have averaged about three-quarters of total
fish exports. Employment is likewise concentrated
in relatively poor fishing communities (380,000 in
non-industrial fishing and 19,954 in industrial
fishing). For certain areas, fishing is therefore
a very important source of employment, and, more
generally, fisheries could play a more important
role in improving some of the grave deficiencies in
domestic protein consumption.
    Brazilian fisheries are likewise important in
comparative terms. Brazil's annual fish catch has
ranked about eighteenth in the world in both volume
and value in recent years, and stands out in having
demonstrated a consistent rise in rank over the
past several decades.[8] It is generally acknowledged
that better Brazilian conservation and harvesting
practices could produce a considerably larger sustained yield. The total value of the annual catch
between $200 and $300 million in recent years, if
not large in terms of the sizable Brazilian economy,
is larger than that of any other Latin American
state.
    Peru, long prominent in international fisheries
affairs, illustrates these contrasting trends. The
Peruvian economy is about ten times smaller than
that of Brazil, and the total value of the annual
catch has likewise been smaller than that of
Brazil although much larger by volume. But Peruvian fisheries exports have been some five times
greater in value than those of Brazil, so it is

understandable that for this relatively small economy international fisheries questions have weighed
very heavily in national ocean policy. For Brazil,
with a much larger economy and smaller fisheries
exports, and consequently with less need to interact with other states in fisheries matters, national
fisheries have had rather limited domestic and
international importance economically.

Brazilian fisheries at times still achieved
political prominence in spite of their rather
limited importance for the national economy. When
fisheries politics has been important for national
ocean policy, this has been because of its symbolic,
nationalistic impact during a crisis rather than
because of intrinsic importance of fisheries for
the national economy. When the crisis receded, so
did the political importance of fisheries. Two
confrontations with great powers over fisheries
issues, one with France in the early 1960s and the
other with the United States in the early 1970s,
further illustrate these findings.

Great Power Challenges and Brazilian Responses

Both great power challenges pitted a developing, coastal fishing state, Brazil, against developed, distant-water fishing states. In each
case, traditional rights involving freedom of fishing were invoked by the great power, while Brazil
vigorously supported new or revisionist fisheries'
interpretations. In each case compromises were
made, but the Brazilian claim largely prevailed.
The resolution of both crises therefore complemented the long-term trend toward more extensive
Brazilian offshore fisheries jurisdiction, a trend
that finds counterparts throughout most of the
world. But, to repeat, neither crisis had a decisive, long-term impact on the larger evolution of
Brazilian ocean policy.

Previous findings in this study about the 1963
Brazilian-French Lobster War were military and
political in nature. Brazilian conventional military superiority in the local theatre deterred
French enforcement of its distant-water fisheries
claim, and contributed to an eventual settlement
favorable to Brazil.[9] The foreign challenge did
have a considerable impact on Brazilian nationalism
at the time, but did not significantly influence
the 1970 decision to extend the territorial sea to

200 miles.[10] We may now relate these findings more specifically to the Brazilian fisheries context.

Some French lobster ships turned to the northeast coast of Brazil because of a decreasing lobster yield in waters off the western coast of Africa, which resulted in some incidents during 1962. Brazil then seized several French fishing vessels in early 1963, on the ground that lobsters were part of the natural resources of the continental shelf, as defined in the 1958 Geneva Continental Shelf Convention, whose exploitation consequently required explicit Brazilian permission. Brazil also argued, as it did in the subsequent shrimp crisis, that predatory foreign fishing practices threatened to deplete the species. In contrast, France argued that lobsters were found in the high seas where freedom of fishing applied, and hence were not part of the natural resources of the continental shelf.[11]

A legal standoff resulted, and the crisis was eventually resolved, after military threats, by diplomacy in Brazil's favor. A settlement was reached setting forth certain regulations for French vessels during a five years period when fishing by contract through Brazilian firms would be permitted.[12]

Previous findings in this study about the 1972 U.S.-Brazilian Shrimp Conservation Agreement were legal and military in nature. The 1972 agreement signalled a more general U.S. policy shift toward acceptance of a geographically extensive, yet carefully defined and circumscribed, economic zone at the Third United Nations Conference on the Law of the Sea (UNCLOS III).[13] Conclusion of the agreement itself was facilitated by close navy-to-navy relations.[14] But sharp differences preceded the 1972 accommodation on the fisheries issue.

Tempers ran high for some time after Brazil declared a 200-mile territorial sea in 1970. Bilateral confrontation over the territorial sea issue involved a number of differences, including navigational rights and naval mobility, but came to focus most particularly on shrimp fishing. One Brazilian military journal, for example, sharply criticized "the protests against the measure /the 200-mile territorial sea claim/, notably from the American government, which at one point even encouraged its own fishing vessels to disregard Brazil's maritime sovereignty."[15]

From the U. S. point of view, the established right of freedom of fishing on the high seas was challenged by the Brazilian claim.[16] The immediate economic issue at stake was an approximate $30 million annual shrimp catch, dominated by American shrimpboats working from Trinidad and the Guianas. Expulsion of the U. S. distant-water shrimp fleet from Brazilian waters and its return to American waters would also have disrupted small-scale shrimp fishing off the U. S. Gulf coast, from whence it had originally expanded.

Brazil's response likewise involved defense of broad interests, as well as more specific fisheries interests. The breadth of the territorial sea was a unilateral sovereign competence, Brazil argued, and since 1970 included national control over off-shore fisheries out to 200 miles. The Brazilian case for fisheries control called attention to alleged foreign abuses. Without knowledge of the Brazilian government, a U. S. research vessel discovered significant shrimp fishing potential off the Amazon mouth, and unauthorized commercial exploitation began by the mid-1960s.[17] Brazilians later charged that without adequate supervision, shrimps and other marine life were being seriously depleted by indiscriminate foreign fishing practices, a charge the U. S. denied by countering that Brazilian shrimp resources were underexploited.

In mid-1971, Brazil began to enforce the 200-mile claim, which allegedly included buzzing of U. S. shrimp boats with military aircraft. By late 1971, Brazil and the United States did begin to seek a negotiated solution to the problem. However, Congress then delayed ratifying the International Coffee Agreement to protest Brazilian enforcement measures in the 200-mile zone. Large Brazilian coffee exports to the U. S. market were threatened, with coffee then about a third of total Brazilian exports and many times the value of the annual U. S. shrimp catch off Brazil. This led to an impasse in the negotiations, with the Brazilian Foreign Ministry expressing its "shock" at the attempt to exert "intolerable economic pressure" by linking the coffee agreement to the question of maritime sovereignty and fishing rights.

Two rounds of negotiations were necessary before a compromise agreement favoring Brazil was concluded on May 9, 1972. President Médici's December 1971 trip to the United States was of considerable assistance in encouraging a calmer negotiating atmosphere for the second round.

The 1972 agreement provided an interim solution to bilateral differences, by permitting 325 registered U. S. vessels to catch shrimp off the mouth of the Amazon river until January 1, 1974, only 160 of which could fish in the area at one time. The United States was to pay Brazil $200,000 yearly to assist it in enforcement of the agreement, and would pay $100 per day for each vessel in violation of the agreement. The shrimp agreement also called for cooperation and joint ventures between the two states for the development of their fishing industries.[18]

The fundamental U.S.-Brazilian difference over the legality of Brazil's 200-mile sea claim was skirted in the shrimp agreement. Both states reserved their juridical positions on territorial seas and fisheries jurisdiction under international law by noting their differences on these matters in a preface to the agreement.

The immediate significance of the shrimp agreement stemmed from U. S. willingness to compromise by submitting to regulations on fishing matters by a state claiming 200-mile offshore sovereignty. For its part, Brazil compromised by accepting an arrangement in which the United States implicitly denied Brazilian sovereignty over the area.

The longer-term significance of the agreement was quite different than expected at the time. At the time, the 1972 United States-Brazilian shrimp agreement was generally expected to be a model for other pragmatic interim fishing agreements between the United States and other Latin American states, especially the CEP states.[19] But this did not occur, and negotiating momentum moved instead toward the global law of the sea negotiations. Fisheries trends at UNCLOS III tended to endorse extensive offshore fisheries rights, as supported by developing states, thereby reshaping the negotiating context. In this favorable international context for national regulation of extensive offshore fisheries, the interim U.S.-Brazilian shrimp agreement evolved toward a permanent offshore fisheries regime.

The U.S.-Brazilian shrimp agreement was periodically renewed pending definitive settlement of the territorial sea issue at the law of the sea conference. Successive renewals reduced the number of U.S. vessels permitted in the regulated zone, increased fees charged, and encouraged joint ventures. The latest renewal in 1977 is to be the last transitional agreement, with the succeeding permanent regime involving U.S. participation in shrimp fishing on a joint venture basis. Similar arrangements were made with other foreign states involved in Brazilian fisheries.

This line of evolution of Brazilian policy toward foreign fishermen was largely unplanned. A high-ranking SUDEPE official (the Brazilian fishing agency) told this author that fishing was a "fifteenth-rate priority" in extending the territorial sea to 200 miles in 1970. Similarly, the 1972 shrimp agreement was limited to interim regulation of foreign fishing, and long-term policy toward foreign fishing was not decided until 1975. Greater emphasis on joint ventures since then will permit continuing foreign participation in Brazilian fishing, but to a lesser degree as fisheries technology is transferred to Brazil and as the Brazilian share of the maximum sustainable yield increases.[20]

Several related southern cone fisheries problems should be mentioned as well. Just as Brazilian ocean fisheries policy evolved somewhat erratically, so did those of Argentina and Uruguay, Brazil's two southern neighbors. Their changing fisheries policies have posed problems for Brazil, like Brazil's 200-mile territorial sea has posed certain potential navigational problems for Argentina and Uruguay. It will be recalled that Argentina went to 200 miles in 1966, Uruguay in 1969, and Brazil in 1970, and that different fishing limits at different times posed problems.

At first, in 1969, the three countries tried to adjust their differences through separate bilateral fisheries agreements providing for mutual access to each others' fisheries, but this approach soon collapsed. Mutual access to fisheries proved not to be a viable solution, since Argentine and Uruguayan fisheries are considerably richer than those of southern Brazil, and neither of Brazil's southern neighbors was consequently sufficiently motivated to sustain a sharing arrangement.

Uruguay has since permitted Brazilian fishing in national waters, but on conditions so strict as to discourage Brazilian fishing there. On occasion, Uruguay has even seized Brazilian vessels not complying with these strict regulations. Argentina has been reluctant as well to grant access to Brazilian fishermen, although direct bilateral clashes have been minimal. Argentina is more distant from Brazil than Uruguay, and the fishing fleet in southern Brazil has difficulty in maintaining operations even in relatively close-lying Argentine waters.

Brazil's own approach to bilateral fisheries negotiations in the 1970s stressing joint ventures with all interested parties was not accepted as a model by its two southern neighbors either. Argentina has shown more interest in joint ventures with developed deep-water fishing states which could transfer fishing technology, than with less developed Brazil. While Brazil's two southern neighbors limit Brazilian access to their national fisheries, both have begun to export considerable amounts of fish products to Brazil.

Fisheries Economics and Politics

Foreign involvement in Brazilian fisheries continues, but now it is on Brazilian terms and is tending to diminish over time. In essence, the changed nature of the foreign presence in Brazilian fisheries has involved a shift from the sphere of international politics toward that of the domestic economy. That is, foreign fishing off the Brazilian coast was a source of international conflict until recent years. More recently, foreign involvement in fisheries on Brazilian terms through joint ventures has been complementary to and increasingly integrated with national development. The situation was reversed in offshore oil, where international oil companies had been excluded and later were invited to participate in exploration, but there, too, recent foreign involvement has been on Brazilian terms and complementary to national development. Both offshore oil and fisheries therefore reflect the trend since 1970, noted earlier, from a politically-oriented territorial sea toward an economic one.

The trend toward an economically-oriented territorial sea should be qualified. The impact of international politics on offshore oil and fisheries has been contained or controlled, it is true, while economically rational exploitation of resources has been given greater emphasis. But domestic politics remains closely linked to exploitation of these ocean resources. Petrobrás continues to be a nationalistic symbol for many Brazilians, one manifestation of which is opposition to risk contracts. As for fishing, more economically rational fisheries exploitation may have little effect on existing regional and social class disparities. Essentially, some of the larger political objections to the Brazilian developmental model have been applied to fisheries. Too much emphasis, it has been argued, has been placed on high-priced fish exports, especially lobsters and shrimp located off the depressed northeast, instead of providing more and cheaper fish, ironically located off the more affluent southern coast, to the lower classes. Emphasis on capital-intensive industrial fishing likewise has tended to have an unfavorable impact on labor-intensive, non-industrial fishing. SUDEPE, too, has been widely criticized as lacking proper organization and planning in these and other matters.

Fishing has been the weak link in Brazil's emergence as a maritime power. Both volume and value of the annual catch have nevertheless been increasing. International problems involving Brazilian fisheries have largely been resolved as well, and better domestic fisheries organization is being achieved. This may permit more satisfactory meshing of the economics and politics of fishing than previously. In particular, planners may have better success in stimulating fisheries exports and cutting down or limiting growth of fisheries imports while improving domestic consumption patterns.

NOTES

1. Glycon da Paiva, a leading Brazilian figure in petroleum affairs and a former Director of Petrobrás, the state oil company, set forth a careful chronology relating on-shore and off-shore development, in response to written questions from this author. Neither on-shore oil scarcity nor off-shore oil potential had a significant impact on the 1970 territorial sea extension. Not until 1970 was it really recognized in official circles that Brazil's on-shore petroleum was very limited, so this was not a significant factor in the 1970 extension of the territorial sea to 200 miles. The most promising avenue at the time appeared to be to develop secure for-

eign supplies of oil, since continuing intensive exploration at home was uncertain and expensive, particularly since domestic politics prevented sharing expenses with international oil firms through risk contracts. Offshore oil exploration since 1968 had been limited and had not indicated significant offshore potential, which only was revealed in the early 1970s. Written response to questions from this author by Glycon da Paiva, Rio de Janeiro, Brazil, August 4, 1975. For a strong public statement by this Brazilian petroleum authority favoring risk contracts, see "A discussão de um monopólio: Talvez seja tarde, diz Glycon da Paiva," Jornal do Brasil, May 25, 1975, page 36. See also Chapter 4, notes 25 and 26.

2. Peter Seaborn Smith has presented a careful account of the politics of Brazilian oil, particularly why Brazil long refused to sanction foreign involvement in spite of pressing domestic energy needs. The book deals only briefly with the recent trend toward greater emphasis on offshore oil exploration, and does not cover recent approval of risk contracts. Peter Seaborn Smith, Oil and Politics in Modern Brazil (Toronto, Canada: Maclean-Hunter Press, 1976).

3. Latin America, June 8, 1973, p. 179. Brazil Today, June 22, 1973, p. 2.

4. Export-Import Bank of the United States press releases of March 19, 1973 and April 25, 1973.

5. Petrobrás News, No. 12, (December 1978), p. 2.

6. See Chapters 2 and 3.

7. Plano Anual de Trabalho: SUDEPE - 1978 (Brasília, Brazil: SUDEPE, 1978), p. 4.

8. Yearbook of Fishery Statistics: 1976 (Rome: Food and Agriculture Organization, 1977), 42: 11; 43:40. Frederick W. Bell, Food from the Sea: The Economics and Politics of Ocean Fisheries (Boulder, Colorado: Westview Press, 1978), Chapter 1.

9. See footnote 31, Chapter 5.

10. See Chapter 2.

11. The relevant portion of the Geneva Convention, Article 2/4, reads as follows: "The natural resources referred to in these articles consist of the mineral and other non-living resources of the seabed and subsoil together with living organisms belonging to the sedentary species, that is to say, organisms which, at the harvestable stage, either are immobile

on or under the seabed or are unable to move except in constant physical contact with the seabed or the subsoil." The basic legal issue involved was whether lobsters were sedentary species as defined in the Geneva Convention which walk on and are therefore natural resources of the shelf (the Brazilian view), or whether they were capable of swimming above the shelf like fish and hence were part of the high seas (the French view). Like Brazil, other Latin American states included crustacea in broad interpretations of shelf rights.

12. The best account of the Brazilian-French Lobster War is by Issam Azzam, "The Dispute Between France and Brazil over Lobster Fishing in the Atlantic," 13 International and Comparative Law Quarterly (1964): 1453-1459.

13. See Chapter 4. Also see Alberto Szekely, Latin America and the Development of the Law of the Sea: Regional Documents and National Legislation, 2 vols. (Dobbs Ferry, New York: Oceana Publications, 1976), 1:195.

14. See notes 76 and 77, Chapter 5.

15. "Soberania Confirmada," Nação Armada, No. 12 (1971), p. 6 (editorial).

16. The best account of the U.S.-Brazilian Shrimp Conservation Agreement is by Bernard H, Oxman, "L'Accord Entre le Brésil et les Etats-Unis Concernant la Peche à la Crevette," 1972 Annuaire Français de Droit International Public, pp. 785-803. Oxman recognizes that in one sense the 1970-1972 shrimp crisis posed exactly the same juridical question as the 1963 Lobster War. That is, both the species are crustaceans which may be viewed as either sedentary species of the shelf (Brazil) or as fish of the high seas (the United States). But the 1970 Brazilian 200-mile territorial sea claim altered the context and made it, not the 1958 Geneva Continental Shelf Convention, the focal point of bilateral disagreement. Oxman, pp. 793-794.

17. A Questão do Mar Territorial Brasileiro, (Brasília, Brazil: Gabinete do Ministro da Marinha, n.d.), p. 11.

18. In practice, this call for mutual cooperation and joint ventures involved transfer of fisheries technology from the United States to Brazil and Brazilian incentives for foreign fishing vessels to engage in joint ventures. For a recent summary of technical cooperation and assistance in the context of the U.S.-Brazilian shrimp agreement, see Relatório Sobre a Reunião Técnica Relativa ao Acordo Entre Brasil e Estados Unidos para a Pesca de Camarão no Norte do Brasil (28/03 à 01/04 de 1977-Miami, USA) (Brasília, Brazil: SUDEPE,

Serie Documentos Técnicos 27, September 1977).

19. "Statement by Ambassador Donald L. McKernan, Coordinator of Ocean Affairs, Before the Committee on Foreign Relations, September 28, 1972," page 14 (mimeographed version). "News in Brief: Brazil," Latin America, May 12, 1972, p. 152.

20. Interview with high-ranking SUDEPE (Superintendência do Desenvolvimento da Pesca) official, Rio de Janeiro, Brazil, August 1, 1975. This analytical chronology of Brazilian policy toward foreign fishing was corroborated by other interviews, including with other SUDEPE officials, and by published and unpublished documents.

8. Shipping

Rapid growth of the national merchant marine
has been a key factor in Brazil's emergence over the
last decade as a maritime power. From a relatively
modest base, Brazilian shipping capacity has grown
to a position of global prominence. The first section of this chapter examines basic domestic and
international problems Brazil faced in developing a
significant national merchant marine, and the nature
of Brazilian responses to the challenge. Particular
attention will be given to the development of
Brazilian maritime transportation policy, which
guided expansion of the national merchant marine
and has had a major impact as well throughout the
Third World and beyond. A final section of the chapter specifies how the major components of national
shipping have implemented Brazilian international
shipping policy.

DEVELOPMENT OF THE NATIONAL MERCHANT MARINE

Rapid growth of the merchant marine was not
easily achieved. Shipbuilding is capital-intensive
and requires considerable technological expertise,
in construction as well as in associated industries.
Brazil's gradual emergence as a respectable industrial power did place it in a better position than
practically all other developing states in meeting
this technological challenge. The established
ocean order still was not amenable to expansion of
national merchant marines of developing states,
Brazil included. The maritime powers dominated
ocean transportation and had fashioned and supported
rules to support their continued domination.
The doctrine of freedom of the seas, already

examined from various perspectives in earlier chapters, had implications for shipping as well. One freedom was freedom of navigation in the high seas, with innocent passage in narrow territorial seas. Developing states have generally tried to extend their territorial seas, including the innocent passage regime, beyond the traditional 3-mile limit, and a consensus has emerged at the Third United Nations Conference on the Law of the Sea (UNCLOS III) for a 12-mile territorial sea. Brazil's extension of the territorial sea to 200 miles in 1970 set it apart from this emerging consensus. But Brazil later softened the 200-mile claim, as noted, insofar as navigation was concerned by signalling that some compromise regime, such as free transit, could be accepted rather than innocent passage.[1] This policy clarification was compatible with Brazil's emergence as a major shipping power, which would naturally lead it to favor easy access to all the seas. Similarly, Brazil has favored equal treatment of ships in ports, including taxes, port dues, and berthing rights.

However, as noted previously, Brazil's territorial sea claim remains extensive, including control over security matters out to 200 miles.[2] Accordingly, Brazil's emergence as a shipping power may not lead it to adopt or conform to interests of established maritime powers. While supporting a legal regime facilitating global navigation, Brazil remains a vigorous supporter of extensive coastal state offshore rights.

The Brazilian attitude toward vessel source pollution suggests the distinctiveness of Brazilian interests as well. Brazil favors the adoption of international standards for vessel source pollution from ships, provided that they are not "too sophisticated" for "the development of the merchant marine of developing countries."[3]

Accordingly, Brazil has come to accept much of the content of the doctrine of freedom of navigation, but it has rejected the corollaries relating to the development of national merchant marines. Insofar as the freedom of navigation doctrine has been used to keep access to world trade routes as free and unhindered as possible, Brazil does not object. The principle of freedom of navigation, however, has also been extended to include freedom of access to cargoes through freedom of competition. This is the corollary Brazil rejects.

Just as state regulation over navigation was carefully circumscribed under the traditional free-

268

dom of the seas regime, so, too, were governments to avoid interference in commercial shipping negotiations. Equal, unhindered navigational access to world trade routes was therefore extended to equal access to carriage of trade, as determined by competitive conditions. Equality of treatment, by this view, would lead to efficiency in world shipping by channelling cargo toward the cheapest, most efficient carriers.

Conversely, the established maritime states have argued that unequal conditions of access to carriage of trade would be both discriminatory and inefficient. Most particularly, a wide variety of measures favoring national flag carriers, if taken irrespective of competitive conditions offered by other carriers, would involve "flag discrimination."[4] Different kinds of subsidies and preferential treatment for national flag carriers have been the most common practices involving flag discrimination.

Brazil, followed by other developing states, has countered by arguing that measures adopted to promote and protect the growth of national tonnage do not involve flag discrimination. Even developed states, this argument continues, often subsidize and favor national carriers and condone ogopolistic practices, such as liner conferences. Shipping is consequently not a freely competitive market, and established carriers from developed states and their governments have unfairly tried to exclude merchant marines of developing states from entering and participating in the market. By this view, discrimination in shipping would instead be limited to unnecessary constraints on navigation and unequal treatment of ships in port. More positively, promotion and protection of national shipping would be urgently required to complement and support general national economic development.

Brazil stands out among developing states, because from a relatively early date it began both to expand the national merchant marine rapidly and to develop such a doctrine to justify this expansion. The evolution and specific content of Brazilian doctrine or theory relating to development of the national merchant marine will now be sketched.

The successive military governments since 1964 have been particularly associated with Brazilian policy stimulating growth of the national merchant marine and urging change in the existing ocean transportation order. Initial attempts in that direction were made in the late 1950s by the Kubitschek administration, including encouragement through incentives for Japanese and Dutch shipbuilding interests to establish shipyards in Brazil, and completion of a number of oceangoing vessels. However, national shipbuilding capacity at the time was limited. The three state-owned major carriers also existed at the time or soon after (Lloyd Brasileiro, the general cargo shipping line; Fronape, Petrobrás' liquid-bulk carrier fleet; and Docenave, the dry-bulk carrier fleet of the Vale do Rio Doce company), but the merchant marine was small and additional funds for expansion were not available. Finally, there was no cohesive Brazilian international shipping policy for vigorously stimulating and defending merchant marine growth, as would emerge by the late 1960s. Prior to 1964, national carriers participated in no more than ten percent of shipping generated by Brazilian foreign trade.

The shipping sector, like all maritime sectors, has been influenced since 1964 by the general policy orientation of the successive military governments. The most prominent general policy guideline has been the security-development doctrine.[5] Several broad implications were derived from this general policy stance for shipping policy.

As for the development side of the doctrine, maritime transportation costs were singled out as invisible transactions constituting a particularly heavy strain on the Brazilian balance of payments. Reliance on foreign shipping affected the final price of the country's exports and imports adversely, and often arbitrarily, and thereby its general competitive position in international trade. Any growth of exports would tend to aggravate the negative service balance, which in turn would make it more difficult to finance needed imports. The lack of a strong national merchant marine therefore tended to limit the growth of exports, as well as imports, with the net effect of constraining national growth.

As for the security side of the doctrine, the national merchant marine has been regarded as an auxiliary of the naval fleet. Growth of the merchant marine also involves heavy responsibilities for the navy in protecting key routes of maritime commerce. In World War II, for example, the early destruction of most of the modest national merchant marine by axis submarines made Brazil's foreign trade and coastal communication dependent on its allies. More positively, since the national merchant marine subsequently came to be regarded as an important stimulus for national growth through support of foreign trade, its expansion would reinforce national security. Because a strong merchant marine supports national growth and reinforces national security, it likewise is an important factor in Brazil's emergence as a major power.[6]

More specific guidelines and justifications were developed as well to stimulate and direct expansion of the national merchant marine. In rejecting the extension of freedom of navigation to include the shipping trade, Brazil countered that every country has a right to carry at least half of its own foreign trade. In particular, cargoes would be reserved on a bilateral basis, in order to assure national carriers at least half of nationally-generated foreign trade. Such cargo reservations would be applied to imports destined for the government and to those involving governmental subsidies of any kind, as well as to certain categories of exports. Since general shipping market conditions were not really free, Brazilian government involvement was allegedly justified in promoting these objectives.

These specific guidelines could be applied flexibly in individual cases, provided that the particular bilateral trading partner conceded reciprocal treatment to Brazilian carriers. The overall objective still would be equal participation by national carriers of the exporting and importing states. In the case of liner conferences, a 40:40: 20 formula would be followed. That is, 40% of each state's trade with another state would be reserved for its respective national carriers, and the remaining 20% would be allocated to third flag countries. Since third flag countries could still participate in a portion of Brazilian trade on an equal, competitive basis, Brazil argued that its policy was preferential with respect to national carriers but not discriminatory to others.

Occasionally, Brazil did conclude bilateral shipping agreements outside liner conferences, particularly with some other Latin American states. These agreements provided for a fifty-fifty division of freight charges between the two trading partners, and thereby excluded any third flag participation. But such arrangements were regarded as exceptions designed to render low-traffic routes viable, and would be converted to a 40:40:20 formula as the market grew.

The two ministries primarily responsible for the formation and implementation of Brazilian ocean transportation policy, the Ministry of Transportation

on the domestic side and the Foreign Ministry
(Itamaraty) for international negotiations, worked
well together in the initial stage during the late
1960s and early 1970s when opposition by developed
states was most pronounced. Two key actors, one
from each ministry, have each analyzed Brazilian
shipping doctrine and policy during these critical
years from their different perspectives in published
monographs. Admiral J. C. de Macedo Soares
Guimarães, the then President of the Merchant Marine
Commission, which was the precursor of SUNAMAM
(Superintendência Nacional da Marinha Mercante), the
national shipping agency located within the
Ministry of Transportation, published his account
in 1969.[7] Minister-Counsellor (later Ambassador)
Murillo Gurgel Valente, the former Head of Itamaraty's
Transportation and Communication Division and a participant in international shipping negotiations,
first published his account in the early 1970s.[8]
Navy influence was more indirect through reserve
officers in SUNAMAM, with Macedo Soares as a case
in point, and through overall responsibility for coordination of ocean policy.

As these and other accounts indicate, Brazilian
international shipping doctrine had been carefully
articulated by the late 1960s and was then implemented quite systematically. This contrasts with
Brazilian ocean policy as a whole and with fisheries
in particular, which have been shown to have evolved
rather erratically, at least up to the mid-1970s.
Naval affairs is the only other major maritime
sector besides shipping in which planned expansion
and modernization began at a fairly early date,
particularly from the late 1960s.[9] Deep seabed
policy, although of less central importance to
ocean policy, also was noted to have exhibited re-
markable continuity.[10]

While Brazilian international shipping policy
has been relatively cohesive and consistent, it
still has been affected by the vagaries of domestic
and international politics. The first significant
policy initiatives and commitment of resources were
in 1967, which, it will be recalled, coincided with
a difficult national period of economic and political
consolidation and stabilization (1964-1967). Successful competition for very scarce resources at
the time ultimately depended on politics. Admiral
Macedo Soares acknowledged, in an interview with
this author, that this initial policy change was
assisted by his close personal relationship with
President Costa e Silva.[11] However, other domestic

political choices involving the development of the
national merchant marine proved divisive. Admiral
Macedo Soares himself later became embroiled in a
rather bitter debate charging that shipping policy
had unduely emphasized the state-controlled sector
of the economy at the expense of the private
sector.[12]

The larger political debate over the Brazilian
developmental model also relates in part to shipping
policy. The major thrust of shipping policy has
been to expand the merchant marine rapidly in order
to complement rapid expansion of foreign trade.
Critics argue that greater emphasis should be placed
on expansion of the internal market and income redistribution, and that priorities and incentives
should be restructured accordingly.

International politics has likewise been
heavily involved with shipping policy, especially
in the initial years from the late 1960s through
the early 1970s. Both Macedo Soares and Gurgel
Valente explicitly recognized that the objectives
of Brazilian shipping policy pointed toward revision
of the entire international shipping structure, and
therefore had potential broad appeal for developing
states in general.[13] The Brazilian challenge to the
existing international shipping order, first undertaken seriously in the late 1960s, gained momentum
by the 1970s and attracted allies throughout the
developing world. As the general principles of
Brazilian shipping policy gained popularity throughout the developing world during those years, developed states were placed on the defensive. The
drive of developing states to build national merchant marines gained momentum, including their
determination to participate more fully in the
carriage of their own trade, while opposition in
principle of developed states to this drive lessened.
However, the established maritime powers did continue to regard such measures by developing states
as inefficient, both in national terms and in terms
of their impact on world shipping in general.

Both of the central actors in the formation of
Brazilian shipping policy who have documented their
experiences, Admiral Macedo Soares and Itamaraty's
Gurgel Valente, implicitly concur that the crucial
period of international political challenge was
from the 1960s through the early 1970s. A brief
review of their writings will allow us to specify
this chronology and draw conclusions therefrom.

Itamaraty's Gurgel Valente entitled his monograph, "Brazilian Maritime Transportation Policy:

Chronicle of a Battle," which, he adds in the body of the text, is a chronicle of a "victorious battle." Writing a subsequent postscript to the revised edition in late 1972, he also referred to the five previous years as constituting "the first and most difficult stage of the implementation of Brazilian maritime transportation policy." Short-term goals of rationalizing Brazil's maritime traffic and increasing participation of Brazilian carriers "have been achieved," while medium- and long-term goals still ahead include continued strengthening of national shipbuilding, expansion of the fleet and lessening reliance on chartered ships, and increased merchant marine support for growing foreign trade.[14]

Similarly, Admiral Macedo Soares, in an article published in 1972, described five stages in the development of Brazilian shipping policy. The first two stages, from 1967, involved acceleration of shipbuilding and rationalization of the structure of the domestic shipping industry, with ships being chartered to fill in gaps until they could be phased out with ships built in national yards. The third period, the "political phase," involved the so-called "freight war," which brought Brazil into open conflict with the major maritime states. Results during this political phase were positive. By 1971, national carriers had made very good progress in increasing their share of freight charges generated by foreign trade (1966: 9.5%; 1971: 42%), even though rapid expansion of trade during those years doubled the size of these costs. To achieve these positive results during the initial five-year period of implementation, 1967-1971, all the major liner conferences were reformulated to conform to national policy, at times only after threats, counter-threats and boycotts were exerted. In spite of all this progress, chartered vessels still carried a considerable portion of the national shipping share. The fourth stage, SUNAMAM supervision of "setting of shipping rates," grew out of the earlier conflicts and generated new ones, although here, too, SUNAMAM's active concern gradually gained legitimacy. A fifth stage involved expansion of the private sector portion of national shipping.[15]

In essence, by the mid-1970s, the battle over principle had largely been won and the conflict shifted towards putting principles into practice.[16] Once broad recognition was given to the right of preferential treatment for national flag carriers, political confrontation tended to lessen in world shipping. The new stage of Brazilian international shipping policy instead involved the economic challenge of building a large and efficient national merchant marine. Development of the Brazilian merchant marine and of those of developing states in general therefore tended to shift from the sphere of international politics toward that of international economics by the mid-1970s. Brazil's fight to gain recognition of rights of developing states in shipping accordingly transcended the national merchant marine.

The Brazilian campaign to restructure world shipping rules was carried out in multilateral negotiating forums, as well as through bilateral channels. Symbolic of the political momentum of developing states was the 1974 UNCTAD Code of Conduct for Liner Conferences. The Code of Conduct approves preferential treatment for national merchant marines, including cargo sharing based on the 40:40:20 formula. Brazilian "ideological leadership" in this movement has been generally recognized,[17] although it is still uncertain to what extent the major shipping powers will accept this particular code of conduct.

Increasing recognition of a right, however, does not guarantee implementation of that right. The argument of the maritime powers cannot be ignored that a national merchant marine, to be useful, must be efficient. The rapid growth of the Brazilian merchant marine stands out in the Third World, but much still remains to be done. Continued expansion of shipbuilding will be required to lessen reliance on chartered vessels, shipbuilding will need to become more efficient, and recent technological innovations, such as containerization, will need to be incorporated into the merchant marine.

The challenge of building an efficient national merchant marine is likely to prove even more difficult for other Third World states than for Brazil. Brazil benefited from a relatively sophisticated industrial base and from rapidly growing foreign trade to sustain expansion of the national merchant marine. In contrast, if a Third World state's foreign trade and industrial base were not sufficiently developed, it is doubtful if its national merchant marine could be efficient. Nor could most Third World states realistically aspire to share in cross-trading, as does Brazil. What for Brazil has been a stimulus for economic development, for them could be a drain on precious investment resources. Therefore, as in the UNCLOS III debates, Brazil will likely be one of the few big winners in the Third

World from the changing rules of world shipping.

THE STRUCTURE OF NATIONAL SHIPPING

Paralleling Brazil's internationally-oriented
drive to restructure the rules governing ocean
transportation has been a domestically-oriented effort to renovate the structure of national shipping.
This has included a series of merchant marine construction programs, institutional reforms affecting
SUNAMAM and Lloyd Brasileiro among others, modernization of ports, and development of so-called export
corridors. To put the principles achieved by the
internationally-oriented drive into practice, such
innovations oriented toward building a strong domestic shipping base are required. The major gains and
problems of the component parts of national shipping
will be discussed insofar as they have an international impact or support Brazilian international
shipping policy.
Shipbuilding was given an initial boost through
the 1967-69 Emergency Naval Construction Plan (Plano
de Emergência de Construção Naval), which was followed by successively more ambitious, regularized
plans. The present $3.3 billion 1975-79 shipbuild-
ing program, for example, has placed almost three
times more orders than the preceding program. As a
result, the shipbuilding industry in Brazil has become the largest in Latin America and one of the
largest in the world. Until 1967, the Brazilian
merchant marine was below one million tons, and had
an average age of about ten years. By the end of
1977, the merchant marine had expanded to well over
5 million tons, and the average age had been lowered
to four years. By 1980, a further jump to ten million tons is expected. From the mid-1960s, national
bottoms also managed to raise their participation in
the carriage of Brazilian trade from less than ten
percent to 50.7%, even though volume soared and
shipping costs generated by the growth of Brazilian
trade almost quadrupled.[18]
Since the share of the national carriage of
Brazilian trade has risen to fifty percent, the major avoidable expense remains chartered vessels.
That is, a sizable portion of Brazil's own share has
been carried in chartered vessels, not nationally-
owned or constructed bottoms. Completion of the
current naval construction program should help ease
the drain of foreign exchange caused by chartered
vessels, with further rapid reduction in chartering

expenses by the early 1980s. The overall invisibles
deficit from freight charges, including chartering
expenses, has already been decreasing since the mid-
1970s. Since Brazilian foreign trade has grown very
rapidly since the late 1960s, the overall freight
charge deficit rose from $146 million in 1967 to a
peak of $901 million in 1974 and then declined to
$552 million in 1977 as shipping gains were made.
Similarly, the expense of chartering vessels increased from $53 million in 1967 to a peak of $562
million in 1974, and then declined somewhat by 1977
to $496 million. Greatest reliance on chartered
vessels in 1977 was by Fronape, Petrobrás' bulk oil
fleet, with nearly $300 million in chartering ex-
penses, followed by Lloyd Brasileiro, the major general cargo shipping line, with $71.5 million, and
Docenave, the dry-bulk carrier of iron ore for the
Vale do Rio Doce company, with $49 million.[19]
    Such disparities between carriers suggest fun-
damental distinctions between the various components
of national shipping. While the entire shipping industry has faced certain common problems and made
advances, different components of national shipping
have faced different kinds of challenges as well.
    For several reasons, initial emphasis in imple-
menting Brazilian international shipping policy from
1967 was placed on expanding participation by Brazilian carriers in the haulage of general cargo.[20]
Prospects were best here for significant results in
the short run, because a relatively high proportion
of total freight charges was involved, although only
a small proportion of overall tonnage. In 1967, for
example, general cargo was only 15.7% of the tonnage
of Brazilian trade, but involved 52.9% of the value.
To the extent that liner conferences could be restructured to permit greater participation by Lloyd
Brasileiro and by other private Brazilian general
cargo carriers, significant short-term dividends
would result. Long-term expansion of both the general cargo and bulk carrier fleets was planned, but
in the short run even a small, if growing, general
cargo fleet could help relieve the strain on the
balance of payments from freight charges. The fixed
schedules of line traffic governed by the liner conferences also facilitated planning and predictable
returns, in contrast with the more erratic bulk carrier trade. Finally, nearly all products receiving
Brazilian governmental subsidies or incentives, and
therefore subject to preferential carriage, were
general cargo.
    A more recent stage in the evolution of Brazil-

ian shipping policy has complemented the emphasis on reform and expansion of the general cargo trade in earlier stages. Primary emphasis was given to the general cargo trade from 1967 through 1973, while from 1974 increasing attention has been given to the expansion of the liquid- and dry-bulk carrier fleets as well.[21] Additional Brazilian carriers were also permitted to enter the bulk trade, and the existing carriers moved to diversify and integrate their respective liquid- and dry-bulk carrier operations.

The choice of transportation of bulk cargo has traditionally been that of the importer, so the Fronape liquid-bulk carrier fleet, which imports oil to Brazil, has not had to surmount political obstacles like those posed by liner conferences for the general cargo trade. While Fronape has been able to transport Brazilian oil imports by general consent, the Fronape fleet has not been able to expand rapidly enough to keep up with growing national demand. Chartered vessels have consequently constituted a particularly heavy expense in this area, and will continue to play an important role for some years because of the very large fleet capacity required to import 80% of the oil for national consumption. The Fronape fleet is still large and growing. Fronape's fleet, including both owned and chartered ships, is projected to expand from three million tons at the end of 1978, to 4.2 million tons by the end of 1979.[22]

Docenave's dry-bulk carrier fleet, particularly involving carriage of Brazilian iron ore exports, relied entirely on chartered vessels until 1967, although it, too, has expanded rapidly in recent years. It totalled 3.4 million tons by the end of 1977, with over a third owned by the company and the rest chartered, and an additional three-quarters of a million tons will be added by 1982.[23]

Docenave has been in a relatively favorable position to maintain a respectable market share of Brazilian iron ore exports for carriage by its dry-bulk carrier fleet. The relationship of supply and demand and the consequent bargaining power of the respective trading partners generally determine choice of carrier in the bulk cargo market. Although Brazil has been an exporter of iron ore, which because of the nature of the bulk cargo market might normally reduce its leverage in influencing the choice of carrier, it still has been in a relatively good bargaining position. Because of fairly steady demand for iron ore (an essential ingredient for steelmaking) and the limited number of suppliers, Brazil has often been able to sell C.I.F. (Cost,

Insurance, Freight) in order to channel iron ore cargoes to Docenave.

Several other recent measures have reinforced Docenave's bargaining position. Purchase of several ore/oil carriers and orders for more have added to Docenave's flexibility, have facilitated cooperation with Fronape, and have even opened up the possibility of some cross-trading. For example, a triangular trade exports Brazilian iron ore to Japan, from whence the same vessel goes to the Middle East to take on oil, and then returns to Brazil. The result is a halving of normal freight charges. Docenave and Fronape have also cooperated in arranging pooling or sharing arrangements.

Through SUNAMAM, the government has balanced and coordinated the interests of these shipowners with shipbuilders. Both builders and owners participate in preparation of SUNAMAM's successive merchant marine construction programs. SUNAMAM assures that shipbuilding capacity will be full and sets ceilings on tonnage for types of vessels, after which there is some bargaining and competition over specifications of general designs and other details.

The Dutch and Japanese shipbuilding firms, Verolme and Ishikawajima do Brasil (Ishibrás), began operations in Brazil in the 1950s, and now operate alongside a number of private Brazilian shipyards. From Verolme's original link to Brazil in the late 1950s of modernizing the British-purchased aircraft carrier Minas Gerais in its Dutch yards and from Ishikawajima's original link through ship sales to Brazil during the same period, they have grown into the largest shipbuilders in Brazil. Both foreign firms have fitted into the Brazilian corporatist type of organization in shipping, particulary as they have become increasingly Brazilianized in personnel and management style, and they have been technological leaders in the national shipbuilding industry.

Exports of ships are promoted and coordinated by Esabrás (Estaleiros Associados do Brasil or Associated Shipyards of Brazil). Verolme and Ishibrás figure among the associated Brazilian shipbuilders in Esabrás. Sales have been growing slowly, and as domestic needs are met more fully by the early 1980s, exports may grow still more, but international competition is stiff. In fact, excess shipbuilding capacity could become a problem for the first time by the mid-1980s, and at that point the challenge of increasing the efficiency of the shipbuilding industry could be put to another hard test. There is

consequently disagreement about the degree to which
reliance on chartered vessels should continue as a
hedge against future excess capacity.

Integrating all these elements of the national
shipping industry in support of maritime transportation policy is SUNAMAM. With many shipping problems
having been resolved both on the domestic and international fronts, shipping promises to continue to be
a key ingredient in building ocean policy.

NOTES

1. See Chapter 4.

2. See Chapters 5 and 6.

3. Third United Nations Conference on the Law of the Sea,
"Delegation of Brazil: Statement at the III Committee on the
question of Prevention of Marine Pollution, July 17, 1974,"
pp. 1-2 (mimeograph copy).

4. For a competent discussion of these issues from a legal
perspective, see Nagendra Singh, Maritime Flag and International Law (Faridabad, India: Thomson Press, 1978). Judge Singh
of the International Court of Justice at The Hague does favor
the view of developing states on these issues, but he also
presents arguments of developed states.

5. Chapter II of a monograph by Murillo Gurgel Valente ex-
plicitly relates national security and economic development to
the need for a strong national merchant marine. Murillo Gurgel
Valente, A Política de Transportes Marítimos do Brasil:
Crónica de uma Batalha (Rio de Janeiro, Brazil: Ministro dos
Transportes, Serviço de Documentação, 1972), pp. 19-27. Also
see an article by Admiral Hilton Berutti Augusto Moreira,
"Transportes Marítimos, Desenvolvimento e Segurança Nacional,"
Revista Marítima Brasileira 91 (October-December 1971): 44-62.
But see Chapter 2 for several qualifications in applying general security-development doctrine to specific maritime sectors.
In particular, each sector has been influence since 1964 by the
general policy orientation of military governments, including
the security-development doctrine, but peculiarities of the
maritime environment and ocean politics and of each sector
therein have required significant modifications and/or exten-
sions of doctrine.

6. Gustavo Francisco Feijó Bittencourt, "Connotações do Poder
Marítimo Necessárias ao Processo de Engrandecimento no Brasil,"
Revista Marítima Brasileira 91 (Oct.-Dec. 1971): 115, 119-121.
Also Hilton Berutti Augusto Moreira, p. 62.

7. J.C. de Macedo Soares Guimarães, Marinha Mercante no Brasil (Uma Opinião) (Rio de Janeiro, Brazil: Livraria Francisco Alves, 1969).

8. Murillo Gurgel Valente, A Política de Transportes Marítimos do Brasil (Crônica de uma Batalha) (Rio de Janeiro, Brazil: Ministry of Transportation, 1972). This is a revised, enlarged edition.

9. See Chapters 5 and 6.

10. See Chapter 4.

11. Interviews by this author with Admiral J.C. de Macedo Soares Guimarães, Rio de Janeiro, Brazil, July 25, 1975 and July 28, 1975.

12. For a summary of this debate, see Ronald M. Schneider, Brazil: Foreign Policy of a Future World Power (Boulder, Colorado: Westview Press, 1976), footnote 33 on pages 224-225. Also see footnote 15 of this chapter.

13. Macedo Soares, Marinha Mercante, pp. 52-57. Gurgel Valente, p. 16.

14. Gurgel Valente, pp. 17, 111, 105.

15. J.C. de Macedo Soares Guimarães, "Transporte Marítimo Internacional e o Comércio," Carta Mensal 17 (July 1972): 47-63.

16. The details of this battle over principles, which are at once complex and quite technical, need not be recounted here. For such accounts, see the works cited above by Macedo Soares and Gurgel Valente. For accounts in English of Brazil's confrontation with liner conferences from the late 1960s through the early 1970s, see Carlos Oswaldo Saraiva, "Brazilian International Shipping Policy," Lawyer of the Americas 4 (February 1972): 28-43; and John J. McDonnell, "Unilateral Regulation of International Trade: U.S.-Brazil Coffee Trade Example," Journal of Maritime Law and Commerce 3 (July 1972): 793-799. Numerous interviews conducted by this author during June and July of 1975 in Rio de Janeiro, Brazil with SUNAMAM officials and officials of liner conferences confirmed the chronology set forth here and assisted in the formulation of conclusions.

17. Susan Strange, "Who Runs World Shipping?: An Experimental Study in International Political Economy," International Studies Notes 3 (Fall 1976): 5. Olav Knudsen, The Politics of International Shipping: Conflict and Interaction in a Transnational Issue-Area, 1946-1968 (Lexington, Massachusetts:

Lexington Books, 1973), pp. 78-79, 129.

18. Navegação Brasileira de Longo Curso, (Brasília, Brazil: SUNAMAM, 1978), pp. 29-32.

19. Ibid., pp. 33-34, 36, 39.

20. Ibid., p. 9. Luiz da Motta Veiga, "O Frete Marítimo. Fretes e Conferências de Fretes. Reflexos sobre a Política de Exportação Brasileira," lecture at the Escola de Guerra Naval, May 20, 1975, pp. 5-6 (mimeograph).

21. Navegação Brasileira de Longo Curso, pp. 26-27. Luiz da Motta Veiga, p. 17.

22. Petrobrás News, No. 11 (November 1978), p. 6. Petrobrás News, No. 12 (December 1978), p. 8.

23. Docenave: Relatório Annual: 1977 (Rio de Janeiro, Brazil: Docenave, 1978), pp. 2-3.

9. Brazilian Ocean Policy in Comparative Perspective

Conclusions reached in previous chapters together present a comprehensive profile of Brazilian ocean policy, and also suggest a number of comparisons. Ocean policy comparisons, using Brazil as a point of reference, will be developed more fully in this chapter and are intended both to complement previous research and to stimulate further inquiry.

BRAZIL AS AN EMERGING MAJOR POWER

A watershed has been reached, both with regard to Brazil's developmental model, including its relationship to national emergence as a major power, and to the academic literature dealing with these events. As for development prospects at this crucial juncture, most authorities remain relatively optimistic that Brazil can cope with current economic difficulties, including serious inflation, mounting import requirements, especially oil, and a very large foreign debt burden. On this basis, they generally project further growth into the late 1970s and 1980s, albeit in less favorable international circumstances than in the late 1960s and early 1970s.

The future of the political side of the developmental model is much more in doubt. Dissent and general dissatisfaction continue to mount for a variety of reasons, including the closed, repressive nature of the political regime, and the highly uneven distribution of rewards and burdens by geographical region and social class. To such critics, pursuit of major power status and burgeoning international contacts merely entrench domestic regional and income inequities while avoiding social reform.

283

Those who stress politics more than economics are accordingly more pessimistic about Brazil's continued emergence as a major power along present lines.

This study contributes a distinctive perspective to the debate over the future of the Brazilian developmental model and its impact on national emergence as a major power. Since ocean policy overlaps domestic and foreign policy, it is an appropriate test case for judging both the nature of domestic economic and political policy impacts and their relationship to international policy dimensions. For example, both general and sectoral aspects of Brazilian ocean policy were influenced by domestic and/or international events at different times, sometimes erratically but at other times in predictable or recurring ways. Comparison of ways in which ocean policy overlaps the domestic and international spheres, or leans toward one or the other at different times, either by sector or as a whole, may lead to hypotheses. Such hypotheses involving Brazilian ocean policy could test economic-political and domestic-international relationships in the maritime sphere and compare them to counterpart non-maritime trends. A related comparison that can rely on the findings of this study would compare the impact of an authoritarian, modernizing regime on ocean policy, domestically and internationally, with other existing studies of ocean policy-making in pluralistic democracies.

Such comparisons go well beyond the scope of this study. But evidence submitted about Brazilian ocean policy does at least suggest that neither the political nor economic interpretations of the Brazilian developmental model sufficiently reflect policy complexities nor their multiple relationships to national emergence as a major power. Hopefully this study can contribute to more integrated hypotheses about such economic-political and domestic-international relationships.

The literature on Brazil's emergence as a major power has likewise reached a decisive point in its evolution. The novelty of a Latin American state emerging as a major power is wearing off, and international actors, including nervous neighbors and interested investors, are accepting it as a reality. By now, ample attention has been called in the literature to this phenomenon, major constraints and opportunities have been analyzed, at least in general terms, and likely overall policy alternatives have been predicted. Now is the time to flesh out these general studies with specific case studies illustrating the foreign policy of an emerging major power.

The current state of the literature is ripe for systematic, well-documented case studies of Brazilian foreign policy, from the perspective of its emergence as a major power. Such a series of specific studies would build on the general theoretical and empirical findings of earlier research by going much more into depth and specificity about problems and opportunities facing Latin America's leading major power candidate. It is on the basis of such specific, systematic case studies that peculiarities and similarities of the various dimensions of Brazil's emergence as a major power can be determined and hence that discriminating generalizations can be made.

This book has purported to offer just such a case study which refines and extends previous inquiries. For example, it has been shown that thinking about Brazil's emergence has focused on land-based power, and that the security-development doctrine shares this bias. But increasingly, continued projection of Brazilian influence internationally must rely on integration of both land-based and maritime power. Brazil's emergence as a maritime power parallels and is complementary to broader Brazilian emergence as a major power. Brazilian maritime interests are already more extensive and varied than those of any other Latin American or South Atlantic state and are continuing to expand.

Some other relevant case studies include energy requirements and responses in the foreign policy of an emerging power and the security policy of an emerging power (military assistance and arms sales, both from established great powers and by the emerging power itself to others; security implications for weaker neighbors, etc.). As Brazil's foreign policy becomes more complex, links between such case studies provide fertile ground for comparisons. Ocean policy is again a case in point. Brazil has moved into a position of Third World leadership and toward national self-sufficiency in maritime affairs; energy policy is closely related since the search for offshore oil has been intensified through risk contracts with foreign firms to help support a larger international role; and, finally, expanding security interests have been evident in the 200-mile territorial sea, growing interest in the South Atlantic, and assertion of effective national control over the riparian network.

Broader generalizations derived from such case

studies would relate to the process of moving from developing toward developed status, conditions for exerting effective Third World leadership and for influencing developed states, and implications for other Third World emerging powers, as well as for lesser powers. The applicability of the findings of this study to each of these areas will now be noted briefly.

DEVELOPING STATES

Like Brazil's emergence as a major power, the broader, related concept of dependency of developing states also needs to be examined in more specific, comparative terms. Developing states on the periphery generally aspire to lessen their dependency on the center, although constraints and opportunities for achieving this result have usually been examined in general or ideological terms. Several recent studies have recognized the need for examining dependency, both in general and in particular the case of Brazil, in more concrete, empirical terms.[1] This study, like them, relies on concrete, empirical analysis and reconfirms their conclusion that Brazil has generally tended to become less dependent in recent years.

Brazil's movement from the periphery toward the center does place it in a distinctive position between the First and Third Worlds. Again, comparisons can suggest to what extent this position is unique. Brazil's relative power easily distinguishes it from smaller, weaker developing countries, but even they, in some ways and for certain purposes, benefit from increased diplomatic maneuverability in an emerging multipolar world. As for more influential developing states, this author has argued that Brazil and India are distinctive Third World candidates for major power status.[2] Unlike Third World oil-producing states, their national development is quite broadly based, if still heavily dependent on foreign oil. Both India and Brazil are subcontinents with large populations, both already occupy positions of great influence within their respective sub-regions, and both have concluded that attainment of paramount national values requires consolidation of major power status. Besides comparing similarities and differences of the emergence of Brazil and India as Third World powers in such general terms, as a case study, Brazilian and Indian ocean policies were compared as well. Both

Brazilian and Indian ocean policies are prominent
among developing states in building maritime capabilities across a broad front.

Several other kinds of comparisons involving
developing states were either explicit or implicit
in this study. Because of Brazil's increasingly
prominent role in international maritime affairs,
this case study provides a particularly important
example of constraints and opportunities for Third
World cooperation.[3]

Brazil gradually moved toward greater cooperation with Latin American and other developing states
in the law of the sea negotiations, and Brazil's
concern with the freezing of power may continue to
associate national interests with those of developing states. For example, Brazilian policy-makers
have expressed determination to extend gains resulting from national maritime transportation policy[4]
and extended offshore jurisdiction to other developing states. To the extent that the advances Brazil
has gained in the maritime sphere can be transferred
automatically to other developing states, such as
general reforms in the law of the sea and liner conferences, they will indeed benefit. But in other
areas, such as the deep seabed and navigational
guarantees, increasing approximation of Brazilian
interests with those of the developed states may set
strict limits on continued cooperation with the
Third World.

Recurring differences have tended to plague
efforts to promote Third World unity. Most Third
World states are either land-locked or geographically disadvantaged or have rather limited coastal
state interests. In contrast, Brazilian ocean interests are extensive and diverse, so that Brazil
promises to be one of the few big winners in the
Third World in both the seabed and non-seabed portions of the law of the sea discussions. This distinctive Brazilian position required serious qualification of revisionist interpretations of the law
of the sea debates.

DEVELOPED STATES

Analysis of Brazilian ocean policy in previous
chapters involved extended analysis of interaction
with developed states, because Brazil's general
diplomatic relations and more specific maritime relations have been and are likely to remain focused
on the industrialized world. More particularly,

relations with the United States have been close and still are extensive, if declining in importance relative to all of Brazil's international contacts. Several perspectives on comparative ocean policy result.

First, Brazilian ocean policy illustrates relations between a state long on the periphery and major powers in the center of the international system. Second, interaction between Brazilian ocean policy and ocean policies of developed states, especially that of the United States, illustrates as well how U.S. ocean policy deals with Third World states. Increasing attention has been given to U.S. ocean policy in recent years, but areas of relative neglect have been U.S. ocean relations with the Third World in general and Brazil in particular.[5] Third, Brazil's movement to an intermediate position between the First and Third Worlds sheds new light on the nature of maritime power status, and more broadly, of major power status. Brazilian maritime interests, both coastal state and deep-water, have been expanding, often in distinctive ways characteristic of neither developed nor developing states.

The distinctive nature of Brazilian ocean interests sets limits on cooperation with developed states, just as it set limits on cooperation with developing states. Expansion of deep-water interests, particularly in the merchant marine and naval spheres, has not been accompanied by more moderate definition of coastal state interests, as one would expect were Brazil to conform to the typical developed state model. Instead, coastal state interests out to 200 miles have continued to be defined expansively, while certain deep-water interests have expanded as well. Deep seabed policy, too, is distinctive in essentially combining elements of typical developing and developed state positions.

Distinctive Brazilian interests have contributed to this anomalous result, which may very well be projected into the future. Brazil does not plan to develop any significant deep-water fishing fleet, and navigational guarantees are regarded as compatible with a 200-mile territorial sea. From this perspective, continued expansion of deep-water interests, especially in the merchant marine and naval sectors, would complement consolidation of national control over an extensive, relatively resource-rich territorial sea. In Brazilian eyes, there is consequently no dichotomy between concomitant expansion of coastal state interests and deep-water interests, as developed states often seem to believe. Brazil's

288

emergence as a maritime power may therefore not necessarily transform national ocean interests into those of a traditional maritime state, just as Brazil's broader emergence as a major power may not conform to past patterns.

Brazilian ocean policy therefore reflects elements of both a deviant and a typical case study, and is accordingly rich in potential comparisons. Comparisons may clarify distinctive and similar aspects of Brazil's rise, both as a maritime power and as a major power, with respect to the established powers.

OCEAN POLITICS IN THE INTERNATIONAL SYSTEM

Previous comparisons may be integrated and extended, in order to suggest needed lines of inquiry about the larger matter of ocean politics in the international system. First, comparisons involving national ocean policy offer a bottom-to-top perspective of the place of ocean politics in the international system. Second, comparisons about interaction between national ocean policies can supply a top-to-bottom perspective of the same matter.

The complex, often arduous process of formation and implementation of national ocean policy has been illustrated through a case study of Brazil. Findings in this study about domestic ocean politics, the dynamics of individual maritime sectors, and overall problems of ocean policy-making are sources for comparison with ocean policies of other national states. Because Brazilian ocean policy is at once typical and distinctive, it offers a particulary fruitful point of comparison with national ocean policies of other states. Again, Brazil's distinctive position illustrates national ocean policy from three perspectives--as a developing state faced with the challenge of forging a national ocean policy, for all practical purposes, for the first time; as a state having made considerable progress in meeting that challenge and gaining entry to the select group of developed states; but still as a state occupying a distinctive position between First and Third Worlds. Some suggestions were made earlier in this chapter about how comparisons involving national ocean policies of these various categories of states might proceed.

Findings in this study about interaction between ocean policies on the historical, legal, economic, political, and military fronts can also serve as a basis for comparisons about international ocean politics of the interstate system. Third World ocean policies have been singled out as deserving greater attention--how they influence the international system; how Third World aspirant powers behave; how Third World ocean policies relate to general diplomatic relations, including similarities and differences in each area; and how Third World ocean policies interact with those of developed states. Comparisons could test and perhaps sharpen and refine established generalizations about center-periphery relations, in general and with particular reference to ocean policy, and stimulate new hypotheses about Third World ocean policies, including their formation, implementation, and influence.

As matters stand, Third World ocean policies tend to be noticed by developed states either because of their increasingly important role in challenging the existing system or because some specific crisis involving them and a developed state arises. Such an orientation regarding Third World ocean policies as a function of developed states fails to appreciate either their complexity or their distinctive dynamics. They should be examined on their own terms as well.

It must be concluded that understanding of the relationships of ocean politics to the international system is quite incomplete, particularly because Third World ocean policies are distinctive yet generally not well understood. Throughout the course of this study, Brazilian ocean interests have been shown to be distinctive, yet comprehensible to the extent that national ocean policy and its policy setting were fleshed in. This national ocean policy profile is likewise amenable to comparison and generalization. Hopefully, this study will contribute to such comparisons, generalizations, and further understanding.

NOTES

1. See note 3, Chapter 1.

2. Michael A. Morris, "Brazil and India as Emerging Third World Powers," paper delivered at the annual meeting of the Latin American Studies Association, Pittsburgh, Pennsylvania, April 5-7, 1979.

3. Two forthcoming annotated bibliographies by this author, "Latin America and the Third United Nations Conference on the

Law of the Sea" and "Comparative Ocean Policy: Africa and
Latin America," complement this study from just such a comparative perspective. These annotated bibliographies are to
appear in 1979 in a special theme issue of Ocean Development
and International Law: The Journal of Marine Affairs edited
by this author on "Influence and Innovation in the Law of the
Sea: Latin America and Africa." Also see the "Editorial Introduction" by this author to the special theme issue.

4. Oswaldo Castro Lobo, "Orgãos e convenções internacionais,"
in Panorama do Poder Maritimo Brasileiro, ed. Mario Cesar
Flores (Rio de Janeiro: Serviço de Documentação Geral da
Marinha, 1972), pp. 210-211. Sr. Castro Lobo at the time was
head of the Division of Transportation and Communications of
the Brazilian Ministry of Foreign Relations.

5. This theme is developed at greater length by this author
in a forthcoming review in Journal of Maritime Law and Commerce of Gerald J. Mangone's book, Marine Policy for America:
The United States at Sea (Lexington, Mass.: D.C. Heath and
Company, 1977). This generally fine survey promises to analyze
both the domestic and international factors that must be considered in the choice of U.S. marine policy, but does not
examine interaction between the United States and developing
states.